CONTEMPORARY DRAMA AND THE POPULAR DRAMATIC TRADITION IN ENGLAND

CONTEMPORARY DRAMA AND THE POPULAR DRAMATIC TRADITION IN ENGLAND

Peter Davison

BARNES & NOBLE BOOKS
TOTOWA, NEW JERSEY

© Peter Davison 1982

First published in the USA 1982 by
BARNES & NOBLE BOOKS
81, Adams Drive, Totowa,
New Jersey, 07512

ISBN 0-389-20232-0
LCN 79-55526

Printed in Hong Kong

For Hugh

Contents

Preface

There are two remarkable ironies associated with the development of English theatre. In Tudor times, the Government's success in bringing to an end the cycles of religious drama, a drama that was popular in two senses, being of the people and enjoyed by them, led indirectly to the formation of a fully professional theatre by the end of the sixteenth century. Thus was a stage provided for Marlowe, Shakespeare, Jonson, and their contemporaries. Then, in the first years of Victoria's reign, the repeal of Walpole's Licensing Act of 1737, which had divided drama into the legitimate and illegitimate, led, paradoxically, to a far sharper separation of these two forms than had been the case whilst that Act was in force. To this day, a music-hall comedian will be said 'to go legit.' when, like Jimmy Jewel, he plays Waters in Trevor Griffiths's *Comedians*. Whereas the first irony stemmed directly from the action of government, the second is not to be laid at Parliament's door. Nevertheless, it is distinctly odd that when the stage was freed, when, as J. R. Planché said, 'free trade in theatricals was established by law',[1] circumstances caused the drama to direct its energies into two distinct channels: music hall and the overheard drama in which disbelief was totally and continuously suspended.

In *Popular Appeal in English Drama to 1850,** I showed how dramatic illusion might be manipulated by medieval and Tudor dramatists; discussed Shakespeare's and Marlowe's relationships with the clowns and their acts; considered the use of the induction by Jonson and Shirley (in the masque as well as the play); and outlined the origins and development of the rehearsal dramas in which the audience was made aware that it was watching a theatrical performance. Even in that long period when the drama written in English was rarely outstanding and often, in literary terms, mediocre, there was nevertheless a tremendously

*Peter Davison, *Popular Appeal in English Drama to 1850* (London: Macmillan, 1982) p.161.

vigorous theatre in London, and sometimes in the provinces. Great actors and actresses on dully-lit stages could persuade audiences, attending in some discomfort in partially-lighted auditoria, fully to suspend their disbelief. But they could also break the continuity of the plays in which they appeared, mock the conventions that made drama viable, and yet regain their hold on the imaginations of their audiences. The theatre was a place of wonder and of make-believe, and if the merely theatrical did get out of hand (as in the pantomime craze of the early eighteenth century), no one doubted that the theatre was a place of excitement.

In this study I try to show how, despite the advent of realistic drama, that sense of wonder and theatricality was kept alive; how audiences retained their capacity for being simultaneously, in the same act, involved in, or detached from, what was going on on the stage; how the Elizabethan and Jacobean dramatic tradition of a mixed drama of overheard and direct address returned, via the Continent (and America) to the English stage; and the effect of the sea-change it suffered on contemporary English drama.

Again, I owe countless debts to those who have studied this subject in the past. Specific indebtedness is acknowledged in the traditional manner, but I made four acknowledgements in the Preface to *Popular Appeal in English Drama to 1850*, and I should like to repeat these here and add a fifth.

The first is to my good friends in the Department of English at St David's University College, Lampeter (among whom I would particularly include the secretary, Elsie Davies), who took upon them my work so that I could have a term free of teaching and administration. The second is to the Rockefeller Foundation, which invited me to spend a month as a scholar-in-residence at its magnificent Study and Conference Center at Bellagio, Como, and in particular to Dr and Mrs Olson who made me so welcome there. Indeed, I owe the Foundation and the Olsons additional thanks for enabling me to spend an extra week at Bellagio in order to complete this book and its companion volume. I am also grateful to the Pantyfedwen Fund for contributing nearly a third of the cost of my travel to and from Italy. Fourthly, I am very grateful to Professor John S. Brushwood, Roy A. Roberts Professor of Latin American Literature, University of Kansas, who not only spared precious time to read a draft of my two books whilst we were at Bellagio, but who later translated and sent me the account of Germán de Campo pulling Pirandello's leg (see pp. 136–7). Finally, I owe a very great debt to my wife, Sheila, who has not only helped me in countless ways to study and write, but who typed out the whole of the first draft from my execrable handwriting when she might instead have been sunning herself by Lake Como, and who also typed out the fair copy. It is owing to such generous help that I was able to accomplish more in a very short time than in years of disturbed and piecemeal effort. I am indeed grateful for the opportunity, peace and encouragement that these people and institutions so freely gave me.

Villa Serbelloni   P.D.
Bellagio

December 1978

1 Introduction

A visit to a theatre in the Restoration period, and right through until the mid-nineteenth century, was particularly unlike going to the theatre today. This was not just a matter of hard boards instead of an inch or two of plush, or even seats without the support of four inches of uncomfortable planking along the back. After all, hard boards survived in the Old Vic gallery until well after the Second World War – they were particularly noticeable towards the end of the second of two parts of *Tamburlaine*. A much more important difference was that of lighting (of stage and auditorium) and also significant was the degree of unruliness common in theatres up until about the middle of the nineteenth century.[1]

Writing in *The London Magazine* in March 1820,[2] William Hazlitt described what he found in the minor theatres – that is, those not classed as 'legitimate', such as Drury Lane, Covent Garden and, in the summer, the Haymarket. He goes to some lengths to explain that he went with limited expectations: 'We were all attention, simplicity, and enthusiasm', he says:

> But we saw neither attention, simplicity, nor enthusiasm in anybody else; and our whole scheme of voluntary delusion and social enjoyment was cut up by the roots. . . . It was the heartless indifference and hearty contempt shown by the performers for their parts, and by the audience for the players and the play, that disgusted us with all of them. . . . The object was not to admire or to excel, but to vilify and degrade everything. The audience did not hiss the actors (that would have implied a serious feeling of disapprobation, and something like a disappointed wish to be pleased) but they laughed, hooted at, nicknamed, pelted them with oranges and witticisms, to show their unruly contempt for them and their art.

Michael Booth, writing of 'The theatre and its audience',[3] gives a number of examples of the rowdiness of audiences in the first part of the nineteenth century. He quotes Charles Kemble's evidence to the Parliamentary Select Committee of 1832 that the shilling gallery was 'commonly very riotous', and the horror expressed in 1826 by the 'fastidious Pückler-Muskau' at the conduct of an English audience in a patent theatre: 'The most striking thing to a foreigner in English theatres is the unheard-of coarseness and brutality of the audiences.' He lays most of the blame on the gallery, and refers to 'some coarse expression shouted from the galleries in a stentor voice', followed by loud laughter or the ejection of the offender. This, he complained, 'happened not once, but sometimes twenty times' and it was, he said, no rarity for remnants of food 'which do not always consist of orange-peels alone' to be thrown on to the heads of those in the pit or into the boxes. But, as Michael Booth points out, the galleries were not alone in creating disturbances. An 'angry gentleman with a sword could be a dangerous person in an eighteenth-century theatre', and early in the nineteenth century 'behaviour in the boxes could be almost as boorish as behaviour in the gallery, and occasionally riotous' (pp. 23–4). That Pückler-Muskau's account is not the result of a visitor's prejudice is clear from what Richard Valpy, the headmaster of Reading School (famous for its performances of school plays in his time), wrote in 1814 of a visit to the Comédie Française in 1788. He was particularly appreciative of the 'great decorum' there: 'None of those riots taking place which disgrace our theatre, but which in England it would be dangerous, perhaps impolitic to prevent.' That decorum was, it should be pointed out, enforced by the presence in the auditorium of no fewer than thirty soldiers![4] Leo Hughes, whilst aware of the danger of exaggerating the degree of violence in the eighteenth-century theatre, none the less concludes 'it is not unfair to say that something near savagery could at times possess some members of the audience, while submissiveness prevailed among the others. It is not always a pretty picture.'[5]

Conditions improved in Victoria's reign though precisely when is open to debate – doubtless because conditions did not improve everywhere at the same time. Booth considers:

It is safe to say that probably by the 1840s, and certainly in the next decade, the manners and general behaviour of audiences began to improve: a natural consequence of the middle-class takeover of the theatre and the increasing sobriety of Victorian middle-class habits. Reports of disorders in the pit and missiles hurled from the gallery dwindle away to almost nothing.

(p. 24)

The first illustration in *Victorian and Edwardian Entertainment from Old Photographs* (by Raymond Mander and Joe Mitchenson) shows a section of a working-class gallery audience of 1860 clearly entranced by the pantomime they are watching; but in his *The Victorian Theatre: a Pictorial Survey*, Richard Southern reproduces two splendid pictures of typical, rowdy galleries. The first is by Cruikshank and the second by Fred Barnard, drawn in the 1860s, showing, as Southern says, that 'the situation was slow to improve'.[6] The whistling and catcalling are apparent although it must be admitted that the gentleman is eating his orange (or apple?) and not, so far, hurling the remnants at those below (see p. 4). That the comments were not always unwarranted is delightfully illustrated by J. R. Planché in his *Recollections and Reflections*. A 'most carelessly represented' and 'wretchedly-written melodrama' attracted from the gallery the rebuke 'We don't expect no grammar, but you might let the scenes meet' (I, 127). Jerome, before earning his living with his pen, was a small-part actor in a number of touring companies. His experiences are very amusingly described in *On the Stage – and Off: the Brief Career of a Would-be Actor* (1885). In this he describes the kind of make-shift scenery against which he and his colleagues competed about 1880, and the response of the audience. On one occasion they were very short of cottage scenery because 'all the virtuous people in the play lived in cottages' (p. 72). The result was that the single cottage design had to serve several settings. 'With a round table and a candle, it was a widow's cottage. With two candles and a gun, it was the blacksmith's house. . . .'

It was no use though. The audience, on the opening night, greeted its second appearance with cries of kindly recognition, and at once entered into the humour of the thing. A Surrey-side Saturday-night audience are generally inclined to be cheerful, and, if the fun on the stage doesn't satisfy them, they rely on their own resources. After one or two more appearances, the cottage became an established favourite with the

THE GALLERY AT DRURY LANE THEATRE, LONDON, ON BOXING NIGHT.

FIGURE 1   Rebuke from the gallery at a badly-presented and wretchedly-written melodrama: 'We don't expect no grammar, but you might let the scenes meet' (J. R. Planché). Drawing by Fred Barnard of a theatre gallery of the 1860s (reproduced in Richard Southern's *The Victorian Theatre: a Pictorial Survey*). A similar rowdy audience was illustrated in Dickens's *The Old Curiosity Shop* (1840).

gallery. So much so, indeed, that when two scenes passed without its being let down, there were many and anxious enquiries after it, and an earnest hope was expressed that nothing serious had happened to it. Its reappearance in the next act (as something entirely new) was greeted with a round of applause, and a triumphant demand to know, 'Who said it was lost?'

(pp. 75–6)

Jerome is not writing a history, but it is likely that he very well hits-off the good-humoured raillery of a 'Surrey-side' theatre – the successors of the minor theatres of the eighteenth century. In such theatres, quiet acceptance of ultra-realism on the stage was not established by the end of the nineteenth century – and by the time it was the rule, such theatres had gone, replaced by cinemas.

Even in a theatre in which Irving was acting, however, response to anything untoward could be lively. Austin Brereton records the reaction of the pit and gallery to a curtailed programme when, following the first night of *The Lyons Mail* on 19 May 1877, the customary farce was done away with and 'the performance ended at the unusual hour of ten o'clock'. 'This was too much – or rather not enough! – for the occupants of the pit and gallery, and Irving had to do his best to pacify the irate members . . . the press advised Mrs Bateman [the Manager] that the prices charged for admission were such that an entertainment of greater length was required.'[7] However Brereton reports that under Irving's management at the Lyceum, which began in the following year, 'There was an absolute frenzy of rage when any one during a performance, the pauses in which were the shortest, took his seat late, or in any other manner made a noise that interfered with the power of hearing what was spoken; and it was easy to imagine that any one creating purposely a disturbance would have had an ill time of it' (I, 273).

That polite patience, even for a poor play or production, was expected by the 1890s is apparent from the reaction of the press to the behaviour of the gallery at the first night of Henry James's *Guy Domville* on 5 January 1895. The first act went well and was warmly received but the second was ill-constructed, full of clichés (including a misjudged drinking scene which James immediately afterwards removed), and was over-dressed. The audience became restless and attention strayed.[8] There was an outbreak of coughing from the stalls and dress circle, and more vociferous comment from the pit and gallery. Thus, when Mrs Edward Saker (as Mrs Domville) came on with an enormous hat she could not manage, 'a voice yielded a line from the popular song, "Where did you get that Hat". . . . Titter succeeded upon titter. The pit and the gallery became unruly, like a group of children facing an object of derision. The audience was now participating in the play, reaching across the footlights to the actors instead of being reached by them.' Although there was some recovery in the last act, it was not enough to prevent the statement, 'I'm the last, my lord, of the Domvilles . . .', uttered by George Alexander 'with a great show of feeling', being received by 'A voice from the gallery burst[ing] into the stillness' with, 'It's a bloody good thing y'are.' At the end of the play, James received an appalling reception. As he put it, he found himself 'in the presence of those yelling barbarians . . . and learned what could be the savagery of their disappointment'. The result was pandemonium.

Although, as Edel says, the press did not accept the verdict of the pit and gallery, even taking 'an intensely British attitude' and decrying 'the poor sportsmanship' of the audience, James and the play did not recover. James thought there had been 'predetermined mischief' but, as Edel says, 'there is no evidence to show that the gallery was anti-American, or that James's personality was in question'. And, of course, not only was the first act well received, but, with the boos and hisses, there was much applause at the end of the play. No, the uproar stemmed from the writing of the second act and its production, and, ironically, as Edel points out, James himself had advocated the hissing of plays disapproved of some twenty years earlier. George Bernard Shaw's comments (it was the third play he had reviewed) are most interesting on the subject of the audience. Whilst describing those who made the uproar as 'unmannerly', yet he 'sorrowfully' admits that 'Mr James is no dramatist, on the general ground that "the drama's laws the drama's patrons give" '. He saw it as the function of the theatrical critic to educate dunces, not echo them; but James's plays were only '*du théâtre* when the right people are in the theatre'. Which is to take us back to Jonson.

It will be apparent, therefore, that by the time Henry Irving took over the Lyceum in 1878, even though an audience might still be restive given cause, it was usual for legitimate drama to be watched in respectful silence – apart from applause and laughter intentionally aroused. This tradition, which we have inherited, is thus not much more than a century old.

The darkened auditorium is also a relative novelty. As long ago as 1598 Angelo Ingegneri had advocated the darkening of the auditorium[9] but it was not for three centuries, according to L. G. Applebee, that playhouse practice caught up with Renaissance theory. This is not quite correct. Nicola Sabbattini's *Practica di fabricar scene e machine ne' teatri* (*The Practice of making Scenes and Machines*), 1637–8, certainly speaks of lighting both stage and auditorium preparatory to a performance:

> After all the spectators have been seated and the time has come to begin the performance, the lamps must be lighted, first those in the auditorium, then those on the stage. Care should be taken that this be done as quickly as possible lest the spectators become uneasy and get the impression that the job will never be finished.

However, in 1683 a description appeared in Paris of the San Giovanni Crisostomo Theatre of Venice. This referred to the lighting of the auditorium.

> The chandelier carries four great tapers of white wax, which light the auditorium and remain lighted until the curtain is raised. Then the whole machine vanishes, and the proscenium returns to its first state. As soon as the opera is ended, this machine appears again to light the auditorium and to allow the spectators to leave at their ease and without confusion.[10]

Although the tone of this report suggests how exceptional was this device, within a century Ingegneri's proposal was put into practice, if not generally. In 1740 a similar method was used in Turin and in 1810 at Ludwigsburg (near Stuttgart), both theatres making 'serious attempts . . . to darken the auditorium during a performance . . . and to differentiate the levels of lighting on the stage and in the auditorium during performance'.[11] It was the installation of gas in the theatre which was to revolutionise the relative brightness of the stage and darkness of the auditorium.

The Lyceum was the first theatre regularly to light its stage by gas (6 August 1817) but it was two days behind Drury Lane in using gas to light the whole theatre in the following month, and perhaps as much as two years after the Olympic in using gas to light at least part of its interior (1815). By 1849, although probably earlier, the gas-plate or gas-table (control panel) had put the gas 'wholly under the control of the prompter'.[12] L. G. Applebee seems to distinguish between being able to control the supply of gas throughout the theatre and actually dimming the auditorium. Certainly the stage light was varied by means of the gas-table from an early date, but there is a certain evasiveness in the accounts about the dimming of the auditorium. Thus, Richard Southern, in his contribution, 'Auditorium' to the second edition of *The Oxford Companion to the Theatre*, says:

> Up to 1823 it had been the custom to keep the lights burning in the auditorium throughout the performance, but at this date it was found possible, by means of a gas chandelier suspended from the roof, to control the lighting. It was then dimmed at the rise of the curtain and the audience was left in comparative darkness during the run of the scene.   (p. 42)

Notice the description, 'comparative darkness'. However, writing in *The Victorian Theatre: a Pictorial Survey* (1970) Southern says: 'The custom of dimming the houselights came in with the installation of gas in theatres about mid-Victorian times' (p. 61). 'Mid-Victorian' would, of course, be rather later than mid-nineteenth century – say 1870 – whereas gas began to be installed in 1817. What is absolutely certain is that with the advent of gas the contrast between the light in the auditorium and that on the stage was very greatly increased. On 7 September 1817, Leigh Hunt wrote in *The Examiner* about the redecoration of Drury Lane Theatre, which had re-opened with full gas lighting throughout the house on the previous evening. He said:

> [we] can promise our Readers much satisfaction with the gas-lights which are introduced not only in front of the stage, but at the various compartments on each side. Their effect as they appear suddenly from the gloom, is like the striking of day-light; and indeed, it is in its resemblance to day that this beautiful light surpasses all others.[13]

Even if the auditorium remained lit, it is apparent from Leigh

Hunt's description that *relatively speaking*, the stage was suddenly very much brighter than had been the case, as compared to 'the gloom' of the auditorium.

Terence Rees, in his detailed study of the use of gas to light the Victorian theatre, gives more specific details of the persistence of auditorium lighting.[14] In part the practice continued to derive financial benefit from the sale of play texts and opera librettos (p. 187). Rees quotes from Clement Scott's account of the première of *Iolanthe* (1882), in which Scott says that he was so interested in reading 'the book' in the undimmed auditorium that he could scarcely watch what was happening on the stage (p. 175). The need for the members of an audience to 'see and relate to each other' was deemed more important than the completion of the dramatic illusion.

> Generally, the lowering or extinction of auditorium lights was accepted only when practised as an intermittent effect; though in the best spirit of British compromise, some theatres *dimmed* the house while the performance was in progress. This was the practice at the Prince's Theatre Royal, Glasgow, in 1849 and by 1858, the editor of *The Builder* could report that the turning down of auditorium lighting during the action was 'sometimes adopted'.   (p. 188)

Auditorium lighting was extinguished at Covent Garden in the 1890s, but that still met with some resistance 'from old *habitués*'. Dr Rees gives a fascinating account of the variations in house lighting for Beerbohm Tree's touring production of *Hamlet* in 1894–5. For this, the auditorium was only completely darkened for Act I, Scenes i and iv. For the rest of the performance the house lights were, in the main, half up (p. 188). In Paris, in January 1893, Strindberg, in his French-language Preface to *Miss Julie*, could still express the wish that the auditorium should be completely darkened during a performance.[15]

The effect of increasing darkness and quietness in the auditorium will be discussed later, but for the moment it will suffice to stress how tumultuous and relatively evenly-lighted were the theatres until well into Victoria's reign. One could not but be aware that one was in a theatre and it must have taken a fine performance to ensure total suspension of disbelief. That an audience might be held in rapt silence was, of course, possible;

but if attention wandered, then performers and audience could not count upon polite indifference, as in the theatre of this century.

In addition to differences in the lighting of theatres and the attitudes of audiences, there is a third characteristic which sharply distinguishes English theatre since the latter part of the nineteenth century – at least in the production of serious drama – from that of earlier centuries. Every modern audience sees all drama, live, or on film or television, with some, and probably considerable, experience of dramatic realism. This may stem from seeing plays that endeavour to be 'realistic' or 'naturalistic', plays that attempt to present the world as it really is (or rather, to present the outward appearance of the world). It may stem from communication through visual media: the photograph, the illustrated paper, the newsreel, actualité film or television. It may even stem from knowledge of the theories of realism. This is not to suggest that prior to Chernishevsky writers were not dealing with 'real' issues of the 'real' world; nor that their art did not represent 'reality' according to one of many conventions. Jonson and Wordsworth both aimed to write in 'language, such as men do use' (Jonson, Prologue to *Every Man in His Humour*, l.21), or, 'a selection of language really used by men' (Wordsworth, Preface to *Lyrical Ballads*, 1802). In the Jacobean theatre the development of citizen comedies in prose was, looked at from one point of view, 'more realistic' than were the poetic romances of Shakespeare – but if more closely identifiable with 'real, contemporary life', they were not necessarily more 'true' than plays set in Arcady. In the eighteenth century, 'the architectural motif was dropped in favour of more realistic locations'; as early as the 1750s, pleas were being made for a stage cleared of spectators, realistic costuming, and complete stage illusion; and Garrick's Drury Lane in 1779 used scenery for a pantomime, *The Wonders of Derbyshire*, based on 'sketches made on location'.[16] Increasingly, if intermittently, 'the simulation of actuality' was aimed for on the stage in the centuries prior to the nineteenth. What so marks off realism as a movement in the mid-nineteenth century is the conscious, thorough-going, all-embracing attempt to represent actuality in the theatre: to persuade the audience it was seeing 'the real thing', rivalling the photograph in liveliness. Whether such drama was more 'true' – to life – is quite another matter.[17]

The advent of realistic drama in the mid-nineteenth century theatre, at a time when the auditorium was becoming darkened and the stage more brilliantly and subtly lit, before an audience quietly attentive, made possible the total suspension of disbelief as a matter of course. It is no wonder that for the naturalistic play *Miss Julie*, Strindberg should have longed for a fully-darkened auditorium. The greater the simulation of actuality on-stage, the more nearly complete must be the break with real life in the auditorium. The way in which the late nineteenth-century audience was transported by means of lighting through the proscenium arch into the world of dramatic illusion, in such a way that make-believe seemed to be reality, is finely evoked by Laurence Irving in his description of the changes his father made to the Lyceum on taking over that theatre in 1878 – over a hundred years ago:

> The working curtain of green baize was retained. When the house lights were lowered and only the lower part of it was softly illuminated by the footlights, this green curtain seemed to fade into infinity – veiling, as Charles Lamb once said, a heaven of the imagination. It was the veil between the world of reality and of make-believe; when it rose the world before and behind the proscenium were blended; the illusory gained substance from the prosaic which in turn reflected something of the glittering imagery of the illusion.[18]

Mordecai Gorelik, as distinguished as practical, man-of-the-theatre as scholar, having pointed to the fact that 'The stage curtain has a history which goes back to the Romans', describes its new role in somewhat similar terms:

> It was no longer a mere device to hide the shifting of scenery. It became the portal of a magic world of illusion, a world whose compelling truth seemed to vie with life itself. It sealed the opening of a lighted peep-box; and when the curtain rose, the contemplative spectator peered into that lighted box with the absorption of one who looks at images in his own mind. . . . You might almost say it caused the theatre building itself to disappear from the mind of the playgoer as he sat there entranced.[19]

The 'contemplative spectator', 'compelling truth', the theatre that has seemingly 'disappeared': and it is through such a peep-box that we view, in our mind's eye, and usually even in the contemporary theatre, the drama of the pre-realistic period. As Anthony Barlow puts it, 'For a short while the audience can leave the realities of their physical existence and enter a surrogate world' (p. 142). This blending of reality and make-believe has become the norm for the modern theatregoer. Randolph and Quinault would mock a modern audience for mistaking fiction for reality with much less reason than an audience of their own times. We have now reached, in 'factional' drama, on film or television, a genre in which fiction can scarcely be distinguished from fact. Indeed, some 250 years after *Pasquin*, the Chilean film director, Raul Ruiz, has unconsciously, if rather labouredly, imitated Fielding's play in his *Of Great Events and Ordinary People* (1979). In this he simultaneously satirises the election process in Paris and 'exposes' documentary film-making.

We now see all drama written before *Caste* and *The Pillars of Society* – that is, all drama written more than about a hundred years ago – through a veil of realism (and we also tend to judge much drama of the past as if it were literature). In his Preface to *Thérèse Raquin* (1873), Zola did not exaggerate how necessary was the advent of realism for the health of the drama; but its near total take-over of the stage inevitably denied the theatre a vital part of its inheritance. Jonson's audiences for his induction plays, Randolph's for *The Muse's Looking-Glass*, Fielding's for *Pasquin*, Foote's for *The Diversions of the Morning*, and Planché's for *The Drama at Home*, could readily slip in and out of involvement with what was performed on-stage. At one moment disbelief could be suspended; at another, the audience could be made conscious it was in a theatre; and then it could again suspend disbelief. Breaking dramatic continuity in this way runs against the essential mode of realistic drama. That the English audience retained its ability to respond multiconsciously[20] was due to those forms of theatre that inherited the illegitimate tradition: music hall, variety, the radio half-hour comedy show, and its television successors.

2 The Music-Hall Tradition

Don't worry about laughter and jokes. There's always somebody who's going to tell you what's funny and how it's funny and why it's funny. Don't worry about that. If it's funny, it's funny, if it's not, it's not. Aristotle tried it and he failed miserably, and he was a pretty smart cat, you know that. Aristotle, Aristotle, poor old Aristotle. You know, there's a peculiar thing, they say that he died in Chalsis, Nubia. I disagree, I think he died – *of* – Chalsis Nubia.

(Shelley Berman)

Towards the end of his essay, 'The Possibility of a Poetic Drama', first published in *The Dial* in 1920, T. S. Eliot says:

> The Elizabethan drama was aimed at a public which wanted *entertainment* of a crude sort, but would *stand* a good deal of poetry; our problem should be to take a form of entertainment, and subject it to the process which would leave it a form of art. Perhaps the music-hall comedian is the best material.[1]

This chapter is not a history of the music hall, although a brief outline of its origin and nature will be given in order that its role might be better assessed. I have discussed the music-hall song elsewhere and so I refer here chiefly to music-hall acts, but my chief concerns are to show how music hall kept alive the tradition of multiconscious apprehension, and how its techniques have been used by English dramatists of the twentieth century.[2] The drama that has evolved in our time may only rarely be poetic, but it is lively and often percipient; much that is interesting about it stems from the music-hall tradition.

Entertainment of a music-hall kind – songs often with choruses, comic turns, clog dancing and the like – existed long before the music hall as an institution developed. In *Popular Appeal in English Drama to 1850* some account was given of the way that Tarlton engaged with his audiences, especially in theming, and how that tradition was still active in the 1630s when Kendal played at Bristol (pp. 37–40). Shakespeare's use of the clown was discussed and nineteenth- and twentieth-century acts were juxtaposed with 'turns' from plays by Shakespeare to suggest how the popular comic tradition had continued. It is just about possible to point to specific moments when that tradition was passed from one clown to another in Shakespeare's day, even though so much of that period is lost to us because not written down. Thus, Kelsaye, who acted The Vice in plays at Bungay, performed also before and after the plays – and was specifically paid for so doing. A little later we find Tarlton doing precisely the same thing: acting a role within a play, but also drumming up interest in what his company was to perform the following day through the presentation of a solo act, and then entertaining the audience after a play in a kind of one-man afterpiece. Randolph's *The Conceited Pedlar* (1627) may be a development of such after-acts.[3]

That Armin was Tarlton's 'adopted son' in the matter of clowning is well known from the account given in *Tarlton's Jests*. It is significant that the occasion that led to Armin's being adopted was a bout of theming between the two men. But it is possible to go a little further and show how Armin developed Tarlton's own technique and material for his acts.

One of the Jests quoted in *Popular Appeal in English Drama to 1850* was that of an incident at Worcester when an attempt was made by a member of the audience to put Tarlton to a non-plus (p. 39). The theme offered to Tarlton was:

> Me thinks it is a thing unfit,
> To see a gridiron turn the spit.

Tarlton was, technically, put down, but he sidestepped neatly:

> Me thinks it is a thing unfit,
> To see an ass have any wit.

Now in Armin's *Quips upon Questions* (1600) we find him using the same material and it is reasonable to conjecture that he is presenting a solo act on the same sort of occasion that Tarlton made his practice. The turns in Armin's book take the form of a question, a discussion in verse (sometimes quite lengthy), and a final quip. They could have been presented in plays – in those plays, for example, like Armin's *Two Maids of Moreclacke* which are singularly lacking in comic turns – or, more probably, they were material that formed a part of a solo act given to arouse interest in a company's performances on tour, or as afterpieces. The item, 'What's Unfit?' offers a sequence of seeming para-doxes, such as that it is unfit that summer should be cold. This is the final stanza:

> The bellows blows out fire, yet makes fire blaze.
> Blow in hot pottage and they will be cooled.
> When thy nails freeze, blow with thy breath apace
> And they will heat again, thou mayst be bold.
>   Things seeming unfit, fitteth to be done:
>   God gives, man uses, since the world begun.

This is followed by the quip – and this, it can be seen, adapts Tarlton's material from the gridiron jest:

> A wonder how, methinks it is unfit,
> To see an iron gridiron turn a spit.
> No, no, methinks that it is more unfit,
> To see a blockhead ass have any wit.[4]

In this way it is possible to show, reasonably convincingly, how material and acts were transmitted from before Shake-speare's time into the nineteenth century, right up to the time when recordings made up in some measure for the loss of the oral tradition. Reading between the lines in this manner it is possible to outline a tradition that takes in Kelsaye, Tarlton, Armin, and even Kendal: all were working the same vein of popular comedy.

Though particular acts obviously come and go, and material for such acts goes in out of fashion, there can be no doubt that the tradition to which Tarlton and Armin were such notable con-tributors continued directly into the age of the music hall. Looked at that way, it is not possible to say precisely when the music hall began. Looked at from a commercial point of view, however, it is appropriate to call the Canterbury the first London music hall and to see it as the progenitor of the vogue for 'the halls'. Certainly its founder, Charles Morton, was known as the 'Father of the Halls', in part because of the way he developed the halls and battled with licensing authorities. What was significant about that hall was that on 20 December 1854 for the first time a charge was made specifically for the entertainment offered. Up until then, entertainment in London might be provided with drink and food but only the drink and food were paid for. It is true that in the transitional period prior to Morton's innovation an entrance fee was charged and a voucher given in return. This voucher – or 'wet money' – could be changed for food and drink. Morton, however, made the essential break: the entertainment itself was sold and bought. But London was not first in the field. Holder's Hall in Birmingham, for example, had charged for entertainment eight years earlier; but it was the Canterbury, and the success of its management, that set the pattern.

Be that as it may, the entertainment offered was no different from what had been provided for years in many taverns in London and the big cities. Indeed, Morton's first star, Sam Cowell, came from Evans's Supper Rooms, his most famous song was 'Villikins and his Dinah', and by tracing back song and supper rooms it is easy to see how the tradition of entertainment came down into the music-hall period. Cowell got this song from Frederick Robson (famous for quick-change acting – getting people to laugh and cry almost simultaneously – and especially in this song 'Villikins');[5] Robson had sung the song at, among other places, the Grecian Saloon in the 1830s; this was next to a tavern known by almost everyone, if only indirectly, the Eagle, which is featured in 'Pop goes the weasel' – 'in and out the Eagle'. Now Evans's supper rooms carried not only the name of their proprietor (W. C. Evans), but the late owner's name – Evans's Supper Rooms – Late Joy's. Joy had been the manager in 1800 and he took over from Lowe who had converted a private house (formerly owned by Sir Kenelm Digby in the reign of Charles II) into a family hotel in 1773.[6] The supper rooms of Evans and Joy have other claims to fame. In the late 1930s The Players' Theatre occupied the building and kept the name 'Late Joys' (which most people imagine means 'Recent delights' – because The Players kept alive old-fashioned music hall). It also seems likely that Evans's Supper Rooms, together with the much less respectable Coal Hole in The Strand and the Cyder Cellars in Covent Garden (inaptly in Maiden Lane), formed the basis for the Cave of Harmony and the Back Kitchen in two of Thackeray's novels, *The Newcomes* (1853–5) and *Pendennis* (1848–50).

Tavern music halls go back at least into the eighteenth century and became increasingly popular in the early nineteenth century. The reason usually given is that people were more affluent (relatively speaking) as a result of the Industrial Revolution. In the 1830s entertainments were developed in beer halls and Mechanics' Institutes around Newcastle upon Tyne. In Birmingham there was a forerunner of the professional music hall at the George and Dragon public house as early as 1825, and the hit song, by a man called Roberts, was 'When Birmingham's a Seaside Town', referring to the concentration of canals near Quay Street. But in Birmingham the principal music hall was Holder's adjoining the New Rodney Inn in Coleshill Street. This hall was opened about 1842 and it foreshadows what happened in London pretty exactly. The hall Holder inherited measured only 30ft by 12ft and was equipped with a small platform and a piano. In 1846 the hall was enlarged to accommodate some six hundred people and an organ costing six hundred guineas was installed. Only eleven years later, so successful was the venture that a third hall was built capable of accommodating two thousand people.[7] These bare facts suggest the growth in popularity not only of this hall but music halls in general, for what happened in Birmingham happened in many cities throughout Britain.[8]

Before going on to say a little about the nature of music-hall entertainment, it might be useful to give some kind of indication of the number of *licensed* music halls in London in the Victorian period. A recent authority states that in 1868 there were thirty-eight 'large and small music halls in London'.[9] Much may depend on the meaning of 'small music halls', but the evidence provided by Diana Howard in *London Theatres and Music Halls 1850–1950* indicates that for the year 1868 there were 40 theatres; 54 music halls as separate buildings; 287 music halls.attached to taverns, beer houses etc.; thirteen 'halls' (often temperance music halls); three pleasure gardens; two concert rooms; one coffee tavern; one song and supper room; and one gallery at which German Reed's entertainments were performed. The 287 music halls attached to public houses were certainly music halls so far as the law was concerned; music-hall artists performed in them, and audiences paid to see them. The *approximate* numbers of theatres and music halls active in each decade of the latter half of the nineteenth century (drawn from Miss Howard's book) would seem to be: 1850–9: 469 (of which 82 were in existence prior to 1850; 13 of these had been established in the eighteenth century, and two in the seventeenth century),

1860–9:	595
1870–9:	441
1880–9:	389
1890–9:	266
1900–50:	191 (plus cinemas)
1950:	70 (plus cinemas)

In 1978 the entertainment guide *Time Out*, boasting of its wide coverage of what's on in London, claimed to cover 45 West End theatres, 35 fringe theatres, and 10 lunch-time theatres, a total of 90. It also reported what was showing at 50 West End cinemas, 105 local cinemas and 18 film clubs, a total of 173. The combined total is 263.

It should, perhaps, be noted that the population of Greater London in 1850 was 2,685,000; in 1901, 6,586,000; and in 1978, about 7,400,000.

Many reasons have been given for the decline of music hall. These have included changes in the Victorian moral climate; performers lazily passing off the same material; competition from musical comedies and films from just before the beginning of this century; and, in the 1920s, the development of radio entertainment. There is little doubt, however, that one reason for the decline in the number of music halls was much more mundane. Under the Metropolis Management and Building Acts Amendment Act of 1878 theatres had to have 'a certificate of suitability' and many small music halls did not meet the fire regulations. A count through Diana Howard's book suggests that as a direct result of that act over sixty halls closed down almost immediately and at least thirty others withdrew applications, had their licences refused, or made no application. Just as illegitimate drama was the unwitting and fortuitous result of one act – Walpole's Licensing Act of 1737 – so another act had the unintentional result of hastening the end of the music hall. Music hall would doubtless have gone the way it did, but perhaps not so disastrously nor so rapidly. Perhaps it should also be borne in mind that the act of of 1878 coincided with the foundation of the Salvation Army.

The staple fare of the entertainment in the taverns and early music halls was made up of songs of various kinds. 'Villikins' was notable for combining pathos and absurd comedy. Nowadays the song is usually guyed, but performed by Frederick Robson it could elicit tears and laughter from an audience almost simultaneously. Robson's technique (much admired by Sir Henry Irving) was named after him. It was applied with particular effect to such moments as when Villikins, a rich merchant who is attempting to make his daughter, Dinah, marry against her will, is walking in his 'garding' – and, as the spoken 'aside' explains, 'It was the back "garding" this time':

> [*Sung*]: He spied his dear Dinah lying dead on the ground
> With a cup of cold pizen all down by her side,
> And a billy-doo which said as 'ow 'twas by pizen she died.
> [*Aside spoken*]: The label was marked, 'British Brandy'.

Robson could extract almost instant pathos out of even the triviality of such a verse, and then raise a gale of laughter from the 'aside'. Here the 'aside' is spoken 'aside from the song', the singer presenting himself as commentator on his own song. What one has in this simple-seeming example is a quite complex use of dramatic illusion and rapid emotional shift. It demands much of performer and audience, but undoubtedly it can work. The problem for the performer is that he must at once get his audience back into the mood for pathos after the laugh. 'Villikins' is typical of those songs or acts which demand of the performer (such as Robson and Cowell) a capacity for controlling the immediate responses of the audience, and that ability has always been required of the music-hall performer to a marked degree. Further aspects of this technique are discussed below.[10]

Another favourite song of the Cyder Cellars and the Supper Rooms was 'Sam Hall'. It is probably to this song that objections are raised in Thackeray's *The Newcomes*: 'If there are any Caves of Harmony now, I warrant Messieurs the landlords, their interests would be better consulted by keeping their singers within bounds' (ch.l). There is little now that would be found objectionable, although in 1928 Chance Newton felt constrained to omit 'Damn' and 'Blast' from the refrain, printing, '—— their eyes'. Like 'Villikins' it can be traced back long before the establishment of the fully commercial music hall, originating, according to David Masson,[11] in a ballad about the pirate Captain Kidd, hanged 23 May 1701.

Although 'Sam Hall' has been sung on the radio in this decade without leading to protests, there is no doubt that much of what was sung in Cellars and Coal Holes would not be acceptable to the BBC, or even perhaps in northern clubs, nowadays. Songsters of the period, such as *The Coal Hole Companion*, *The Cyder Cellar Songster*, *Nancy Dawson's Cabinet of Choice Songs*, and *Fanny Hill's Bang-Up Reciter* are explicit without being witty. Henry Spencer Ashbee, writing under the pseudonym *Pisanus Fraxi* in 1877, said:

> the death blow to these jovial, smutty ditties was struck when the doors of the Canterbury and Weston's Music Halls were opened to women; the entertainment had then to be modified, and suited to female ears; vice was not checked, but its aspects changed; and instead of being places of resort where men could indulge in coarse and bawdy songs, the music halls became meeting-places for prostitutes.
>
> A certain force and rough humour pervade all these effusions, but they are always coarse and lewd, and many are written in a slang which is now obsolete.[12]

By no means all the pre-music-hall songs were like this and a cheerful, innocent example, which suggests also the kind of spoken act that was to play a large part in the music halls, is 'The Steam Packet', published in 1820. This gives an account of a day-trip to Margate before the railways had opened up the south-coast resorts.

> The wind gets up, the waters swell,
> The steward's man comes with his bell;
> Whilst 'Steady! Steady!' quick does chime,
> Announces that 'tis dinner time.
>
> One by one we slowly go,
> To the cabin down below,

When seated, eating sweet delights,
Soon settles all our appetites,

[*Spoken*] Well, this mutton is fine; Southdown I suppose –
mouthdown; O yes sir, 'tis certainly down in the mouth – my
dear, don't you eat too much of the turnips, perhaps you'll be
sick – fie papa, you might say unwell – but I think I could eat a
bushel – very strange I have such an appetite, 'tis the sea air I
suppose – sea *hare*, ma'am, I don't think there is such an animal
. . . *and so on. And on.*[13]

But Ashbee was absolutely right in so far as Morton's
Canterbury was to change the tone of the halls. Just as the
theatres performing 'straight' plays were becoming more
ordered and more middle-class in ambience (which is not to say
that the audience was made up of only the middle class, for the
gallery alone would prove otherwise), so the halls 'became more
respectable'. In the early days a chairman was always present to
try to keep some kind of order, and although music halls with or
without chairmen could be rowdy, and poor acts could get a
roasting (as could even Marie Lloyd), Morton worked hard to
develop a family entertainment. By the end of the nineteenth
century, the lavish music halls looked not dissimilar from the
'regular' theatres, a world away from their tavern origins.
Nevertheless, the songs and acts were identical in theatrical
terms, though their content had been much modified, despite
frequent complaints of 'ceruleanism', or 'blue', risqué, jokes.
Paradoxically, as Ashbee noted, some halls did attract prostitutes –
however a full history of the halls in their social context is beyond
the scope of this chapter.[14]

Although songs were important throughout the history of the
music hall, as the 'patter' of 'The Steam Packet' indicates, a kind
of comic monologue made its appearance long before the halls
were established. This developed very considerably so that an
act, by Dan Leno or Little Tich, for example, late in the
nineteenth century, might be mainly monologue but introduced
and concluded by all or part of a song. So much was this the rule
that in 1892, when F. Anstey produced *Mr. Punch's Model Music-
Hall Songs & Dramas*, he could give an example of song-and-
patter act rather condescendingly headed 'The Frankly Canaille',
which describes the 'little spoken interlude' as customary. There
are seven stanzas with choruses and synopses of seven

'interludes'. The whole parody is worth repeating (especially the description of the tea) but the first verse, interlude and chorus will suffice to show how well established was this routine by 1892.

The Poor Old 'Orse

We 'ad a little outing larst Sunday arternoon;
And sech a jolly lark it was, I shan't forget it soon!
We borrered an excursion van to take us down to Kew,
And – oh, we did enjoy ourselves! I don't mind telling *you*.

This to the Chef d'Orchestre, who will assume a polite interest. Here a little spoken interlude is customary. Mr P. does not venture to do more than indicate this by a synopsis, the details can be filled in according to the taste and fancy of the fair artiste: – 'Yes, we did 'ave a time, I can assure yer.' The party: Me and Jimmy 'Opkins; old 'Pa Plapper' – asked because he lent the van. The meanness of his subsequent conduct. 'Aunt Snapper'; her imposing appearance in her 'Cawfy-coloured front.' Bill Blazer; his 'girl' and his accordion. Mrs Addick (of the fried-fish emporium round the corner); her gentility – 'Never seen out of her mittens, and always the lady, no matter how much she may have taken'. From this work round by an easy transition to –

The Chorus – For we 'ad to stop o' course,
                  Jest to bait the blooming 'orse,
                  so we'd pots of ale and porter
                  (Or a drop o' something shorter),
                  While he drunk his pail o' water,
                  He was sech a whale on water!
                  That more water than he oughter,
                  More water than he oughter,
                      'Ad the poor old 'orse![15]

In the 1930s and the 1940s Max Miller was still involving the conductor of the orchestra in the same manner, and Frankie Howerd had exchanges with the conductor, Billy Ternent, that developed into a feature of his act. In effect, a 'hidden' part of the theatrical event (like the camera in a television show) was made apparent, something which would not be done in a 'straight' play in the days when a small orchestra would 'accompany' the performance (but compare the reference to the accompaniment

to the Pages' song, 'It was a lover and his lass', *As You Like It*,
v.iii.36–40).

Max Miller would claim to have written the songs he sang, or
that he had had them written by a relative. He would explain,
ingenuously, that he was singing them at the request of his
recording company, or his mother. He would often announce an
outrageous title and then sing something totally different, or
reverse that procedure. This is from an act recorded at Holborn
Empire during the 1939–45 War. As in all the Max Miller
examples reproduced in this chapter, (L) indicates, however
inadequately, laughter. It should be stressed that the audiences
were made up of regular attenders at the music halls where the
recordings were made, not special 'studio audiences'. 'Sydney' is
the conductor of the orchestra:

I'll make another change in the programme tonight, ladies an'
gentlemen, I'm goin' to sing another brand new number, a
little number entitled, er, 'Just because I roll my eyes'. 'Just
because I roll my eyes' (L). Dedicated to me, lady, because I
wrote it myself (L). An', an' you've been very nice tonight, an'
that's why I'm going to sing it for you. After which I shall
definitely dance, after this number (L). You never know when
I'm kiddin' do you? Now, shall I start it off Sydney? [*guitar
arpeggio*] Shall I? An' will you creep in?

Sydney: Certainly.
Miller: Will you (L).
Sydney: Yes.
Miller: I'll give you the key, see (L). Look, I'll tell you what
I'll do tonight, Sydney, I'll do two choruses of
'Rambling Rose' with the boys, and then I'll do
'Sally' by meself (L) (L). [*Arpeggio*] Naow, shuddup,
whadsamadder with yer?
[*Sings*]: A girl stopped me in Leicester Square,
wearing a little green hat,
All because I roll my eyes – I'll have to break meself
of that.

It is this kind of act that John Osborne recaptures in *The Entertainer*:

And now I'm going to sing you a little song, a little song, a little song written by the wife's sister, a little song entitled 'The Old Church bell won't ring tonight, as the Verger's dropped a clanger!' Thank you, Charlie!

And he sings, 'We're all out for good old number one'.[16]

The music-hall act, even more than farce, depends upon the performer. The act as written means little. Baudelaire in 'On the Essence of Laughter' (1855), described a performance by an English pantomime troupe in Paris. This involved a clown being guillotined and then stealing his own head and running off with it – a scene not out of place in such an expressionist play as Hasenclever's *Humanity* (1918). Baudelaire then concludes:

> Set down in pen and ink, all this is pale and chilly. But how could the pen rival pantomime? The pantomime is the refinement, the quintessence of comedy; it is the pure comic element, purged and concentrated. Therefore, with the English actors' special talent for hyperbole, all these monstrous buffooneries took on a strangely thrilling reality.[17]

A good enough example of how little of an act's effect may be interpreted from the text alone can be gathered from Arthur Roberts's description of an impromptu encore to a duet called 'Not a Word' which he gave with Teddy Payne in 1893. This was a dialogue made up as they went along and, having quoted the dialogue they improvised, Roberts describes the effect so:

> There may not sound anything particularly humorous about the . . . dialogue, but the fact remains that it went so amazingly well with the audience that it was kept in ever afterwards, never failing to prove one of the big hits of the evening.

And this is the dialogue that proved so amazingly effective that it proved a big hit:

Roberts: Oh! they say the British lion!
Payne: Not a word! Not a word!
Roberts: Oh! they say the British lion!
Payne: Not a word! Not a word!
Roberts: Oh! they say the British lion, yes, they say the

British lion! Oh! they say the British lion!
Both: Not a word![18]

It is for this reason that I have, so far as practicable, selected for comment examples from acts recorded before genuine audiences even though, as in this instance (Max Miller at Holborn Empire) it is very difficult to 'see' what is the source of the laughter:

We started to walk across the desert (*titter from audience*). Naow, turn it up – what's the matter with you? (*Laughter*). Naow – well (*More laughter*). Naow, when a chap's talking (*Miller's own fruity chuckle followed by audience laughter*). No, true (*Audience laughs*). Well (*Laughter*). Gid aht of it, what's the matter with you? (*Laughter – Miller chuckles – Audience laughs*). We started to walk across the desert . . .

Frankie Howerd once discussed how apparent spontaneity was achieved:

What one tries to do is to arrange the script in the first place so that it has the appearance of spontaneity about it. A patter act is usually written so that the lines sometimes don't finish, that they're left in mid-air. Most people talk in short spasms and they interrupt each other like you going 'Um' now to me halfway through a sentence. In a patter act you try to leave pauses as though you're talking to somebody and they're saying 'Um', 'Ooouah', and making all these things in between, and one's answering them. One of the great exponents of this was Norman Evans, the northern comedian, who did a very famous thing called *Over the Garden Wall*. 'Did she really? What? With the coalman? Ooh, I think it's . . . Ooh, when? . . .' I get an awful lot of amateur writers sending me scripts which very often consist of going 'Ooh, no, not on your nelly, ah, fearless Francis!' with no content at all, just a lot of surface expressions. But I go very much on jokes or lines, and I put in the surface spontaneity of going 'Well it depends how you . . . well . . . oh . . . ooouah.' What I want is the meat, some funny lines.[19]

It will be very apparent how different is this technique from that of the 'smoothed realism' of the 1930s and 1940s *théâtre de boulevard* drama. In such seemingly realistic dialogue the Ums and Aahs and the *non sequiturs* are excised. Harold Pinter uses just these inconsequential elements of speech dramatically (see the discussion of *Last to Go*, below, pp. 60–4).

Spontaneity is, therefore, carefully considered and what might seem like *ad lib* is often very carefully positioned and rehearsed. When Max Miller asks a lady how her memory is (see below), it may *seem* like an *ad lib*, but may well be carefully placed to help build up the performer's relationship with the audience, to prompt laughter, or to play its part in 'controlling' the audience. Some comedians can and do *ad lib* well (Tommy Trinder did), but others are not so gifted and *ad lib* action can, in fact, lead to trouble. There is a good, and therefore oft-repeated, story about Marie Lloyd that illustrates this. She was appearing as Red Riding Hood in a Drury Lane pantomime in 1892–3, with Dan Leno, Herbert Campbell and Little Tich. When Marie Lloyd was ostensibly saying her prayers, in her nightie, by her bed, one of these three (said to be Leno, but more probably one of the others) called from the wings, 'Look under the bed, Marie'. Marie was 'on' at once.

> She looked under the bed and the audience roared. She did not leave it at that. Having got her 'laugh' she wandered all round the stage looking for an article which, in those days at least, was usually found in a most inconspicuous place – under the bed. The gag was an enormous success with everybody but the management. There was an inquest and Gus Harris was furious. Never before had such indecency been seen at Drury Lane, well, not since the days of the Restoration comedies, anyway. . . . It was touch and go whether Marie was sacked or not. She survived but never did the gag again.[20]

Henry Irving's theatre manager, Bram Stoker, said:

> I can understand the basic wisdom of George Frederick Cook when on the Liverpool stage he stopped in the middle of a tragic part and coming down to the footlights said to the audience: 'Ladies and gentlemen, if you don't applaud I can't act.'[21]

Every theatrical event demands an audience, that goes without saying, but in the music hall, the relationship 'across the foot-lights' is so direct that absence of response kills an act and eager response makes one.[22] J. S. Bratton has shown how comic songs belonged to the audience as much as the performer,[23] and the way the involvement of the audience is engineered can be seen from the stage directions in *Sleeping Beauty and the Beast*, a Drury Lane pantomime of the 1900–1 season, starring Dan Leno and Herbert Campbell. The scene is a lesson in arithmetic (a subject that figures in many music-hall acts) and the King (Herbert Campbell) is demonstrating his prowess with the help of the Queen (Dan Leno) at the blackboard.

Queen: Give me the chalk [*takes chalk and goes to blackboard*]. Now then!

King: Will any gentleman kindly give me a number?
[*This scene should be played very rapidly – King shouting real or imaginary numbers that audience give him, and Queen writing furiously on blackboard. When board is full of figures –*]

Queen: His Majesty will now give the figures on the board categorically and in rotation.
[*King reels off figures rapidly, all very apparently wrong, while Queen points to them on board; at the end they bow*]

Queen: While I am adding up this little sum his Majesty will tell you the day of the week any given date fell upon during the last seventeen thousand years.

King: [*To audience*]. Will any gentleman give me a date?
[*This scene should also be very rapid. King keeps saying 'Tuesday' 'Saturday', etc. etc., to real or imaginary dates given him, and often before they are given him. While he is doing this, Queen is adding up sum anyhow. When she has finished –*]

Queen: Ready! [*She has chalk in one hand and the duster in the other*]. His Majesty will now give the correct answer [*King reels off a lot of figures*]. Quite right! [*Immediately wipes out all figures with duster*].[24]

It is significant that early recordings should have sometimes endeavoured to create a sense of audience – just as do contemporary television producers who apply the cheers of 40,000–50,000 spectators to a football match watched by what is obviously a handful of perished spectators. Thus, Burt Sheppard recorded a little sketch in 1899 in which he purported to be a prospective Member of Parliament. As he announced each item of his platform there were cheers, followed by a voice calling out 'Louder'. This is the act:

> . . . I am not going to make a lengthy speech. (*Cheers*) When I
> get into Parliament – there'll be plenty of work for everyone –
> (*Cheers*) –   'Louder' –
> Short hours and double wages –
> Your clothes will cost you nothing –
> Ham will sell at 4 pence a pound –   'Louder' –
> Flour and bread will be distributed free of charge –   'Louder' –
> And in conclusion I would say, that in the last great day, when
> graves will open and thunder rolls, and the Angel Gabriel with
> one foot on dry land and one foot in the sea   'Louder' –
> Shall with his golden trumpet proclaim that the time shall be
> no more   'Louder' –
> There'll be some damn fool who'll holler –   'Louder' –
> Thank you sir! (*Laughter*)

And the band played 'God Save the Queen'

One of the problems the music-hall performer faced was controlling his audience. Although the rowdy audiences seem to have lasted longer in the music halls than in the theatres where 'straight' drama was performed, the music-hall performer had certain advantages over the legitimate actor. It did on occasion happen in the legitimate theatre that an actor had to plead with an audience for a hearing, but that inevitably broke the dramatic continuity. In the halls there was a chairman in the early years, but in any case the performer could 'naturally' address his audience; he was already doing so. The music hall did not adopt the fully-darkened auditorium as quickly as the theatres presenting realistic drama. As late as 1948 I recall the houselights being raised and members of the audience being invited by the comedian (Tommy Trinder, I think) to 'inspect' one another. Setting one part of an audience to sing in competition with another – pit versus gallery, or right versus left, or men versus women – is practised to this day, especially in pantomimes. Thus, consciousness of being in a theatre, 'at a show', lived on in the music halls much longer than in *théâtres de boulevard*, but, just as in the eighteenth-century theatre, involvement in the act and awareness of the surroundings could go hand in hand. What developed, as audiences became better behaved, was the use of control to raise laughter. George Robey was particularly adept at this, raising his prominent eyebrows, looking direct at the offenders, and sternly commanding: 'Desist!' A. E. Wilson has described the technique:

> A hoarse laugh rings out in the audience. [Robey] directs a stony glare upon the interrupter. Really! I meantersay! Such heartiness is out of place; it is unfitting in such an environment. So might some clerical dignitary regard brawling in a cathedral. He is surprised and hurt at such unwonted behaviour. It is not to be tolerated. Whatever next? All this is expressed in the raising of eyebrows, in that minatory, reproachful glance, and the raising of a hand: 'Desist!', he commands. [25]

And the theatre would be convulsed in laughter and firmly in the palm of George Robey's hand.

One of the devices for gaining audience sympathy is by the presentation of one of a duo or trio as witless. Thus, in *Happidrome*, a BBC radio show that was quite popular for a while during the Second World War, one 'character', Enoch, who had a catch-phrase, 'Let me tell you', spoken rather slowly in a Yorkshire accent, was set up as the fool:

Lovejoy:	. . . Come here, gormless
Enoch:	Let me tell you, I live by my wits.
Lovejoy:	Well, poverty's no disgrace.

Here incongruity (the fool living by his wits) and sympathy with the speaker of a favourite catch-phrase are combined. Invariably (as with Laurel and Hardy or Abbot and Costello) the 'gormless one' can turn the tables. Enoch's girl has just run off with another man:

Enoch:	It's no joke to be thwaaarted.
Lovejoy:	Thwaaarted? Nay you mean thworted.
Enoch:	No, thwaaarted. Me mother says its thwaaaarted, so it must be thwaaaarted.

> *Lovejoy:*   No, no. When you were a little lad, what did you
>   have on the back of your hand?
> *Enoch:*   Mook.
> *Lovejoy:*   No, no, you had worts.
> *Enoch:*   No, they're waaarts. Me mother says they're
>   waaarts, so they must be waaarts.
> *Lovejoy:*   Now listen autumn crocus, if you went into a dairy
>   for some milk, you wouldn't ask for a quaaart,
>   would you?
> *Enoch:*   No.
> *Lovejoy:*   Then what would you ask for?
> *Enoch:*   Two pints.

Dialect differences (and here they are slight enough) have been a source of comedy since at least the time that Mak adopted 'a southern tongue' in the *First* and *Second Shepherds' Plays* (see *Popular Appeal in English Drama to 1850*, pp. 12–13).

Some music-hall comedians made a feature of establishing direct contact with their audiences at once and 'in their own (public) person'. They would then present an act in which reference would be made to mythical mothers, brothers, girl friends and, inevitably, mothers-in-law. Tommy Trinder began his act regularly in the manner of this performance recorded at Peterborough during the war:

> Ladies and Gentlemen, the name is 'Trinder' – T-R-I-N-D-E-R, pronounced 'Chumley' – and I'm going to sing to yer – [*laughs*] you (*audience choruses:*) lucky people. Would all the orchestra please stand up a minute, I've lost a pair of trousers out of my room (L).

The fact that an audience could, in the first moment of an act, join in with the catch phrase 'You lucky people' is indicative of how readily taken up was the device. Trinder repeated the name-gag a little later, just before telling a joke about his 'brother', and did so in a way that seemed to make contact with an individual member of the audience. He told how a Home Guard challenged him with the customary, 'Who goes there?'. Trinder then broke the continuity of the story, reverting to his own persona:

> Don't look in the programme sir, the name's Trinder (L).

Gentleman doesn't believe I'm Tommy Trinder. If I'm not Tommy Trinder, I'm having a hell of a time with his wife (L).

The act included a song.

Perhaps no one was better than Max Miller in getting on terms with his audience. He broke off singing a song at the Metropolitan with: 'Oo! (L) There's a lady got opera glasses on me (L). She thinks I'm a race 'orse (L).' The script as such has little in it to raise laughs, but Miller readily succeeds in doing so. This act began with a song, introduced almost abruptly and followed up by his technique of 'preparing' his audience. He then told a story, insisting by repetition on its funniness – skilfully prompting laughter from his audience. He also interjected 'asides' to the audience, almost (but never quite) insulting, in the manner practised by Bruce Forsyth.

Thank you very much ladies an' gentlemen, thank you very much. So off we go, with the first song, a little song entitled, 'Last night I was in the mood, tonight I must get some sleep' (L).

He then sang 'Passing the Time Away', about young couples in the park. At a performance at Finsbury Park Empire, Max Miller introduced the song as, 'We've had a lot of fun, no harm done, and thanks for the memory'. Note the use of repetition.

I know exactly, I know exactly what y'r saying to yerselves. Y'r wrong (L). I know what y'r saying (L). Oh you, you wicked lot (L). You're the kind of people that get me a bad name (L). Here's a funny thing, now this is a funny thing. I went home the other night – there's a funny thing (L) and I went in the back way, through the kitchen, through the dining room, into the drawing room, an' there's a feller standin' there, not a stitch on (L). Can you imagine that, lady? (L). How's your memory, girl? (L). 'E 'adn't got a stitch on. I called the wife in. I said, 'Who's this?' She said, 'Don't lose your temper Miller, don't go ravin' mad.' I said, 'I'm only asking a fair question, who is it?' She said, 'He's a nudist, an' he's come 'ere to use the phone.' There's a clever one from the wife, eh? (L) (L). So tonight, I'm goin' to do for you something entirely different. I'm going to do a monologue, a monologue tonight, entitled, 'What Juju wants, Juju must have' (L). I don' know what it is, an' I'm really not bothered (L).[26]

Needless to say, there was nothing entirely different about Max Miller performing a monologue and nothing novel about the one he chose. It was all part of his technique for preparing his audience, getting them ready for laughter.

Miller was adept at combining his own flamboyant self (he was always exceptionally colourfully dressed) with the persona he adopted for whatever story he was telling. At Holborn Empire he created a very effective mental image of the desert in the minds of the members of his audience, despite frequently breaking the continuity of his story.

I went to Africa, the North of Africa, where the camels are. I stayed on the desert five weeks, five weeks on the desert. I'm a real sheik. I'd go in anybody's tent tonight (L). You put a tent up lady and try me (L). I'd go in, I'm no trouble (L). I carry me own fan. Here, Ooo (L). Lissen, d'you know the first thing I saw in the desert? A mummy. I think she was looking for a daddy (L). She came straight up to me an' she said, 'Pharaoh my Pharaoh'. I said, 'I'm not yer Pharaoh.' She said, 'Who are you?' I said, 'I'm Mrs Miller's youngest son an' I've come here for peace an' quietness.' She looked at me. She kept lookin' into my eyes (L). What was she after? Me lashes? (L). Naow, naow, 'cos I've got big eyes, haven't I? Look (L). Naow, naow. I 'ave got big eyes. Look (L). That's me mother's fault, lookin' all over England for me father. Here (L) (L). Lissen, lissen, she looked into my eyes an' she said . . .

The first thing to notice here is the way that Max Miller controls his audience – not in terms of keeping them in order, but in ensuring they laugh just where he wants them to. The 'Here' after 'fan' and the use of 'Look' draw the laughs from all the audience at once. Then, to direct the audience's attention to his next story, he will repeat (sometimes three or more times) 'Listen'.

The second thing to notice is the way in which members of an audience can 'see' Miller as a comedian, a man in the flesh before

their very eyes, as it were, and simultaneously in whatever role
he is describing to them in the stories he tells, however fanciful
they are. He needs no set and no props; he wears a costume
totally inappropriate to the desert. Furthermore, he and his
audience can readily switch back and forth, in and out of the
story. It is this plunge back after the momentary suspension of
disbelief, this reinvolvement in the story, that makes it so
difficult to work the Brechtian alienation technique with an
audience accustomed to this tradition (and since then, inured to
television commercial breaks, perhaps). In the extracts from
Frankie Howerd's 'Common Market' act (pp. 43–4) and Max
Miller's 'Swimming Instructor' act (pp. 41–2), the performers
lose their places (Miller making a *double entendre* of it). In
'straight' drama this would be embarrassing and call for an in-
trusive prompt; but not so with Howerd and Miller. The audience is immediately gathered back into the act. Two parallels
might prove illuminating.

George Robey, in his autobiography *Looking Back on Life*,
recalls the 'ludicrous irrelevance' of the backcloths in front of
which music-hall singers performed. 'Picture me,' he says,
'singing such lines as:

> You can tell her by the pimple,
> The pimple on her nose!

in front of a cloth that depicted Melrose Abbey by moonlight!'
After giving several more examples, he comments:

> These back-cloths were part of the queerness of the halls in
> those early 'nineties, and I can't think why we tolerated them
> so long. In the [legitimate] theatres such anomalies wouldn't
> have been tolerated for ten minutes. Can you imagine Henry
> Irving asking 'Is that a dagger that I see before me?' in front of a
> cloth representing the Epsom racecourse on Derby Day? Or
> Ellen Terry, as Ophelia, going mad in front of a painting of the
> beach at Margate?[27]

That such anomalies were tolerated may be no more than a
product of insensitivity or artistic unconcern on the part of
performer, producer and audience. Nevertheless, once expe-
diency, thoughtlessness and insensitivity had permitted such

ludicrous irrelevance, it is clear that, for the most part, audience and performer were able to dissociate what was irrelevant to that act from what was relevant.

Film editing uses a technique which may well have developed from the capacity of music-hall audiences to respond to breaks in the continuity of a story. From very early in the history of the silent film, editors would cut between two actions going on simultaneously, but far apart. D. W. Griffith has been incorrectly credited with the innovation, but it has been traced back much earlier by Barry Salt. He quotes two examples from 1906. In one there is cross-cutting between an aerial rescue and what is happening on the ground (*Rescued in Mid-Air*, Arthur Melbourne-Cooper); in the other, there are 'repeated cuts between a speeding car and events at its destination' (*The Hundred-To-One-Shot*, Vitograph).[28] I would suggest that an audience's capacity to respond simultaneously to what in effect are two events (related though they are) stems from the music-hall audiences' ability to respond simultaneously to two or more planes of reference, emotions, or events.

Although it can be argued that all drama, legitimate and illegitimate, can demand a multiconscious response – what might simply be termed 'theatricality' or 'self-conscious drama-turgy' – it does seem to me that, *after* the legal distinction between legitimate and illegitimate was abolished, a distinction can be drawn between a drama that involves total suspension of disbelief and one in which continuity can frequently be broken whilst the act retains its integrity.[29]

The catch-phrase, such as Trinder's 'You lucky people', or Enoch's 'Let me tell you', is the outstanding example of a few words which often, in themselves, are irrelevant (as those quoted by Hamlet in the Bad Quarto) but which are invested with special significance by performer *and audience*. Successful catch-phrases come to have a life of their own outside the theatre – so much so that their repeated use on-stage itself becomes an intrusion into the theatre world. The catch-phrases of *ITMA*, for example, could not have been injected into a 'straight' play of the period without breaking the dramatic illusion. As W. S. Gilbert puts it (in the mouth of the sad jester Point) "Tis ever thus with simple folk – an accepted wit has but to say, "pass the mustard", and they roar their ribs out.'[30]

Some catch-phrases have been evolved by accident. Sandy

Powell's 'Can you hear me, mother?' first occurred when he dropped his script during a radio broadcast:

> . . . while picking up the pages he kept things going by ad-libbing; anything that came into his head. During this he repeated the phrase 'Can you Hear Me Mother?' many times not thinking of it as a particularly funny line, but an appropriate one while he gathered the pages together. Having got over that little spot of bother, they carried on normally, and the matter was soon forgotten. . . .

A few days later, the manager of Coventry Hippodrome complimented Sandy Powell on his new catch-phrase, and, once the surprised comedian had identified it, he made it part of his act.[31]

The catch-phrases of *ITMA* were much more deliberately planned. They served, in part, to identify the large number of characters who came and went. One of the most famous was Mrs Mopp's 'Can I do yer now, sir?' (which began as 'Can I do for you now, sir?'[32]). It so happens that there are publicly available recordings of a very early (1941–2) and a much later (13 January 1944) use of this catch-phrase. In the first recording the studio audience does not respond at all; in the second the applause (admittedly by a very responsive naval audience at Scapa Flow), is overwhelming. First, Handley as Mayor of Foaming-in-the-Mouth, is arranging a theatre show:

Signor So-So:	Mr Handley, Mr Handley. Everyone is coming to the Handleydrome tonight. The theatre will be filled to calamity.
Handley:	Calamity! (L) You mean capacity.
So-So:	Every seat is sold twicely.
Handley:	Nightly twicely? Well that will do me nicely (L).
So-So:	Yes, even the boxes will be crumbed.
Handley:	Crumbed? I won't have anybody eating sponge cakes in my theatre.
So-So:	Yes, in all the shops I have hung up great big blackguards.
Handley:	Ha, Ha, Ha (L). Well it's time some of them were hung up. I can name three for a start. Oh, you mean placards, do you?

So-So:	Yes, blackguards.
Handley:	I see.
So-So:	In every way I have stuck up boosters.
Handley:	Boosters! (L)
So-So:	Come to the Handleydrome [*singing*]
Handley:	. . . [*joining in*] Come to the Show! Chase me down the mountain side, eeeny-miney-mo. Well listen (LL). We should have a big bumper house, So-So (LL)
Mrs Mopp:	Can I do yer now sir? (*No reaction from audience*)
Handley:	Go away Mrs Mopp, can't you see I'm dressing.

Then in 1944, Handley with the Navy:

Handley:	Here's the orders for the day. 5.0 am, Show a leg, don't like the look of it, put it back again (LL). 10 o'clock, cup of tea served to self and wife in twin hammocks (LL). 10.5 wake up (L). 11.00 am, censor captain's letters (LL). Copy out all the new words (L). 12 noon, manicure big toe with anchor. (L). 1.5, cast off from buoy and tie up to girl (LL).
Mrs Mopp:	Can I do yer now sir? (*12 secs laughter and applause, interrupted by:*)
Handley:	Well, if it isn't Mrs Mopp, the mascot of the marines . . .

Elkan and Dorotheen Allan make an interesting point about the *social* significance of the radio catch-phrase. The examples given all come from *ITMA*.

The essential requirement of a catch-phrase is that it should slip naturally into ordinary conversation. Embarrassment disappears from many awkward social problems if one can be employed. Bowing a friend through a gate seemed to be eased by the use of 'After you, Claude'. Many a bearer of awkward news has been helped over the start of his story by 'Gee, boss, something terrible's happened.' A resentful, 'Hey, don't forget me', sounds petty and slightly childish, but 'Don't forget the diver' was apparently accepted. But catch-phrases age quickly. There would not be much of a smile today awaiting a wit who remarked, 'Well, for ever more', or, 'It's me noives.' They, together with the rest of the *ITMA* originals, have a quaint, period flavour.[33]

Some characteristics of cross-talk acts are shared with clown acts of the Shakespearian period. There is much use of the device of 'mistaking the word' in the golf lesson which Jerry Desmond gave with the great Midlands comedian, Sid Field.

Desmond:	. . . Now make the tee.
Field:	Make the what?
Desmond:	Make the tee.
Field:	I thought you were goin' to play golf?
Desmond:	So we are.
Field:	Well what's it all about making the tea for then?
Desmond:	No, make the tee with sand.
Field:	Uh? Well I'm not drinkin' that stuff.
Desmond:	What stuff?
Field:	Tea with sand,? Don't be foolhardy. Tea with sand – more like cocoa.
Desmond:	Yes yes, very very comical. Come on. Take your stance.
Field:	Take my what?
Desmond:	Take your stance.
Field:	Ah, you've got me there. Which is that one out of these [*pointing to golf clubs*]?
Desmond:	Oh for heavens sake, get a stick in yer haaaaaand.

There was much more to the act than this kind of humour (and this short extract has two catch-phrases which would now need to be pointed out, 'What's it all about?' and 'Don't be foolhardy'). The climax (curiously not even included on the recording[34]) was a moment on a par with Falstaff's explanation as to why he ran away (see II.iv.299 ff., and see *Popular Appeal in English Drama to 1850*, pp. 63–4). It was, for all who saw it, one of the supreme comic moments of theatre, and, as with Falstaff's in *I Henry IV*, always a surprise, always funny. After many preliminaries Jerry Desmond would finally tell Sid Field to address the ball. A look of incredulity would slowly fill his countenance and then, unhurriedly and deliberately, as if humouring a madman, he

would get down on his knees, put his face close to the ball on its
tee, and say, as the audience held its breath, 'Dear ball!' As
Baudelaire said a hundred years or so earlier, 'Set down in pen
and ink, all this is pale and chilly . . .'.[35]

Mistaking the word developed in an interesting way in the
1930s. In 1934, Jeanne de Casalis appeared at the Alhambra in
London in a revue sketch in which she had trouble conversing by
telephone. This was developed into a solo variety sketch which
became very popular and which was ideal for radio. In the part of
Mrs Feather she would get the words right but mistake the
intent. Thus, a young man comes to the door and she assumes he
has come to mend the roof.[36] But she is mistaken; his name is
Hoover – so naturally she thinks he has come to mend the
vacuum cleaner. This also is erroneous:

> But the man said he wasn't Hoover – at least he *was* Hoover,
> but not the Hoover Hoover.
>   'Whose Hoover are you then?' I asked.
>   'I belong to the *Evening Post*,' he replied, 'and I've come
> about the fire!'
>   'You're too late,' I said, 'they've put it out.'
> It then transpired that what he really wanted was for me to give
> him a story for his paper.   (p. 19)

Harry Worth has adapted this as a situation-comedy routine for
radio and television. In this extract, Worth persuades a very
unwilling bus conductor to help him carry all his impedimenta,
including a deck-chair, from the bus-stop to a shop outside
which he intends to keep vigil all night. In this way he will be first
in the queue for a sale that begins in the morning.

Worth:	Just a minute. I wonder if you could help me?
Conductor:	[*warily*] What do you want now?
Worth:	I always have difficulty putting the deck-chair up. Perhaps you'd give me a hand.
Conductor:	[*angrily*] Now look, I've got a bus-load of passengers waiting over there.
Worth:	Well, there's no need to disturb them. I'm sure we'll manage it between us.

A couple more examples will confirm how old are traditional

techniques and even content. Flanagan and Allen had a special act for King George V's Jubilee (1935). It should be borne in mind when reading this act, that, in theory at least, the education of the music-hall audience for which it was intended was neither as intensive nor as comprehensive as our children now enjoy.

Allen: Well, you have some nice wares there.
Flanagan: What's that?
Allen: I say, you have some nice wares there.
Flanagan: 'Wares there'? You can't say that.
Allen: No [*very deliberately*] you have some nice wares there.
Flanagan: You can't say that. 'Wares there', full stop! If you get six months, you can't walk out of prison in the middle of it.
Allen: What d'ye mean, walk out of prison in the middle of it?
Flanagan: Well you must –
Both: Finish the sentence, finish the sentence.
Allen: I have finished the sentence, you have some nice wares there. Wares a noun.
Flanagan: Eh?
Allen: Wares a noun.
Flanagan: In a convent, who doesn't know that.
Allen: In a convent! A noun, not nun!
Flanagan: There's English for you, 'not none'. Fancy putting a verb to follow a plural. It doesn't go.

The nun/noun joke appears somewhat earlier, and doubtless unknown to Flanagan and Allen, in *Eastward Ho!* (which Jonson helped write in 1605):

Security: . . . for she had a great desire to be a Nun, an't please you.
Gertrude: A Nun? What Nun? A Nun Substantive? Or a Nun Adjective?
Security: A Nun Substantive, Madame, I hope, if a Nun be a Noun. But I mean, Lady, a vowed maid of that order.

(D1^r, modernised)

And the manuscript of the aristocratic William Percy's piscatory drama, *The Aphrodysial* (*c.* 1605) has this little dialogue, amongst an exchange full of puns:

> *Harpax:*   Will you none?
> *Balene:*   Non*
> *Proteus:*   Says, 'tis high noon.
>
> (f. 128ᵛ, modernised)

The asterisk in the original refers to this marginal note: 'Pronounced nown in French'. John Day's *Humour out of Breath* (1608) goes in for the same sort of wit:

> *Boy:*   He is likewise a nominative case, and goes before his mistress.
> *Octavio:* That's when the verb he goes before, his mistress, and he can agree together.
> *Boy:*   If not, he turns accusative and follows his master.
>
> (ii.i)

This form of 'wit', it will be noted, comes from all levels of society, and appeals across class boundaries – to this day.

The response to much of this humour is immediate and, to the catch-phrase, almost automatic. Often, however, and particularly when innuendo is involved, there must be a degree of thought and this can lead to the development of considerable powers of imagination in the audience. Max Miller was so good at having his audience complete the innuendoes he implied that there was some basis for his complaint that it was his audiences who were to blame for his being regularly banned by the BBC. Often his jokes had sexual implications of a kind still not *quite* acceptable on the BBC, but, as is essential to such humour, the language had a completely innocent primary meaning:

> Did I tell you about the Yorkshireman who came to London? He couldn't get any Yorkshire puddin'. He went 'ome and battered himself to death. Now, I tell you (L). It's all clever stuff you know, all clever (L). You can't go wrong with it. Oh, I must tell you this one (L).

All the laughs came in the linking passages and, in addition to responding to what has been said, these ensure that the audience is ready to laugh at the next joke. Furthermore, the comedian can gauge just how far he dare go (in the days when the pleasure of daring could be part of the thrill of an act). Because of his reputation and the twinkle in his eye, Max Miller could imply far, far more than he said. Even taking into account the more restrictive times, the words in his acts said, as he claimed, nothing which could give offence. What he relied upon was the imagination of his audiences – what he would call *their* dirty minds, not his. A developing story is ideal for building up implications which the imaginations of the individual members of the audience can variously develop.

> Listen, I was goin' home the other morning, at daybreak, daybreak – I wouldn't venture out at night (L). Just goin' along the country road, saw this young lady; she was coming towards me. When she got right up near me, I looked at her and said, 'Can I see you home?' She said, 'No, I'm going the other way'. I said, 'I can turn round'. See? (L) So I turned round, see, I turned round, and we started to walk in the middle of the road. I said, 'Let's get up on the path'. So we get up on the pa– and there was all grass on the path, all grass. So I bent down and I felt the grass. I said, 'Some dew', and she said, 'Some don't, good morning'. Now lissen (L)(L)(L).

One of the best of Max Miller's acts that depends for its effect upon the audience's imagination is Max as a swimming instructor.

> I used to be a swimming instructor myself at Brighton. I used to take the girls out to teach them to swim – if they couldn't swim I didn't go out with them – I'd no time to waste (L). And I remember many years ago, in the middle of July, I took a young lady out – she couldn't swim – I went out three miles with her – I don't mess about on the shore – and when I got right out (L) – when I got right out I said to this beautiful woman: 'Now what would you like to do?' And she said 'I'll do the breast stroke to start with.' So I said 'Go on, I'll stand and watch you' (L). So I stood on me stilts and she did the breast stroke. Then she said, 'Now I think I'll turn over' (L). And she turned over, may the sand get in my eyes if I tell a lie

(L), as she turned over, I slipped my hand underneath to hold her up – otherwise she'd go down (L). I'm entitled to do that because I'm the swimming instructor y'see (L). I got my hand underneath; she's lying on her back on the top of the water – her head'll be about here, her feet there, and my hand'll be about (*pause*) (L) Nah! Lissen, lissen, lissen, and all of a sudden, she gave a scream – not a very loud scream – she went [*he moans*] (L); [*he chuckles*] (L). Twice. I didn't hear her the first time – I was creeping up on her (L). I said, 'What yer screaming for?' She said, 'A shrimp's bitten me' (L). I said, 'Don't be a mug it's me'. I said 'You want confidence'. She said 'You want handcuffs'. Now lissen (L). . . .

Building up a complete and complex mental picture is but a short step from this. Askey and Murdoch's *The Proposal* (see *Popular Appeal in English Drama to 1850*, pp. 58–60), depends in part upon the audience recalling in the second part of the sketch the various imaginary 'props and settings' of the first part. One of the possibilities of an act that depends upon mental images is that it can go beyond the limitations of actuality. The late Joyce Gren-fell's brilliant monologues could conjure up real, almost palpable, nursery schools. Here a visitor is being shown round.

Who is making that buzzing noise? Well stop it please Neville. Hazel, dear, come away from the door and get something to do. *I do love to see them all so happily occupied, each little one expressing his own personality.* George, don't do that. And this is my friend Caroline and Caroline's painting such a lovely red picture, aren't you Caroline? I wonder what it is. Perhaps it's a lovely red orange is it, or a sunset? Oh, it's a picture of Mummy! Oh, for a moment, I thought it was an orange, but now you tell me I can see – it's Mummy. Um, aren't you going to give her a nose? No? No nose. *I think it's so interesting, the way they see things, don't you?* Sydney, stop blowing at Edgar and get something to do. Yes, I know I said you could choose what you are going to do but you cannot choose to blow at Edgar. Well, because I don't think it's a good idea. Well, because I – I'm not going to discuss it with you Sydney, now go over there and join Susan at her sand table. Yes there is room, Sue, there's heaps of room, just move up – Susan, we never bite our friends. Now say you're sorry to Sydney. No you needn't kiss him. No, you needn't hug him, Susan! Put him down! Sydney Aaa! *I'm afraid that some of our egos are a little on the big side today.*[37]

Contrast the actuality of Joyce Grenfell with the almost surreal world of John Tilley, the first comedian of the Windmill Theatre, who died, after a professional career of only three years in August 1935:

And talking of mocking, I had a very painful experience only yesterday. I went over a mock turtle factory. I don't know whether you've ever been over a mock turtle factory. A big factory with a huge room with the turtles comfortably seated all round the room. Then in came the chief mocker, and the things he said to those turtles. I mean personal things, cruel things. Oh, I was livid. There was one awfully nice little turtle, a shy retiring little turtle [*confidential, very quiet*] – er, very sensitive about its shell, it had some sort of [*slight pause*] malformation of the shell. [*Normal tone*] This brute of a chief mocker came up and cracked all the petrol jokes – 'That was a good Shell that was'. Well, the poor thing was almost soup by the time I left. You see, that's what they *do*, that's the way they make their soup. Oh I *was* so annoyed.

This technique is still very much alive. A record of Frankie Howerd at The Establishment on 26 September 1962 has on the 'B' side a very interesting act played before a BBC audience, in which Frankie Howerd discusses the Common Market. He wants to illustrate Italy and he compares the country with the shape of a leg. This enables him to engage intimately with the audience, direct attention to a pun that the audience has missed, and also get over a fluff in reading his script. The most important aspect in this context, however, is the way he builds up an image in the minds of his audience, so that the comic points he makes will raise laughter. A small 'l' indicates light laughter and a capital 'L', general laughter.

Now Italy (l), now Italy, ladies and gentlemen, now Italy is that country in the Mediterranean, it's sort of shaped like a leg. Now you think of that, see, imagine that, shaped like a leg. With the Apennines crawling up it (L). Now listen (L), no listen now, no, please. Now Milan comes somewhere around where the suspenders would be (L). Have you got the picture? Because if you haven't it's very difficult if you haven't got a map, you see (L). Now look at your legs (l), your own legs mate, not hers (L). Now Rome comes about where the er – I've turned over two pages there (L). Let's go back again. Now, go again. Now Rome comes about where your kneecap is you see, it's sort of built on seven hills – so you can imagine a knobbly knee covered in heat bumps, that's Rome (L), the eternal nobbly city (l). Now, listen (l) come on hurry up, you're taking your time over these, 'cos there's some good stuff here you know (l). Don't waste it (l). Now Naples (l), now Naples comes about where the top of your sock is and Florence comes half way up your thigh (l). Now (LL). Now (l), don't look now madam, take my word for it (l), will you, please? (L).

It will be noted how successfully Howerd builds a titter, as he would doubtless call it, into a full laugh, simply by prompting his audience with 'filler' words.

Possibly one of the most important contributions the music hall has made to drama – and not only music hall, but its continuation in radio – has been to keep alive the fanciful and absurd during a period when drama was concerned to be realistic – even naturalistic – and when the film, by its very nature, *seemed* to present the world as it actually was. The force of the realistic movement in drama and film (and in pictorial newspapers and magazines) has conditioned generations to interpret the world as it is filmed and photographed. This outward realism implies a rational world, and even perhaps suggests that we live in rational societies. The fact that in Britain expressionist drama made little headway, and that the few films that denied realism (such as *Helzapoppin* and *The Cabinet of Dr Caligari*) often only attracted minority audiences, meant that the chimera of realism held sway over the minds and imaginations of many people. One counteracting force was the music hall and its successors. There are, for example, the absurdities of Little Tich's 'One of the Deathless Army', satirising the newly-formed Territorial Army in the first decade of the twentieth century. Describing the 'horribleness of war', he says:

Then the enemy clustered around us, and the colonel went clean off his chump. And the horses drew horse and stampeded, and the camels had all got the hump. Well I was having a whisky and soda, sir, when a shot struck me, er, somewhere behind. As I could not pull it out in the street, sir, I went in and pulled down the blind. And the shells lay around me in thousands, and still they continued to drop. So I payed for the dozen I'd eaten and walked out of the oyster shop. And the shots they were buzzing around me, and one nearly blew off my head. There were cannons to right of me, cannons to left of me – so what did I do? Went in off the red.

Mark Sheridan's 'The Fire Was Burning Hot' depicts absurdly a less-than-effective fire brigade:

> The fire was burning hot,
> And the water was perishing cold;
> Our gallant lads all parched and dry,
> Watching from the pub close by;
> And when the fire was out,
> Like heroes they behaved,
> And every soul in that empty house
> That didn't get burnt got saved![38]

Willson Disher, writing about Harry Tate, asked, 'Why all that fuss made about "expressionism" on the stage? Far from being a novelty made in Germany, it had been Harry Tate's stock-in-trade for years.'[39] He then discusses 'Golfing', but what he says could as well be applied to 'Motoring', an act of the pre-1914 period.

Son:	We have broken down Papa.
Tate:	[*angry*] Well I know that, that's the very point I'm trying to find out. What has broken down.
Son:	The circumference of the gear wheels should be three pie r.
Tate:	Three pie r?
Son:	Yes. But yours are four pie r.
Tate:	That means I've a pie too many?
Son:	Yes.
Tate:	Well the chauffeur had better get out.

Son.	I don't mean him, Papa.
Tate:	Oh, what d'ye mean?
Son:	It's really the co-efficient of the tangent.
Tate:	What is?
Son:	Pie r.
Tate:	D'ye hear what he says?
Chauffeur:	Yes sir.
Tate:	Well, what d'you think?
Chauffeur:	Well sir, they're very expensive.
Tate:	What are?
Chauffeur:	Er, what he said, sir.
Tate:	Well what did he say?
Chauffeur:	Oh, er, ask him.
Tate:	D'you think I've come out to ask him? I want to know from you, you've got a motor cap on, you ought to know something about it.
Son:	*They can't be bought, Papa.*
Tate:	What a fool you are, of course they can't. What is it?
Son:	It's really 22 over 7.
Tate:	What is?
Son:	The coefficient of the tangent.
Tate:	22 over 7?
Son:	Yes. You see, three sevens are twenty-one.
Tate:	Well what's that got to do with 22 over 7?
Son:	Well, you can't go.
Tate:	Oh, three sevens are twenty-one and you can't go!
Son:	You must borrow one to make it twenty-two.
Tate:	Well, how d'y make it 22?
Son:	You see this car won't go.
Tate:	That's the point we're coming to it.
Son:	Well, you must borrow one [*Slap*].

Pearl Binder, discussing English humour, has argued that:

English humour is essentially children's humour. It has its being on three planes, the verbal, the practical, and the fantastic. All three types are relished and understood from one end of our society to the other. What makes the House of Lords laugh will also make the dockers laugh. . . . It is to be expected that a literary country like England should excel in verbal wit. What is unique with us is that the wit is not what would be considered wit in other countries. Rather it is verbal buffoonery, a juggling with the sound and sense of words, a peculiarly English, childish delight in mystification, secret meanings, and the appreciation of sound without sense for its own sake.[40]

Music hall, and its descendants, radio (*ITMA*, *Round the Horne*, *The Goon Show*) and television (*Monty Python*), exploit this buffoonery and juggling with the sound and sense of words, but the part payed by music hall has been the more vital because it existed during the most intense period of realistic 'serious' art. Possibly the most appropriate way to end this brief analysis of this kind of act – for much more could be said – is by printing a monologue and a section of a cross-talk act which deal with as serious a subject as one can imagine in the years between the two world wars. Flanagan is making a speech to persuade the electorate to vote him into Parliament; he then answers a few questions from his partner, Allen.

When the warime time come, the fine big strong strapping fellows they take 'em away 'an put 'em in the stenches, tch-tch, and the sick ones they leave at home to enjoy themselves. I ask you what th', what's the use of being healthy? Citizens and Citizenesses, any day, any day you can pick up your table-cloth and read that the edumacation authorimatries ts-st, they say that little childrens don't get sufficient too much a lot. They put forward a new digestion that the museums from art should be open after hours, so little childrens can go along Sunday. Now just for instruments, a little girl, five years of old age, goes into the museum of art and the first thing it sees is a picture of Venus. Well he's got to learn sometime. . . .

After referring to the Geneva Confidence, he goes on:

Flanagan: . . . And look at the, look at the Chancellor from the Exche – Exche – Chan – the Exch – Neville Chambermaid, he said, 'Save the pennies and the pennies'll turn into shillings; save the shillings and the shillings'll turn into pounds, save the pounds and he'll take it away from you. Oi! . . .'

Allen:	Are you aware, sir, we spend fifty million pounds a year on education?
Flanagan:	Sure. Fifty million pounds a year on edumacation and one hundred million pounds a year on the ammunition. You know why?
Allen:	No, why?
Flanagan:	We spend fifty million pounds a year to shoot the brains in to yer and a hundred million pounds a year to shoot them out again.
Allen:	But you must bear in mind, sir, people in this country are very brave. Stoic.
Flanagan:	Stoik?
Allen:	Stoic.
Flanagan:	Stoik?
Allen:	You know what Stoic means!
Flanagan:	Yes, I had it for my dinner today.
Allen:	Had what?
Flanagan:	Stoik and chips. But they need to be brave in this country, look at the Parliament we got.
Allen:	Why, what's wrong with the Parliament?
Flanagan:	Vy, the Parliament is the finest body of men dat money can buy.

The transition from music hall (or, in America, vaudeville) to radio, and thence to television, warrants a book in itself. A good, succinct account is provided by Elkan and Dorotheen Allan in chapter 12 of *Good Listening*. They discuss the beginning of 'relayed vaudeville', *Monday Night at Seven* (then *Eight*), *Bandwaggon*, *ITMA*, and so on. It would not be inaccurate to say that the kinds of technique and content discussed with reference to music hall have continued and been developed by radio and television, as some of the examples quoted may suggest.

By and large film reinforced realism in art. It *seemed* to show how things actually were, however false appearances might be. There were one or two interesting exceptions which show the influence of music hall (or vaudeville) techniques. The most extreme example of the exposure of film techniques (equivalent to the satirisation of every aspect of play-writing and production in *Pasquin*) was *Helzapoppin* (1941). The film was a less-than-wholly-successful adaptation of a Broadway show which had made free with dramatic illusion as only a show in the illegitimate tradition can.[41] Adapting the show for film, therefore, not only ran into the inevitable difficulty that Hollywood, like Whitehall, knows best, but also met the problem of how to present strictly theatrical jokes in film terms. Paging Mr Jones in order to deliver to him a potted plant was easy enough, but it was not possible to reproduce on film a woman seeking her husband in the audience.[42] Furthermore, film techniques are technical, a mystery more removed from general understanding than techniques of writing or acting, so that some of the breaks in illusion did not come across. (They do not seem so puzzling today.) Pushing a frame back into rack, or the recall of the mysterious 'Rosebud' of *Citizen Kane*, were too 'in', cleverly conceived though they and similar instances were. There were, however, similarities with rehearsal-type plays, particularly the argument with the director as to the kind of film Olsen and Johnson, the two zanies, wished to make. The film director, concerned to change things to the way Hollywood conceives of 'entertainment', was, in effect, a latter-day Mr Puff. Some of the strictly film gags appeared in one guise or another in other films, and what once was strange is now readily accepted by a mass audience. When Olsen and Johnson discuss the 'story' of *Helzapoppin* with the scriptwriter, it is visualised on paper, the paper becomes a screen, and, as Leonard Maltin puts it, 'The picture fades into this story-within-a-story, and the actual film begins' (p.250). In the Laurel and Hardy film *Thicker than Water* (1935), a large still of the next location was mounted up as a screen, pulled into view by an actor (who once let go, as if the spring he was pulling against were too strong), and then a jump-cut was made from the still shot to live action. This device is now a commonplace of television. The influences of such devices, akin in filmic terms to exposures of the 'mechanics of the theatre', have been pervasive. It can be argued, indeed, that the influence of the stage version of *Helzapoppin* (which opened on 27 September 1938) reached the screen before the film version. Paul Rotha has said:

> It is often said that *World of Plenty* began a new technique of film argument, derived from the American stage *Living Newspapers*. This is only partially correct. The first film in which I tried this technique of using every trick and device of the movie medium – stock library footage, diagrams, cut-in

interviews, an argumentative voice track, trick optical effects and so on – was in *New Worlds for Old*, written and made in 1938 on my return from New York. It was a curious combination of *Helzapoppin* and the *Living Newspaper* that suggested to me that in film one could take this 'argument' approach even further than on the stage.[43]

The most commonly-used music-hall technique in film (and television) is undoubtedly the direct address to the audience. Despite the fact that the performer is not there in person, there is an attempt to establish contact with the audience 'through the medium'. This device was used from the early days of gramophone recordings (for example, by George Formby Snr and Billy Williams) and as late as the 1930s. Thus, Bud Flanagan, at the end of his oration as an MP (see above, pp. 47–8), says:

This is my final verds to you before I go on to the other side, we are now coming to the intermission. Ta–ta–ta–ta–ta–ta– [*imitating fanfare*]. That's the music for the intermission. Goodbye, I'll see you on the other side. Oi!

Olsen and Johnson, Hope and Crosby, and the Marx Brothers were all involved in talking to the audience in the cinema in the tradition of the music hall. Thus, in *Road to Bali*, Hope turns to the audience as Crosby is about to sing and says, 'He's going to sing folks; now's the time to go and get your popcorn.' According to Leonard Maltin, the origin of this is to be found in the Marx Brothers' *Horsefeathers* (1932). Harpo and Chico sit down at the harp and piano respectively for a serious musical interlude. Groucho walks up to the camera and says to the audience, 'Listen, I have to stay here, but why don't you folks go out to the lobby for a smoke until this thing blows over?'[44] Rather more subtle, and, as appearing in a less anarchic film, more intriguing, is a line in *His Girl Friday* (1940; directed by Howard Hawks). This is a comedy on a serious subject: the press coverage of an execution in an American jail. Cary Grant, playing a newspaper editor, sends a young woman to find a character called Bruce Baldwin, played by Ralph Bellamy. The girl asks how she will recognise Baldwin. 'He's like that film star' says Grant, 'what's he called ?' A momentary pause and then: 'Ralph Bellamy' comes the answer to his own question, and off she goes.

Such instances were very much the exception, taking into account the vast number of films made, although breaks in the world of illusion continue to occur in films from time to time, and often quite unexpectedly. In the film *Deadfall* (1968) – not a comedy – a pretty girl says to Michael Caine, 'I want to get into films'.

Caine: Oh, you're an actress then?
Girl: [*Surprised*] No! I want to get into films.

In general, however, the weight of influence of the film re-inforced realism. The countervailing influence of challenges to the integrity of the illusion in film was nothing like as strong as that of music hall, even as late as the 1930s, with respect to *théâtre de boulevard* drama. In general, it would be fair to say that, despite films using music-hall performers (such as George Formby Jr and Tommy Trinder), one was not as conscious of the two traditions in the film as one was in live theatre. Nevertheless, the tradition was not wholly without effect in films of the 1930s and 1940s.

Despite its lack of literariness and, at its worst, its banality, repetitiousness and clumsiness (all of which might be said of some legitimate drama), the music hall had certain virtues which are more to be valued than those for which it is traditionally held in esteem. That it had vigour and cheerfulness, and that it was often very great fun is certainly true. What is more important for drama as a whole, however, is what gave it its unique character in terms of theatre and art, especially in the light of the tremendous movement and influence of realism in drama from about the middle of the nineteenth century. Realism arrived early in English drama, through Robertson (from 1865), received the impact of Ibsen's social dramas rather late (e.g. *Pillars of Society* and *A Doll's House*, 1889), and missed the full influence of his later, less realistically-oriented plays. Thus, realism continued on as 'the genre' through Granville-Barker, Galsworthy and the 'Manchester Realists', well into the twentieth century. Expressionism made little impact on English drama – Reginald Berkeley's *The White Château* (1925; broadcast by the BBC on Armistice Day), and O'Casey's *The Silver Tassie* (1929) are exceptional and in the main realistic. It is hardly surprising that it was in documentary film that English dramatic art (to use the term broadly) achieved so much, from Grierson's *Drifters* (1929) onwards.[45] It was the music hall (and later variety on radio), that, until some twenty years ago, gave expression to something other than the attempt to reproduce 'reality'.

Although music-hall songs and acts made great use of materials and events of everyday life, these were always subsumed within the theatrical experience. There was never any danger of judging an act as good because it was like life, even though Harry Tate's 'Motoring' or Sid Field learning golf were drawn from life. In the music hall the audience was always being 'invited to disbelieve' rather than continuously to suspend its disbelief; art and life were never confused. Never did music-hall or radio comedy (such as Hancock or the Glums), however much it derived humour from its life-like experience, give the false impression, as did Hollywood and the West End, that it was offering a representation of actuality. It therefore did not deceive, as Hollywood and the West End so often did, by passing off a would-be, never-never world as a representation of life as actually lived.

Music-hall audiences were always aware that they were witnessing an act, a performance. They were not so lost in the drama of the brightly-lit stage that the fall of the curtain brought them back to reality with a shock, like an afternoon film audience streaming into a sunlit street. The music-hall audience was for ever being reminded that it was at a performance – and 'What a performance!', whether by 'Mrs Miller's youngest son', or a comic who insistently repeated, 'Trinder's the name'. The exorbitant price of programmes would be referred to; the hardness of the gallery seats; this performer was to be admired; that 'autumn crocus' was gormless. The flavour of a pun would be discussed, and all would delight in its badness. No music-hall audience confused Little Tich's Territorial, Arthur Roberts's QC, Bert Sheppard's Candidate, Bud Flanagan's MP, John Tilley's Scoutmaster, or Arthur Askey's Proposal, for the real thing. Music-hall, radio and film audiences could automatically distinguish between art and life in Handley's *Tomtopia*, or on *The Road to Morocco*, or during *Hancock's Half-Hour*. It was this same capacity that an Elizabethan audience experienced when it attended plays by Shakespeare or Jonson or Heywood. Involvement was possible, but it was the capacity to apprehend the act and actuality simultaneously – not apron stages, nor artifice in acting – that made viable, and so intensely theatrical, the soliloquy, the monologue and the aside. It was not the theatre, not the players, not even the text in Shakespeare, but the audience's complexity of response that was so vital. It was *this* which the music hall sustained through a long, exciting period of realistic drama that was nevertheless inherently inimical to theatricality. It is in its capacity to dramatise the absurd (long before the word was coined for drama) that this can perhaps be most easily seen. Compare, for example, Henry Tate's game with π with the intellectual absurd in Strindberg's *The Dream Play* (which anticipates by over fifty years Ionesco's number-play in *The Lesson*)!

The direct influence of music hall on drama (and on poetry) can be seen in a number of ways. T. S. Eliot's interest in music hall led to his using the context and the form of the music-hall act. *The Waste Land* (first published in 1922, about the time Eliot was writing on music hall in *The Dial*) has a 'Gert and Daisy' act, almost as it might be given in a music hall – or perhaps, even, a tavern music hall, with the interruptions, 'Hurry up please it's time.'

> When Lil's husband got demobbed, I said –
> I didn't mince my words, I said to her myself,
> HURRY UP PLEASE IT'S TIME
> Now Albert's coming back, make yourself a bit smart.
> He'll want to know what you done with that money he gave
>   you
> To get yourself some teeth. He did, I was there.
> You have them all out, Lil, and get a nice set,
> He said, I swear, I can't bear to look at you.
> And no more can't I, I said, and think of poor Albert,
> He's been in the army four years, he wants a good time,
> And if you don't give it him, there's others will, I said.[46]

Music-hall influence can easily be seen in *Sweeney Agonistes* (first published 1926), although the scatterbrained telephone act devised by Jeanne de Casalis (as Mrs Feather) cannot be a source, as is sometimes supposed, for it dates from 1934. Most interesting in Eliot is the use of direct address by the four Knights at the end of *Murder in the Cathedral* (1935). Eliot employs this brilliantly to tempt the audience to accept the Knights' action and thus, in effect, to share their guilt. Although analysis of the text is

difficult because of the radically different roles of the fourth
Knight (doubling the Fourth Tempter) in English and American
editions, there is no doubt that in performance the juxtaposition
of overheard drama and direct address works brilliantly.[47]

O'Casey's use of popular dramatic techniques, music hall and
melodrama, was, unlike Eliot's, unconscious, but what he
achieved has been far more influential. To O'Casey must go the
credit for evolving a new kind of tragedy. It is possible to see its
origins in Synge's *Playboy of the Western World* (1907), and even in
W. S. Gilbert's *Pygmalion and Galatea* (1871), both seeming
comedies that end in loss, bitterness and tears. (It will be noticed
that all three dramatists are Irish.) O'Casey's *Juno and the Paycock*
(1924)[48] begins as a sort of comedy of tenement manners with a
virtual music-hall duo, Boyle and Joxer, ever fearing being
caught out by the long-suffering Juno, but comically interrupted
by the Coal Vendor.

Boyle:	. . . Ofen, an' ofen, when I was fixed to the wheel with a marlin-spike, an' the win's blowin' fierce an' the waves lashin' an' lashin', till you'd think every minute was goin to be your last, an' it blowed, an' it blowed – blew is the right word, Joxer, but blowed is what the sailors use . . .
Joxer:	Aw, it's a darlin' word, a daarlin' word.
Boyle:	An', as it blowed an' blowed, I ofen looked up at the sky an' assed meself the question – what is the stars, what is the stars?
Voice of Coal Vendor:	Any blocks, coal-blocks; blocks, coal-blocks!
Joxer:	Ah, that's the question, that's the question – what is the stars?
Boyle:	An' then, I'd have another look an' I'd ass meself – what is the moon?
Joxer:	Ah, that's the question – what is the moon, what is the moon?

(p. 23)

What follows is sheer pantomime, as Joxer rushes to hide – just as is his eventual reappearance at the end of the act.

The watershed that separates farce and tragedy comes near the end of the second act when Mrs Tancred enters. Boyle, hypo-critally, will have nothing to do with the problems of others; Joxer supports him by a line from the opera *Maritana*, and Juno falls – tempted to agree:

Boyle:	Here, there, that's enough about them things; they don't affect us, an' we needn't give a damn. If they want a wake, well, let them have a wake. When I was a sailor, I was resigned to meet with a wathery grave; an' if they want to be soldiers, well, there's no use them squealin' when they meet a soldier's fate.
Joxer:	Let me like a soldier fall – me breast expandin' to th' ball!
Mrs Boyle:	In wan way, she deserves all she got; for lately, she let th' Die-hards make an open house of th' place; an' for th' last couple of months, either when th' sun was risin' or when th' sun was settin', you had C.I.D. men burstin' into your room, assin' you where you were born, where you were christened, where you were married, an' where would you be buried!
Johnny:	For God's sake, let us have no more o' this talk.

(p. 47)

Only, Johnny, the son to be illegally executed for giving away Mrs Tancred's son, realises how empty is the jollity. The comedy and farce are now left behind. Such humour as there is is satirical and bitter. Johnny is dragged away; Mary is pregnant and deserted; Juno mourns; but Boyle, like an absurd, comic inversion of Horace's ideal hero, can face the collapse of his world with a kind of equanimity. O'Casey has shifted the ground from under our feet. He has related music-hall comedy and melodrama (complete with wills, bequests, unmarried mothers and bailiffs) in such a way that the result is a deeply-moving tragedy. But his masterstroke is to come – so innovatory that it has on occasion been omitted from performance (including the Abbey Theatre recording). After Juno has recalled Mrs Tancred's earlier quotation from Ezekiel 11:19 ('take away our hearts o' stone, and give us hearts o' flesh'), she leaves with Mary to view the body of her son. The stage is empty – the play could end here – but, after a pause, steps are heard shuffling up the stairs. In come Boyle and Joxer and the play ends with an 'ol' drunks' act from the music hall. 'Captain Boyle's Captain Boyle' (ironically recalling 'I am Duchess of Malfi, still', from a play well known to O'Casey) and 'th' whole worl's . . . in a terr . . . ible state o' . . . chassis!' (pp. 72–3). It is even easier to take Boyle to our hearts again than it is to be seduced by the arguments of Eliot's Knights, but that is to fall as did Juno, but even more seriously – for we have now experienced the full tragedy. O'Casey uses a genuine comic act, very familiar from the halls, but we must not respond – unless our hearts are of stone. Out of melodrama and music hall O'Casey creates tragedy and his alchemy has, probably unwittingly, influenced English dramatists of the next generation. *Juno and the Paycock* develops Robson's technique. It induces laughter but leaves us open to tears. There is no real comfort at the end of the play for we come to realise that in Boyle we see the apotheosis of Hollow Man, and that is tragic. It is this technique that Pinter develops even further, first allowing us to laugh, and then surprising us by making us realise what we are laughing at.

Samuel Beckett's *All that Fall* (1957) draws on many sources, even a perversion of laws of language,[49] but as a play designed for radio it is not unreasonable to look for likely influences in that medium. *All that Fall* depends greatly on sound effects – cartwheels, a neighing hinny, dragging feet, bicycle bells, squeaks of brakes, motor-van and car sounds are but a few. The following passage is exceptional only in that the sounds are brought together in so concentrated a fashion:

> [*Silence*]
>
> *Mrs Rooney:* All is still. No living soul in sight. There is no one to ask. The world is feeding. The wind – [*brief wind*] – scarcely stirs the leaves and the birds – [*brief chirp*] – are tired singing. The cows – [*brief moo*] – and sheep – [*brief baa*] – ruminate in silence. The dogs – [*brief bark*] – are

hushed and the hens – [*brief cackle*] – sprawl torpid in the dust. We are alone. There is no one to ask.
[*Silence*]

(p. 29)

The use of sound effects throughout the play has a great deal in common with the radio show which gave sound effects 'character'. In *ITMA* they were no longer a means of scene setting, like the BBC's famous seagulls that denoted a seascape or a cliff top, or merely decorative. They were a means of punctuating the rapid progress of events, especially the introduction of characters, doing the work of words, and permitting an extraordinarily economical drama for a medium that relied upon words – and sounds. In this brief extract, which takes less than a minute to perform, six characters are involved, four of them (Dorothy Summers, Funf, the Voice and Horace Percival) being introduced and 'exiting' during that time; there are seven effects (F/X), and six 'items' or incidents (monster, funfair, Funf, business of the day, lunch, shaving):

Tommy Handley:	. . . Councillor Cheese-cake, I'm surprised at you.
Dorothy Summers:	We're all surprised at you. You're not a Mayor, you're a monster.
Tommy Handley:	You must have seen my Lochness in the paper. The proposition I put before you today concerns a funfair to be held in and around the Lighthouse.
Fred Yule:	A funfair – it's preposterous.
Tommy Handley:	It isn't – it's Easter.
(F/X)	[*Phone*]
Tommy Handley:	Hullo?
Funf:	This is Funf speaking.
(F/X)	[*Machine gun*]
Tommy Handley:	Missed him. Now gentlemen, I will proceed with the business of the day.
Voice:	Your lunch, sir.
Tommy Handley:	Thanks.
(F/X)	[*Pop, then drinking sound*]
Tommy Handley:	What's for afters?

Voice:	This, sir.
Tommy Handley:	Oh, thanks.
(F/X)	[*Pop, then drinking sound*]
Tommy Handley:	Swallowed unanimously. Having disposed of that, the moment has now come when I –
Horace Percival:	Shave, sir?
Tommy Handley:	Thank you. Why it's Dan Druff my barber. Come in, Dan.
(F/X)	[*Stropping noises*]
Tommy Handley:	Now gentlemen – start the shave, Dan – with your approval this is what I propose to do.
(F/X)	[*Lathering noises*]
Tommy Handley:	I – er – [*coughs*] that's rather nice shaving soap that, Dan . . . Make it vanilla next time. I propose to –
Horace Percival:	Lift your chin, sir.
Tommy Handley:	Oh, right.
(F/X)	[*Sandpaper noises*]
Tommy Handley:	I propose to –
Horace Percival:	What's the razor like?
Tommy Handley:	Razor? I thought it was a broken bottle – Ooh . . .[50]

ITMA not only demonstrated how sound effects could be used, it speeded up even more the rapid responses of audiences[51] and sharpened their capacity to create scenes in their own imaginations. It is no exaggeration to say that *ITMA*, and some later radio programmes, did a great deal to train audiences to be able to respond effectively to post-1955 drama.

There is, I believe, a case to be made for seeing in Harold Pinter's Davies of *The Caretaker* (1960) something of the persona adopted by Tony Hancock in *Hancock's Half Hour*. It is as if Hancock in his more lugubrious moods is dispossessed, and finds himself in a real, nightmare world. Davies describing the convenience at Shepherd's Bush, or the wonderful account of how he tried to get some boots from a monastery at Watford (which can stand as a monologue in its own right), seems to have something of Hancock lurking underneath. Mick's speeches about his uncle's brother, or his friend in Shoreditch (who lived in

Aldgate), or his offer of an unfurnished flat could almost be the kind of rapid monologue with which Arthur English used to conclude his music-hall act.[52] Pinter marvellously translates elements that could stem from the music-hall tradition into a different milieu and for different purposes. The result is that, as with O'Casey, our assurance is undermined, old certainties no longer hold, and fear threatens us with we know not what.

A particularly interesting use of music-hall techniques by Pinter is to be found in what Martin Esslin calls 'the most mysterious and difficult of Pinter's writings'.[53] It is easy to sympathise with Esslin, for *Landscape* (1968) and *Silence* (1969) are difficult to pin down, especially if the plays are studied or performed without an awareness of the use of innuendo in the music-hall tradition. It is particularly surprising that Harold Pinter, who so infrequently explains what his plays 'mean', should have given an explanation of *Landscape*:

> . . . the man on the beach is Duff. I think there are elements of Mr Sykes in her memory of this Duff which she might be attributing to Duff, but the man remains Duff. I think that Duff detests and is jealous of Mr Sykes, although I do not believe that Mr Sykes and Beth were ever lovers.
>
> I formed these conclusions after I had written the plays and after learning about them through rehearsals.[54]

As puzzling as 'meaning' is an explanation of the reason why these plays grip an audience as compellingly as they do. Hearing professional performances, and more especially, participating in several readings of the plays with students in Britain and Canada, have convinced me of their theatrical power. It is apparent that they can work on an audience, and I think it likely that their 'meaning' is only to be understood in terms of performance. Of all Pinter's plays, these most clearly demonstrate his power as a master of writing for theatrical performance and, simultaneously, they demonstrate the impossibility of isolating 'meaning' adequately, in the form of a paraphrase of the words on the page, apart from performance. In these plays the meaning is the dramatic experience, and in *Landscape* and *Silence* this can only be accomplished with the participation of an audience.

What goes on in the silences and pauses of Pinter's plays has been variously explained, and Pinter gave the most amusing, if not the most enlightening, commentary on his use of the dots and dashes, which preceded his use of the pause:

> I've had two full-length plays produced in London. The first ran a week and the second ran a year. Of course, there are differences between the two plays. In *The Birthday Party* I employed a certain amount of dashes in the text, between phrases. In *The Caretaker* I cut out the dashes and used dots instead. So that instead of, say: 'Look, dash, who, dash, I, dash, dash, dash,' the text would read: 'Look, dot, dot, dot, who, dot, dot, dot, I, dot, dot, dot, dot.' So it's possible to deduce from this that dots are more popular than dashes and that's why *The Caretaker* had a longer run than *The Birthday Party*.[55]

Martin Esslin offers as succinct a differentiation of Pinter's pauses and silences as anyone:

> When Pinter asks for a *pause*, therefore, he indicates that intense thought processes are continuing, that unspoken tensions are mounting, whereas *silences* are notations for the end of a movement, the beginning of another, as between the movements of a symphony.[56]

In *Landscape* and *Silence*, however, and sometimes elsewhere, there is more to such pauses and silences. Mr Esslin is absolutely right when he says that 'dramatic dialogue is not necessarily the dominant element in the playwright's armoury: it may be equally or even less important than the non-verbal actions of the characters, and, indeed, their silences'.[57] Mr Esslin also makes a good point a little earlier when he says 'What matters in most oral verbal contact therefore is more what people are *doing* to each other through it rather than the conceptual content of what they are saying'.[58] These arguments can, I think, be taken much further. What is particularly significant is what the members of the *audience* do (or rather, think) within the silences. Many variations are possible, but analysis of four passages, one each from *Landscape* and *Silence*, and two from a much less significant work, the early sketch, *Last to Go*, will illustrate the sort of thing that is going on within the silences.

Last to Go (1959), as well as being a comic revue sketch with affinities to a Harry Tate routine, demonstrates several of Pinter's linguistic techniques. One of the most interesting of these is the way characters who think at different rates are dramatised. The newspaper-seller tells the coffee-stall barman that, having discovered which was the last of his newspapers to be sold, *The Star*, *The Standard* or *The News*, he went to Victoria to find George.[59] The barman is still thinking of the time the newspaper-seller had passed by his stall after he had sold his last newspaper, a time when trade was busy. The dialogue runs as follows:

Barman: I mean, you didn't stop here and have a cup of tea
         then, did you?
Man: What, about ten?
Barman: Yes.
Man: No, I went up to Victoria.
Barman: No, I thought I didn't see you.
Man: I had to go up to Victoria.
         [*Pause*]
Barman: Yes, trade was very brisk here about then.
         [*Pause*]
Man: I went to see if I could get hold of George.
Barman: Who?
Man: George.

                                                    (p. 129)

Two things might be noticed here in this context. One is the different rates of thinking of the two men, and it is this that, in part, gives the comic effect; secondly, there is what happens in the two pauses. In both, the audience's expectancy is tricked (and the effect of that is comic), most obviously in the first pause. In this first pause the audience is left to consider the significance of 'Victoria'; the word sets in train (one might say) thoughts in the minds of individual members of the audience, to be interrupted by the barman's 'Yes'. This might confirm whatever is going on in the minds of the members of the audience, but as the barman almost immediately reverts to his own original line of thought, there will almost certainly be a contradiction with what the members of the audience contributed to the silence in their minds. The resulting dislocation has, as I have said, a comic effect. The pause, however, is clearly 'working' dramatically – and so is the audience. Such a pause might almost be dignified by being termed a silent pun, even a sort of zeugma.

This effect is even more expertly achieved towards the end of the sketch, in the third of the pauses in the following passage:

Man: He never suffered from arthritis.
Barman: Suffered very bad.
           [*Pause*]
Man: Not when I knew him.
           [*Pause*]
Barman: I think he must have left the area.
           [*Pause*]
Man: Yes, it was the 'Evening News' was the last to go
           tonight.

                                                        (p. 130)

In the third pause the audience will almost certainly continue the line of thought prompted by the Barman's, 'I think he must have left the area', and this will seem to be confirmed by the news-paper-seller's 'Yes', which immediately follows the pause; but in what then follows expectancy is again tricked.

This usage of the 'silent pun' is, of course, comic but what is more important is the way that an audience participates in the dramatic action within the silence – the way in which the audience 'makes' the dramatic moment. The technique and the participation are a commonplace of the music-hall tradition. They are essential elements in any act which depends upon innuendo for its effect. What the audience of this sketch is doing is what is done by an audience of a Max Miller sketch.

If one turns to *Landscape* and *Silence* there will be found a sophisticated use of this simple device, a use that involves the audience deeply in the dramatic action and the 'meaning' of these two plays. In the first example, from *Landscape*, the use of silences and pauses is significant; in the second example, from *Silence*, the technique is taken a stage further, silence itself almost being dispensed with.

In *Landscape*, Beth describes an experience with a man which took place on a beach. In the passage which follows, a passage as self-contained as any can be from so closely-knit a play, her lines – the first and the last – can be spoken as if in sequence. They are,

however, separated by Duff's lines in which, as Pinter's Note to
the play directs, 'Duff refers normally to Beth, but does not
appear to hear her voice', whilst 'Beth never looks at Duff, and
does not appear to hear his voice'.[60]

Beth:	He moved in the sand and put his arm round me.
	[*Silence*]
Duff:	Do you like me to talk to you?
	[*Pause*]
	Do you like me to tell you about all the things I've been doing?
	[*Pause*]
	About all the things I've been thinking?
	[*Pause*]
	Mmmnn?
	[*Pause*]
	I think you do.
Beth:	And cuddled me.
	[*Silence*]

(pp. 20–1)

In the first silence the audience will inevitably begin to take
further the relationship which Beth suggests in her statement,
'He moved in the sand and put his arm around me.' Duff speaks
in the main of the present time and his words are appropriate to
the present, but there is a suggestion that he is, as it were,
continuing the relationship begun on the beach, and one can see
why Pinter should respond to this, as he listened to the play in
rehearsals, by thinking that 'the man on the beach is Duff'. We
may think this is so as we participate in the performance of the
play. But one cannot be positive that this is the true relationship,
despite Pinter's own interpretation. It is noticeable that Pinter
derives his own interpretation *from his experience as a listener to the
work in rehearsal;* he does not tell us what Pinter the writer
believed to be the relationship. Within the minds of individual
members of the audience will be created a tension between
possible interpretations – possible innuendoes – springing from
what each individual member of the audience has contributed to
the silence. Discussion with those who have heard the play soon
establishes that there are several different tenable relationships
within the play. Here there is nothing of the comic which is

found in *Last to Go*, but there is the same demand made on the audience that it contribute to the action, silent though that action is.

The pauses between Duff's lines not only show him exercising his mind but continue the opportunity members of the audience have to exercise their imaginations. After Duff's last words, 'I think you do', there is, significantly, no pause, and Beth's 'And cuddled me' strikes sharply against not only Duff's line of thought, but, almost certainly, the lines of thought pursued by individual members of the audience. The silence which follows 'And cuddled me' provides an opportunity for that conflict to be momentarily resolved, that is, resolved until assumptions are again challenged. Duff's new line of thought which immediately follows this silence – 'Of course it was in his own interests to see that you were attractively dressed about the house, to give a good impression to his guests' – has just this effect. As has Beth's next speech – 'I caught a bus to the crossroads . . .'.

It is by careful management of the pauses and silences that performers can enable an audience to participate in *Landscape*. What is so remarkable about this play is that it demands an audience's silent but active participation to make it complete, and this participation is what provides the chief, dramatic tension, and, ultimately, the 'meaning' of the play. It is this use of 'innuendo' that makes the experience of the play so moving and a paraphrase so thin. In the demand made of the audience, a demand ancient enough in popular entertainment, there is a shift in legitimate theatre which is novel, if not revolutionary, in the degree and quality of the participation required of the audience. It has a parallel in the epic theatre when an audience is expected to think (and often prompted in the direction it should think). Where *Landscape* triumphs is in the way that a performance demands, simultaneously, an individual response from each member of the audience, and yet the audience can still enjoy its corporate experience. There is a tension built up between the stage dialogue and the thoughts of each individual member of the audience and, implicitly, between each member of the audience. It is this implicit tension which gives the play its strange theatrical power.

The same technique is to be found in *Silence*, especially towards the end of the play when the action is repeated but the demand upon the individual imaginations of members of the audience is taken a stage further, Pinter using word–association rather than silence to achieve his effect.

Ellen:	He sat me on his knee, by the window, and asked if he could kiss my right cheek. I nodded he could. He did. Then he asked, if, having kissed my right, he could do the same with my left. I said yes. He did. [*Silence*]
Rumsey:	She was looking down. I couldn't hear what she said.
Bates:	I can't hear you. Yes you can, I said.
Rumsey:	What are you saying? Look at me, she said.
Bates:	I didn't. I didn't hear you, she said. I didn't hear what you said.
Rumsey:	But I am looking at you. It's your head that's bent. [*Silence*]
Bates:	The little girl looked up at me. I said: at night horses are quite happy. They stand about, then after a bit of a time they go to sleep. In the morning they wake up, snort a bit, canter, sometimes, and eat. You've no cause to worry about them. [*Ellen moves to Rumsey*]

(pp. 43–4)

The two silences allow for the audience's imigination to work, but here it is the repetitions of words and ideas within and between speeches which more significantly prompt the imagination. Thus, Ellen's 'could', spoken three times, conflicts with Rumsey's 'couldn't' and more directly with Bates's 'can't', which is itself contradicted by his 'can' in the same line. Bates picks up Ellen's 'yes' and Rumsey's 'hear'; 'said' begins with Ellen, is taken up three times by Rumsey as 'saying' or 'said', and twice by Bates before the second silence, and once thereafter; Bates insistently asserts that he didn't hear, and Rumsey in each of his three speeches refers to looking, and that, too, Bates takes up. Apart from such obvious links, one cannot but be aware that four of the five senses are referred to. Thus there are lines which are extremely closely interconnected, with an insistent repetition of certain words, yet where the logical relationship of the speeches is obscure, and much of what is said refers to an inability to hear.

Whilst an audience might simply let the words flow over it, careful pointing of the words and skilful use of the silences will encourage the active participation of the imaginations of the individual members of the audience. It is this then that makes the repetitions of the dialogue at the end of the play a genuine theatrical climax and not simply a literary trick. Furthermore, the climax is one for which the audience is itself partially responsible.

These techniques are not exclusive to *Landscape* and *Silence*. They are to be found in *Old Times*, though less concentratedly, and occasionally in earlier plays, though much less frequently and often with less assurance, something which Pinter seems to have noticed. Thus, the first edition of *The Lover*, has this passage:

> *Sarah:* She doesn't mind, she wouldn't mind – she's happy, she's happy.
> *Max:* Don't talk so wet.
>   [*Pause*]
> *Sarah:* I didn't know you were a Northerner.
>   [*Pause*]
>   I wish you'd stop this rubbish, anyway.[61]

The lines, 'Don't talk so wet' and 'I didn't know you were a Northerner' fall between the music-hall technique appropriate to *Last to Go* and the development of that technique which is to be found in *Landscape*. The result is uncertain and therefore inappropriate in *The Lover*, and Pinter excised the lines in revision.

Despite the 'look of the texts on the page', *Landscape* and *Silence* are very moving plays, but it can only be in performance that they can generate the quite extraordinary degree of tension latent in them. They are not simply plays for two or three characters respectively, but plays for characters and audience – just as a music-hall act or song is for performer and audience. These plays are remarkable dramatic and theatrical experiences which make the most subtle use of the well-tried music-hall technique of innuendo.[62]

3 The Continental By-Pass: from Tieck to Brecht

'There are', she said, 'a kind of folk
Who have no horror of a joke.'
(Lewis Carroll, *The Three Voices*)

A full analysis of the effects of Continental influences upon English drama cannot but be complex and encyclopaedic. It should not be limited to those influences that have affected the writing of dramatic literature but must refer also to acting, production, stage design, lighting, and so on. My concern here is very much more limited. I seek to trace, as succinctly as I can, the path by which certain devices that break the dramatic illusion were re-introduced into English drama from the European Continent some twenty years ago, and the effect they may have in productions in England. I shall, exceptionally, include a discussion of three American plays – those by Wilder – which have made an important contribution to the use and revitalisation of such devices.

A strong case can be made that Continental influence on English drama is only effective if there already exists in England a somewhat similar, if latent, tradition. Allardyce Nicoll remarked that English drama was independently moving towards a 'renascence' at the end of the nineteenth century, but the movement was 'certainly stimulated and strengthened' by developments in Europe.[1] Robertson's serious, realistic, socially-conscious drama did much to prepare the way in England for the effective influence of Ibsen's social dramas; Shaw, though early influenced by Ibsen, and a sponsor in England of such dramatists as Brieux,[2] developed his form of comedy from the old melodrama, as he himself pointed out in his Preface to *Three Plays for Puritans* (1901). To go further back, the influence of Molière on Restoration and eighteenth-century drama (with translations and adaptations by such dramatists as Davenant, Wycherley and

Fielding) was anteceded by the work of Fletcher and Shirley (whose *The Lady of Pleasure*, 1635, has many of the characteristics of the later drama, characteristics which remained in fashion until Sheridan).[3] Even earlier, although Daniel's *Queen's Arcadia* (1605) and Fletcher's *The Faithful Shepherdess* (1608) are indebted to Guarini's *Il Pastor Fido* (published 1590; performed 1595), the propensity for tragicomedy can be traced back for almost two centuries. What Ibsen, Molière and Guarini did was 'to stimulate and strengthen' existing or latent characteristics. It is noticeable that the powerful movement of expressionism in all forms of art, including drama, never took root in the English theatre, even though, in America, O'Neill's drama was more deeply affected. There was nothing then latent in legitimate drama to be stimulated. Although music hall might have provided fertile ground (see pp. 44–8), the two forms, legitimate and music-hall, had just been 'divorced' as it were.

With the resurgence of dramatic writing in England some twenty or so years ago, two strong Continental movements seem to have influenced English drama: Brecht's epic (particularly its alienation effect) and what has been conveniently tagged 'the absurd'. If Brecht's influence has seemed particularly alien (and it is on that that I wish to concentrate), the absurd has seemed relatively at home in England, despite the assumption often made that the Anglo-Saxon temperament responds only to the logical, rational tale. The evidence is otherwise.

It is correct that drama which tells a story rationally, and which has a well-defined beginning, middle and end, appeals very strongly to an English audience. But that seems eminently reasonable, just as it is to feel cheated if the end is left 'up in the air' because the dramatist is playing a game with his audience or the censor intervenes. Medwall, it will be recalled, came down quite clearly on the side of the man who was noble through his own achievement in *Fulgens and Lucres*, and had Lucres make the choice. In both he went beyond his source, and had he not done so his audience would, rightly, have felt cheated. Delight in a well-told, carefully-wrought story is perfectly proper, but it is not a bar to enjoyment of the absurd.

Pearl Binder's statement that the English delight in verbal buffoonery and 'the appreciation of sound without sense for its own sake' has already been quoted (above, pp. 46–7). Richard N. Coe, writing on Ionesco, has pointed out that:

Even before the end of the century, there were major writers (such as Dostoevsky and Rimbaud) and minor ones (such as Edward Lear and Lewis Carroll) whose concept of the nature of man either simply failed to be contained within the bounds of rationality, or else preferred to side-step them altogether, and to seek refuge (as did W. S. Gilbert) in a world of mock logic and childish fantasy.[4]

It is rather doubtful if the music hall was much affected by a struggle with the concept of the nature of man, but the absurd has been a vigorous element in such entertainment. Little Tich and Mark Sheridan are clear ancestors of The Goons, and the language of *ITMA* is frequently fantasy-based. Nevertheless, it may be that it is to Lear, Carroll and Gilbert that we should look for a literary tradition of the absurd which the Continental movement (centred on Ionesco as much as anyone) stimulated in England after the Second World War. This is particularly so because the drama of the absurd, though it can rouse laughter, is not essentially comic, as is music-hall and radio absurdity. As Elizabeth Sewell has explained:

> Laughter is incidental to Nonsense but not essential to it. Many people confuse the two, but a moment's recollection of the work of Lear or Carroll shows that much that happens in the world of Nonsense is not comic at all.[5]

It is not difficult to find parallels between the work of those dramatists loosely called 'absurdist' and earlier nonsense literature. Thus, Vladimir's 'How time flies when one has fun!' in *Waiting for Godot* (1955)[6] cannot but go back to a scene in *The Mikado* (1885) when the newly married Yum-Yum is endeavouring to believe that she can compress time so that she shall enjoy thirty years of married happiness in a month:

> Yum-Yum: [*still sobbing*] Yes. How time flies when one is thoroughly enjoying oneself![7]

Although Yum-Yum is sobbing and Vladimir is not, there is no doubt which is the more 'serious' usage of the same idea. The undercurrent of humour in Beckett is enhanced (as doubtless he realised) for those who recall *The Mikado*. The difference is apparent between the two works in a way that it is not between *The Goon Show* and N. F. Simpson's, *A Resounding Tinkle* (1957).[8] The idea of parking a motor scooter 'on that piece of waste ground behind Rachmaninov's Second Piano Concerto' is pure Goonery, as is this attempt to start a conversation (though it harps back also to Flanagan and Allen):

Mr Paradock:　Well, let's start this conversation. How was it we broke the ice at the Wordsworths'? What was it we began with? A noun clause each, wasn't it?

Don:　That's right. We were all given a noun clause each – in apposition – and then we had to go round asking everyone in turn for the noun it was in apposition to, till we found the right one.

Mrs Paradock:　I suppose John was as much in demand as ever with his adverbial clauses?[9]

Lewis Carroll, charming though much of his writing is, does suggest serious, and sometimes disquieting undertones. The 'Alice' books have been subjected to considerable analysis, so I should like instead to draw attention to his poem *The Three Voices*.

Carroll's real name – it need scarcely be mentioned – was Charles Lutwidge Dodgson. He was a professional mathematician who wrote fiction, and it is not really surprising that he should have shared some of the anxieties of a great novelist with an interest in mathematics: Dostoievsky. Dostoievsky's *Notes from Underground* (1864) seems to show, in a much simplified form, the non-Euclideanism of Lobachevsky (1792–1856):

And who can tell, perhaps the purpose of man's life on earth consists precisely in this uninterrupted striving after a goal. That is to say, the purpose is life itself and not the goal which, of course, must be nothing but twice two makes four. And twice two, ladies and gentlemen, is no longer life but the beginning of death. At least, man has always feared this twice-two-makes-four, and it's what I'm afraid of now . . .

. . . Yes, man is a comical animal, and there's obviously a joke in all this. Still, I say that twice two is an unbearable notion, an arrogant imposition. This twice two image stands there, hands in pockets, in the middle of your road, and spits in your direction. Nevertheless, I'm willing to agree that twice-two-makes-four is a thing of beauty. But, if we're going to praise everything like that, then I say that twice-two-makes-five is also a delightful little item now and then . . .

. . . I know, for instance, that suffering is inadmissible in light stage plays. . . . Nevertheless, I'm certain that man will never give up true suffering, that is, chaos and destruction. [10]

Carroll's *The Three Voices* is not a work of art of the order of *Notes from Underground*, but it is very revealing of the state of mind of some intellectuals at the time it was written (a few years before Darwin's *On the Origin of Species*, 1859). Furthermore, the way in which Edward, of Pinter's *A Slight Ache* (1959), is overcome by events bears a striking resemblance to the fate of the man in *The Three Voices*. [11] The poem first appeared in *The Train* (November 1856) and was published with five additional verses (those beginning 'He saw them drooping here and there') in *Rhyme? And Reason?* in 1883. [12] The poem is – very significantly – a bitter parody of Tennyson's *The Two Voices*. Carroll imitates the topic, metre and rhyme-scheme. Tennyson's poem ends, after wrestling with depression, on an exuberant note of affirmation. The speaker goes forth into the fields, where '. . . Nature's living motion lent/The pulse of hope to discontent.' 'So variously seem'd all things wrought' that the speaker wonders how the mind can be 'brought/To anchor by one gloomy thought', and how it could be that he could have communed with 'that barren voice' rather 'Than him that said, "Rejoice! rejoice!"' [13]

Carroll's poem has a completely different conclusion. His character disintegrates, concerned with such questions as 'Shall Man be Man?', and, overwhelmed, is left to the oncoming tide.

The Three Voices tells the story of a man gaily walking along a sea-shore (from the illustrations it looks something like Eastbourne), happy and carefree. He 'trilled a carol fresh and free' and 'laughed aloud for very glee'. The wind then blows off his hat, and in this simple incident there is the beginning of a process of disintegration remarkably similar to Edward's in *A Slight Ache* or Choubert's in Ionesco's *Victims of Duty* (1952). The hat is blown

> All to the feet of one who stood
> Like maid enchanted in a wood,
> Frowning as darkly as she could.

When she stops his hat by spearing it with her umbrella, he mildly complains of the damage done to it, whereupon she attacks him with verbal savagery. '"There are", she said, "a kind of folk/Who have no horror of a joke".' A little later she menacingly accuses him, in a manner that anticipates the horror that can underlie the banal of Ionesco and Pinter.

> 'The man that smokes – that reads the *Times* –
> That goes to Christmas Pantomimes –
> Is capable of *any* crimes!'

The discussion between these two is very one-sided, nearly as one-sided as that between Edward and the Matchseller. So 'Ceaseless flowed her dreary talk' that he had no time to answer her questions, even if he knew how to. Then at last,

> Wrenched with an agony intense,
> He spake, neglecting Sound and Sense,
> And careless of all consequence:

> 'Mind – I believe – is Essence – Ent –
> Abstract – that is – an Accident –
> Which we – that is to say – I meant –

Not to our surprise, 'She looked at him, and he was crushed'. Having stripped his views to the bone, she 'proceeded to unfold her own', asking the questions still being asked in the drama of the absurd:

> 'Shall Man be Man? And shall he miss
> Of other thoughts no thought but this,
> Harmonious dews of sober bliss?'

At length she stops and he leaves her:

> He sat and watched the coming tide
> Across the shores so newly dried.

He wonders why he has for so long been willing,

> To hang upon her every word:
> 'In truth,' he said, 'it was absurd.'

But this is not the end of the poem, only of The Second Voice,
For now The Third Voice begins.

> Not long this transport held its place:
> Within a little moment's space
> Quick tears were raining down his face:

He now hears a voice within his head,

> In words imagined more than said,
> Soundless as ghost's intended tread.

The wretched man

> . . . sickened with excess of dread,
> Prone to the dust he bent his head,
> And lay like one three-quarters dead.

As time passes, Dawn, Noon, Eve and 'leaden Night', he is
dashed to earth, 'Tortured, unaided, and alone'. Finally he asks:

> 'Shall Pain and Mystery profound
> Pursue me like a sleepless hound,
>
> With crimson-dashed and eager jaws,
> Me, still in ignorance of the cause,
> Unknowing what I broke of laws?'

Then comes the answer. 'Her fate with thine was inter-
twined . . . Each unto each were best, most far':

> 'Yea, each to each was worse than foe:
> Thou, a scared dullard, gibbering low,
> AND SHE, AN AVALANCHE OF WOE!'

And that is all. A gay opening, an inexplicable visitation full of menace, the disintegration of a man, and a sense of fortuitous horror, an avalanche of woe. Rhyme? Or Reason?

The Three Voices is an early example of the absurd applied to existence (and that is not putting it too portentously). Lear and Gilbert may be 'light nonsense' in an absurdist tradition, but at times Carroll's humour has a grimness that is not dissimilar from that found in the tragic farce of some of the drama of the absurd. It is not difficult to see the 'absurd' of European dramatists striking a chord in post-war England, bearing in mind the English nonsense traditions, comic and grim.

However, such is not the case with the influence of Brecht from the time of *The Threepenny Opera* (1929) onwards. Indeed, the reverse is the case. The tradition of breaking continuity in English drama (and from the middle of the nineteenth century until a decade or so after the Second World War, that meant music-hall and radio comedy) led to a *deeper* involvement in what followed the break (given that the performer knew his job – see pp. 33–4). Thus the problem Brechtian alienation techniques can present in England is that instead of detachment they can lead to deeper involvement – say, to put it crudely, greater sympathy with Mother Courage. These techniques – the acts of *The Enter-tainer* (1957), the ballads of *Live Like Pigs* (1958), the placards and sayings of *Oh What a Lovely War* (1963) – cannot be guaranteed to effect detachment, and may well have a contrary effect. The interventions of the Stage Manager in *Our Town* (1938) certainly do not prevent the very deepest involvement of an audience in the fortunes of those living at Grover's Corners, and I suspect the same might even be said of the alienation techniques used in *The Skin of Our Teeth* (1942). I have not, however, had an oppor-tunity of seeing this play. No performance I have witnessed of *Waiting for Godot* (not a play obviously Brechtian, of course) has failed to keep me involved in the predicament of Vladimir and Estragon, even though an audience may (and should) be amused by the breaks in continuity.

> *Vladimir:* [*triumphantly*]. It's Godot! At last! Gogo! It's Godot! We're saved! Let's go and meet him. [*He drags Estragon towards the wings, Estragon resists, pulls himself free, exit right*] Gogo! Come back! [*Vladimir runs to extreme left, scans the horizon. Enter Estragon right, he hastens towards Vladimir, falls into his arms*]

There you are again!
Estragon: I'm in hell!
Vladimir: Where were you?
Estragon: They're coming there too!
Vladimir: We're surrounded! [*Estragon rushes wildly towards back*] Imbecile! There's no way out there. [*He takes Estragon by the arm and drags him towards front. Gesture towards auditorium*] There! Not a soul in sight! Off you go. Quick! [*He pushes Estragon towards auditorium. Estragon recoils in horror*] You won't? [*He contemplates the auditorium*] Well, I can understand that. [14]

Though the tradition has been much used, in a curious way it has remained on the whole alien, even though its origins are English. There are signs, in some of the work of Tom Stoppard and Peter Nichols for example, that different planes of dramatic reality can co-exist in contemporary drama, but the influence of breaking continuity in the music halls still seems too strong for the use of that technique in the way Brecht intended it for any but an intellectually-prepared – or coterie – audience. This is understandable but strange, given the ultimate origins of Brecht's techniques. These go far deeper in English drama than *The Beggar's Opera* (1728), and it may be that the English drama from which they originate could no longer itself be presented today with the degree of detachment its authors would have wished. I propose, therefore, to sketch the more obvious sources of Brecht's use of breaking continuity, in so far as they relate to English drama. My concern is not with Brecht's work as such (which may seem perverse) but with its relation to, and production in, English theatre.

The origin of Brecht's alienation technique is to be found in Jonson's induction plays. These were known to Ludwig Tieck (1773–1853) and there seems to be little doubt that he wrote his play, *Puss-in-Boots* (*Der gestiefelte Kater*, 1797), under Jonson's influence. [15] It is, of course, quite possible that other traditions were involved. There was no need for Tieck to go to English drama for breaking continuity, asides to the audience, nor for the induction device, or contrasting planes of dramatic illusion. The Latin play *Cenodoxus* (1602), for example, has action on three planes, heaven, hell and earth; continuity is broken; and there are asides to the audience.[16] Calderon's *Life is a Dream* (1635) sees theatre as reality and life as illusion.[17] *The Theatrical Illusion* (*L'Illusion Comique*, 1636), though successful in Corneille's own day, and 'promptly forgotten after his death',[18] presents two plays, one comic and one tragic, within a frame. The tragedy gives the impression that Pridamant's son, Clindor, is dead, but the magician who has arranged this 'television' dramatisation (after the manner of Greene's *Friar Bacon and Friar Bungay*, 1589) explains that the 'dead' son is a successful actor, and the curtain is raised to show the actors and door-keeper counting the takings. Pridamant, though relieved that his son is alive, is distressed to think he is an actor, and Alcandri, the magician, then speaks in praise of the stage, concluding with:

> Besides, if standing's rated by one's wealth,
> The theatre's a profitable line;
> Your son's extracted from this pleasant trade
> More affluence than had he stayed at home.
> Discard this common error, finally,
> And do not mourn for his good fortune.
> (p. 280; 11. 1665–70)

Closer to Tieck's own day was Goldoni's *The Comic Theatre* (1750), a rehearsal play.

There is no reason therefore why Tieck should not have written *Puss-in-Boots* out of the European Continental tradition. However, the certainty is that the greatest influence upon him was Shakespeare and his contemporaries, especially Jonson. Tieck studied Elizabethan drama whilst at university and by the time he was twenty, in 1793, he had translated (and rather freely adapted) *Volpone*.[19] In 1800, three years after *Puss-in-Boots* was written, he translated *Epicoene*. Although Tieck is sometimes understood to have translated much of Shakespeare, he really acted as kind of general editor, supervising the work of his daughter, Dorothea, and that of Graf Baudissin. In a letter to Graf Baudissin in 1829 he mentions his studies at Göttingen (1792), where he says he had read Massinger, Fletcher and Jonson. He mentions repeatedly that among Shakespeare's contemporaries he most admires Jonson, and therefore translated two of his plays in the following years. He does not mention specific titles of non-Shakespearean plays in his letter to Graf Baudissin, but as he used

Dodsley's *Collection*, he would have had available there, of plays mentioned in *Popular Appeal in English Drama to 1850*, *The Downfall of Robert Earl of Huntingdon*, *Mucedorus* and *The Two Angry Women of Abingdon*. He refers in his letters and criticism to several of Jonson's plays, including two with inductions: *Volpone*, *The Alchemist*, *Epicoene*, *Every Man in His Humour*, *Every Man out of His Humour*, *Tale of a Tub* and *The Staple of News*. He does not appear to mention *The Knight of the Burning Pestle*.

It is not possible to identify all the non-Shakespearean plays read by Tieck, but his admiration for, and translation of, Jonson's work, together with the ready availability of his plays, can leave no doubt that he knew of Jonson's use of inductions and intermeans. In his Introduction to his translation of *Puss-in-Boots*, Gerald Gillespie says:

> the devices of Beaumont and Fletcher's *The Knight of the Burning Pestle*, Ben Jonson's comedies, and Gozzi's farcical fables were familiar to him. But his vast reading makes it difficult, and in many ways useless, to widen the speculation beyond obvious or acknowledged stimuli.   (p.22)

In *Puss-in-Boots*, Tieck seems to share with Jonson a highly critical view of the theatre of his own day, the critics themselves and the audiences. One wonders, indeed, whether he knew of Fielding's plays (which were available to him in Göttingen University Library).[20] The ostensible fairy-tale subject of *Puss-in-Boots* is unlike the subject-matter of the Jonsonian plays with inductions and intermeans, but the format is strikingly similar. Further, the induction to *Every Man out of His Humour* and the Prologue to *Puss-in-Boots* both not only feature critical discussions of drama, but have a similar appeal for acceptance by the public. Cordatus cannot guess how this strange new play, *Every Man out of His Humour*, 'of a particular kind by it selfe . . . will answere the generall expectation' (ll. 231–4). In *Puss-in-Boots* there is the ever-present criterion of 'good taste' (e.g. Prologue, pp. 39 and 41) and Fischer and Müller begin by trying to work out what kind of play is to be presented. However, neither of the critics are 'in the know', whereas Cordatus is the author's friend. Cordatus also 'has the place of moderator', according to Jonson's Characters of the Persons, and that might have suggested to Tieck the role of Pacifier (Ein Besäuftiger) for his play. The splendid caricature of a kind of critic still with us, Bötticher, gives an account of the use of masks by the ancients, together with self-approving comments on the research he has undertaken. Cordatus is less satirically treated in the induction to *Every Man out of His Humour* (as befits the author's friend), but he also has a lengthy speech on the origins and development of Classical comedy. There is nothing in Jonson's play equivalent to Tieck's Author who begs for a hearing, although the induction to *Bartholomew Fair* has the agreement between audience and author. Nor is there any indication that Jonson's audience stamps impatiently (unlike Fielding's device of having the author's friends catcalling and tapping with canes prior to *Don Quixote in England*), but Cordatus does express a wish that the play would begin: 'this protraction is able to sowre the best-settled patience in the Theatre' (ll. 287–8). *The Staple of News* has in its induction and intermeans a complete group of critics (Tattle, Censure, Mirth and Expectation) called aptly by Jonson 'Gossips', and it is precisely their roles that the gossips, or critics (Bötticher, [21] Schlosser, Fischer and Müller), play in Tieck's play.

Tieck presents his author as a disastrous failure. Like Macilente (the Presenter of *Every Man out of His Humour*), Tieck's Author closes the play, but whereas Macilente begs 'a plaudite for God's sake', Tieck's Author completes 'The Final End' (Völliger Schluß) with a rebuke to the audience:

> No, the gentlemen out there are better than I am at farce. I withdraw. [*He exits. Those left go home*]
>
> (p. 131)

The nearest Jonson might be said to come to admission of failure is in the intermean between Acts IV and V of *The Staple of News*:

Tattle:	*Why? This was the worst of all! the* Catastrophe!
Censure:	*The matter began to be good, but now: and he has spoyl'd it all, with his Begger there!*
Mirth:	*A beggerly* Iacke *it is, I warrant him, and a kin to the* Poet.
Tattle:	*Like enough, for hee had the chiefest part in his play, if you marke it.*
Expectation:	*Absurdity on him, for a huge ouergrown* Play-maker! *why should he make him liue againe, when*

	they, and we all thought him dead? If he had left him *to his ragges there had beene an end of him.*
Tattle:	*I, but set a begger on horse-back, hee'll neuer linne till* *hee be gallop.*

Damplay is always prepared to give twenty-shillings-worth and more of censure for his two-shilling seat, but he is well placed – and answered – by Jonson's Boy, in *The Magnetic Lady*.

It would be wrong to press such similarities too hard. It is not likenesses of comment and argument that are so revealing as the general pattern of induction with intermeans forming a critical frame to the play. Tieck is much more concerned to satirise critics and audience, whereas Jonson, though he uses satire, is more concerned to have the critics interpret his plays aright. However, Tieck's play, in its criticism of the theatre and its exposure of theatrical illusion, has a great deal in common with the Fielding of *Pasquin* of fifty years earlier and of his *The Author's Farce* (1730), which featured a cat which the author within that play, Luckless, intended should read the play's Epilogue (see *Popular Appeal in English Drama to 1850*, p. 136).

It will be realised that, up until the time of Planché's *The Drama at Home*, that is, up until the time that *Puss-in-Boots* was belatedly performed for the first time in 1844, theatrical illusion was regularly shattered in the English theatre. Sheridan's *The Critic*, for example, was written in 1779, and Reynolds's *The Dramatist* in 1789. Tate Wilkinson presented *The Rehearsal* between 1777–83, *The Muse's Looking-Glass* in 1782, and *The Critic* between 1781–90 – and his was but one provincial company. The breaking down of dramatic illusion – the making aware to the audience that it was in a theatre – which seems so unusual in Tieck, was commonplace in the English theatre at the end of the eighteenth century.

Puss-in-Boots received its première only in 1844. It seems then to have been forgotten until revived in Berlin in 1921 by Jürgen Fehling, and then again in Tankred Dorst's adaptation (*Puss-in-Boots, or How the Play is Played*) in 1963.[22] It is the revival of interest just after the First World War that is of particular interest here. Pirandello, who studied at the University of Bonn from 1888 to 1891, had been interested in the relationship of the dramatist to his creation, and the unavoidable intervention of the actor, a dozen or fifteen years before Fehling's revival.[23] Whether

Puss-in-Boots was a major influence on *Six Characters in Search of an Author* (1921), 'or whether Tieck was only one of several known stimuli for Pirandello after the latter's studies in Germany, has been mooted but never adequately explained', says Gerald Gillespie. Pirandello, he goes on, was instrumental in 'emancipating imagination in the drama', and his influence was felt especially in France, by Thornton Wilder and, 'stimulated by Wilder's theory and practice of the destruction of illusion', by such playwrights as Frisch and Dürrenmatt.[24]

What was so striking about Pirandello's *Six Characters* was not that its ripping away of the fiction of the fourth wall was innovatory, nor, as Felicity Firth says, that Pirandello held a mirror up to art, stripping 'the mask off the theatre itself' and so showing it 'the unbearable truth that it can no longer convince'[25] (which is hardly correct), but that his play created such interest when presented in Paris and Berlin in 1923 and 1924. It seemed innovatory, rather than being the *reintroduction* after eighty years of a time-worn device. Indeed, what was then still an innovation in English drama was the kind of play that dealt realistically with serious issues, especially those dramatising life in the unfashionable north of England.

Nor was *Six Characters* particularly unusual (as Peter Rink suggests, p.5.) in attacking naturalism at its centre. Jarry, Wedekind, Kokoschka, Hasenclever and Reinhard Goering had all done that. No, apart from the undoubted worth of the dramatic and, paradoxically, *theatrical* experience it gave, *Six Characters* was important because it showed the young Brecht the way that the old tradition of English drama worked: the way direct address could be contrasted with theatrical illusion. As Brecht himself puts it at the end of the First Appendix to the *Messingkauf* Theory:

> The A-effect is an ancient artistic technique; it is known from classical comedy, *certain branches of popular art* and the practices of the Asiatic theatre [*my italics*][26]

Brecht's theory, as explained by him at the beginning of that same Appendix, is relatively simple: 'It deals with the traffic between stage and auditorium: how the spectator must master the incidents on the stage' (p. 101). That Brecht understood how aware an Elizabethan audience must have been that it was at a performance can be gathered from his description of a Shakespearean production and by the old-fashioned actor's response:

> *Dramaturg:* . . . Add to that the fact that they acted (and also rehearsed, of course) by daylight in the open air, mostly without any attempt to indicate the place of the action and in the closest proximity to the audience, who sat on all sides, including on the stage, with a crowd standing or strolling around, and you'll begin to get an idea how earthy, profane and lacking in magic it all was.
>
> *The Actor:* So that *A Midsummer Night's Dream* was played in daylight and it was daylight when the ghost in *Hamlet* appeared? What price illusion?
>
> *Dramaturg:* People were supposed to use their imaginations.[27]

Brecht came across Pirandello's *Six Characters* when it was produced in Berlin in 1924 by Max Reinhardt (for whom he was working). Brecht had by then written *Baal* (1918), in effect a satire on expressionism; *Drums in the Night* (1919), which won him the Kleist Prize in 1922; *In the Jungle of the Cities* (1923); and an adaptation of Marlowe's *Edward II* (1924). There was virtually a Pirandello cult in Berlin at this time. In 1925, six of his plays were produced in German translations (including one in which Helene Weigel, whom Brecht married in 1928, appeared), and Pirandello brought his Teatro d'Arte from Rome to perform three of his plays in Italian.[28] In 1924 Reinhardt produced, in addition to *Six Characters*, Shaw's *St. Joan* (1923) and Goldoni's *The Servant of Two Masters* (1740) and Brecht attended rehearsals. The immediate effect for Brecht, coupled with his interest in a curiously assorted mixture of English literature – Marlowe, Gay, Kipling and Shaw – was the writing of *A Man's a Man* (1924–6), set somewhat vaguely in British India; the essay 'Three Cheers for Shaw' (1926), which contains amid some sharp insights into Shaw's work, the significant sentence, 'Probably every single feature of all Shaw's characters can be attributed to his delight in dislocating our stock associations';[29] the *Domestic Breviary* (1927), ballads and satires which show Kipling's influence; and *The Threepenny Opera* (1928).

The use to which Brecht was to put this rediscovery that the two dramatic traditions could co-exist – that theatrical illusion and the disruption of this illusion need not be destructive but form an artistic whole – was in some ways very similar to the use to which Fielding put that conjunction of opposites. Fielding's chief concern in his irregular dramas was political and social satire; Brecht's was the same and, through The Philosopher in *The Messingkauf Dialogues*, he described its effect in this way:

> If empathy makes something ordinary of a special event, alienation makes something special of an ordinary one. The most hackneyed everyday incidents are stripped of their monotony when represented as quite special.   (p. 76)

But, as the Dramaturg warns:

> There's no A-effect when the actor adopts another's facial expression at the cost of erasing his own. What he should do is to show the two faces overlapping.   (p. 76)

Brecht's drama and his theories stand in their own right. The problem they present for English theatre will be obvious. Whereas in Fielding's time, a measure of detachment was possible for the audience at a play like *Pasquin* (1736), the break in that tradition, caused by the coming of realism, changes in stage and theatre lighting, and the composition and manners of the audiences, has meant that what one might call a 'native English tradition' has returned not only unrecognisable as such, but to a very different theatrical situation. The development of music hall techniques which exploited the audiences' capacity for multiconscious response, and the ability of audiences to slip back into the play-world after a break, indeed their capacity to use their imaginations, has worked against the kind of detachment that Gay and Fielding could count upon and which a play like *Mother Courage* needs.

The political ends which Brecht sought to serve through his epic drama and the A-effect should not disguise the fact that he was an intensely theatrical dramatist. It is partly this, indeed, as well as the music-hall tradition, that causes us to react more sympathetically to Mother Courage than is Brecht's intention. There is a possibly unintentional tribute to the dramatist in Brecht in Günter Grass's address on the Quatercentenary of

Shakespeare's birth, 23 April 1964, and in his play, *The Plebeians Rehearse the Uprising* (1966).[30]

Grass's play shows the striking construction workers interrupting a rehearsal of *Coriolan* and asking 'the Boss' to help them draft a statement and also to give them his support. Is he not a friend of the workers and one capable of influencing the government? Grass points out that no authentic statement by Brecht has been published: 'His heirs and his publishing house have kept these documents under lock and key'; and Brecht 'emerged without visible harm from the workers' revolt' (p.34). Grass suggests a failure of political nerve in Brecht, and perhaps an inability to live up to the kind of actions for which his drama (in its political aims) had argued. On the other hand, one can also see the essential dramatist in the Boss rather than the essential politician:

> In my play the Boss does not refuse out of hand to write the statement the workers hope for. He agrees to compose it as soon as the masons and carpenters have shown him exactly what happened at the beginning of the workers' revolt; he wishes to derive benefit from current events for his production of *Coriolan*, for his uprising of the plebeians.   (p.34)

In the play, the dramatist can be seen taking over from life when the Boss breaks into a 'real' quarrel to rehearse it so that it is more – what? Dramatic? Real? True?

> [*The Carpenter, the Road Worker, the Mason on one side, Rufus and Flavus on the other, come to blows. The rest of the workers and plebeians try to make peace*]
>
> Hod Carrier: Don't let them provoke you. Our enemies are someplace else.
> Brennus: Hold your people back.
> Foreman: Stop it, do you hear? Stop it!
> Plasterer: No excesses! Remember, that's what we decided.
> Podulla: If this is the practice, his theory was wrong.
>   [*The Boss enters left, followed by Volumnia and Erwin*]
> Boss: Now that I call class struggle. A drunken wedding

	Between the plebs and proletariat.
Erwin:	An exemplary image!
	[*The brawl begins to break up*]
Boss:	[*Leaps in among the workers, grabs hold of them*]
	Good! Do it again. The same position, please.
	Here, you grab him and you punch him.
	He ought to sweat, his tongue should be hanging out,
	And you look pained. His knee is in your groin!
	Plebeians' rags, inextricably mingled
	With masons' white sleeves, trouser legs.
	This neck, this back, they're cracking,
	Because that knee, that forearm . . . Apply the thumb!
	And now hold still a second
	Like statues, like Laocoön.
	If only we could cast you all in bronze.
	And put you on a pedestal with the
	Inscription: Socialism, scorning pain
	And muscle cramp – Well, what does socialism do?
	Behold – it conquers! Well, that's that. And now,
	Plebeians and proletarians, relax,
	And tell me all about the uprising

(pp. 62–3)

It is almost as if we are back with Garrick's Glib in *A Peep Behind the Curtain* (1767), furious that his rehearsal should be spoilt by an elopement (see *Popular Appeal in English Drama in 1850*, pp. 151–53). The Boss, like Vapid and Glib, shows such single-minded devotion to drama that the normal human responses are dulled even to the extent of 'rehearsing life' as if it were drama. It might be noted also that in the *Messingkauf Dialogues* Brecht echoes an irony from the Prologue to Villiers's *The Rehearsal*:

For (changing Rules, of late, as if men writ
In spite of Reason, Nature, Art and Wit)
Our Poets make us laugh at Tragoedy,
And with their Comoedies they make us cry.

In the *Dialogues*, Brecht's Dramaturg also talks of different styles (changing rules):

> *The Dramaturg:* . . . On top of that our acting can be natural-istic one night and stylized the next. Our actors can speak blank verse or gutter lan-guage, both equally well. Our musical come-dies quite often turn out to be tragic, our tragedies include songs. One night the stage can show a house that is realistic down to the last detail, to the last stove pipe; the next night a wheat market can be represented by a few coloured poles. Our clowns make the audi-ence shed tears, our tragedies reduce it to helpless laughter. With us, in other words, everything is possible. Should I add 'alas'?
>
> (p. 13)

It is not that Brecht is actually picking up what Villiers wrote, even if he knew it, but that he is very much a man of the theatre, despite his political interests, very much concerned for the theatre. Far from exposing naturalism, or realism, or expres-sionism or any other -ism, Brecht uses all the dramatic tech-niques at his disposal and (whatever his ostensible aims) revivifies drama.

The use of Brechtian techniques in English theatre has faced another difficulty besides that of audiences attuned to a theatrical response different from that which Brecht expected. His technique has been seen as a means of getting across in the English theatre (as in Germany) political and social messages. This is understandable, but it would be more rewarding to theatre (and more effective in influencing audiences, perhaps) were his techniques seen as a means of writing a drama capable of giving a vigorous theatrical experience based on the English audience's capacity to respond in the same work to the legitimate and illegitimate traditions. It is no accident that two of the liveliest dramas which have hit the English theatre since 1956, *The Entertainer* (1957) and *Oh What a Lovely War* (1963), have used both these traditions. It is possible to see from her experience in pre-war street theatre (which used the techniques of the Living Newspaper[31]), how Joan Littlewood could have evolved *Oh What a Lovely War*,[32] but the influence of Brecht (and she was the first to produce *Mother Courage* on the stage in England, at Barnstaple in 1955) affected this . . . what? Show? For example, the Newspanel carries the headlines:

300,000 ALLIED CASUALTIES DURING AUGUST

A girl
calls out: Chocolates, vanilla ices, bonbons; next week at this theatre, a special double bill: the great American comedy Teddy Get Your Gun and He Didn't Want to Do It, featuring Whata Funk, the conchie. Chocolates, vanilla ices, bonbons [*Enter male dancer with sheet music*] Have you got your copy of Gwendoline Brogden's latest hit – complete with pianoforte parts included –

(pp. 34–5)

The jolly song, 'Hitchy-Koo', is then sung and during the girl's announcement and the song, four slides are shown. Three of the slides show advertisements for tonics – Carter's Little Liver Pills, Phosperine and Beecham's Pills (depicting a cyclist who has just been run down by another cyclist, and the legend 'If you are run down, take Beecham's Pills'). There is a touch of ironic humour in this last advertisement, for it has an incongruous link with the 300,000 casualties. The fourth slide is not an advertisement for a tonic, but offers a more bitter comment on the commercial advantage to be gained from the war:

Beware of umbrellas made on German frames. When you Buy an Umbrella Insist on Having a Fox's frame.

The great difficulty of getting English audiences to think politically in the theatre (and perhaps at any time) is well illustrated by *Oh What a Lovely War*. Despite Living Newspaper and Brechtian influence, it was 'a great show'. Its pierrots and gaiety, its newsflashes and bitter ironies, may well have affected attitudes, but not through 'thought', 'detachment', the A-effect. It was not just a romp, it did touch nerve centres; but its message came across through subconscious feeling, not detached thought. It was, for that reason, far more successful theatrically and 'politically' than plays more overtly attempting Brechtian techniques with the intention of directly effecting changes of response.

The recovery of past techniques was not always a direct result of Continental influence. O'Neill's many experiments included a number that attempted to adapt old techniques to the needs of the twentieth-century theatre. In *Strange Interlude* (1928), for example, the actors on-stage would 'freeze' whilst one of their number unburdened himself or herself of unspoken or sub-conscious thoughts. Despite certain confusions and dramatic awkwardness, this development of the aside was effective in this play, though hardly capable of general use. More significant, and anticipating English practice by a couple of decades, was the work of Thornton Wilder.

At the end of his Preface to his three plays, *Our Town* (1938), *The Matchmaker* (1938, as *The Merchant of Yonkers*) and *The Skin of Our Teeth* (1942), Wilder says very modestly that he is 'not one of the new dramatists we are looking for . . . I am not an innovator but a rediscoverer of forgotten goods and I hope a remover of obtrusive bric-à-brac'.[33] Wilder is certainly a redis-coverer, not in the sense of reminding us that there was a great Austrian comic dramatist called Johann Nestroy, still less that there was a farceur called John Oxenford (the work of both of whom underlies *The Matchmaker*),[34] but in the way he successfully and convincingly restored to the legitimate stage, in a viable form, the techniques of direct address. Further, he showed to the world in *Our Town* how the false illusion of the theatre could be swept away, without destroying the theatre's unique power for making us feel intensely. Wilder's earliest attempts at effecting this combination still have quite remarkable theatrical power. *The Happy Journey to Trenton and Camden* (1931), a one-acter, is almost naively simple on the surface, so much so that in directing a cast of American students presenting the play to an English audience in 1981, my chief problem was convincing the performers that they would not be laughed off the stage. I was myself convinced enough that the play would work but I confess to being taken by surprise at just how effective it was, especially when played before the kind of audience not usually susceptible to such seemingly simple fare.

The play dramatises to perfection that finding 'value above all price for the smallest events in our daily life' in which Wilder so strongly believed. Décor is irrelevant. Wilder demands that there be no scenery – take the stage as it is. The stage manager is required to make a car out of four kitchen chairs and he reads most of his lines from his script making little attempt at characterisation. He plays men, women and children – but also takes on the role of a petrol filling-station attendant. Elmer, the loved but somewhat dominated father, mimes his driving because to Wilder the slightest human actions are so much more precious than the mechanisms they set in motion. The journey itself covers a mere thirty miles or so, passing the township, Laurenceville, where Wilder worked as a schoolteacher for a time – the school is pointed out in the play – and the play lasts some twenty-five minutes. Yet, in its quiet, 'undramatic' way it is intensely moving as it celebrates how every fleeting moment of our living is to be treasured.

The effect on the audiences, the sympathetic laughter, the stillness, especially at the end, were clear evidence of the play's power to touch the heart, even in 1981. Less public, but even more striking, was the way it moved some of those who performed it. With its two companion pieces, *The Long Christmas Dinner* and *Pullman Car Hiawatha*, *The Happy Journey* was performed on a number of occasions as part of the Federal Theatre Project between 1936 and 1939. Bearing in mind that amongst those who gained early experience of the theatre in this project were such people as Orson Welles, Arthur Miller and Joseph Losey, it is not too outrageous to suggest that these one-acters played a part in bringing about major changes in approaches to drama in the United States.

Our Town has, it must be admitted, something in common with a Norman Rockwell painting for the *Saturday Evening Post*. They both show superb craftsmanship; Rockwell's is traditional; in Wilder's, tradition is modified in an important way by its frame. Both can be regarded as reflecting a rather over-simplified view of values passed or passing: a time that was. Yet Rockwell at his best, and Wilder in *Our Town*, achieve what Wilder says was his aim: 'to find a value above all price for the smallest events in our daily life' (p.12). In a manner typical of him he goes on, 'I have made the claim as preposterous as possible . . . But it is not preposterous.' The *Washington Post* said, in an editorial tribute to Norman Rockwell shortly after his death at the age of 84, 'Mr Rockwell addressed and nourished a down-home American sentimentality that he recognised as deep and serious'; he was a man 'genuinely awe-struck by the mysteries of simple acts'; and it instances a Thanksgiving Day cover for 1945 'showing a mother and her soldier son peeling potatoes together in the kitchen'. The borderline between touching deep well-springs of feeling and triteness is extraordinarily narrow and such an artist's task is today the more difficult in societies reluctant to express such sentiments. Although in America Wilder's *Our Town* has become hackneyed through countless amateur performances, its freshness is still apparent in England. Wilder avoids much of the danger of the kind of sentimentality into which Rockwell can slip by the use of a dramatic frame. The direct address of the stage manager, the empty, half-lit stage, ensure that from the beginning we sense that this is 'just a story'. Our emotions need not be involved. We are to observe, to be detached. But it is not possible.

Brigid Brophy once analysed her reactions to sentimentality in a discussion of Louisa M. Alcott's *Little Women*.[35] Being herself an almost wholly unsentimental writer, she was not afraid of Louisa M. Alcott's example. It was as a reader she feared her; because she made her cry. In the course of analysing the novel and the way it worked on her, she made a number of very interesting points. The true artistic impulses she described as relentless if not cruel; the sentimentalist would not take the responsibility for being ruthless; instead 'he appears to hold his hand in compunction'. Secondly she pointed out how:

> The weepiest of trashy movies is the one which throws in a moment or two of genuine newsreel. And then, having invoked the reality of the real world, sentimentality does the one thing neither morality nor art can stand for – it is hypocritical.

Thirdly, she referred to an incident in J. M. Barrie's *Peter Pan* (1904) which she categorised as the ultimate sentimental immorality:

> The most unforgivable of all the occasions when sentimentality has burst through the artistic conventions is the one when Peter Pan bursts through the proscenium and invites the audience to keep Tinker Bell alive by affirming that they believe in fairies.

'If I could see any sense in censorship at all' she commented a little later, '*Peter Pan* would probably by my first and only candidate.' Using these criteria it is possible to see not only how *Our Town* avoids overall sentimentality, though coming close to it, but what dangers lie in wait for those using techniques of direct address.

Emily dies in childbirth and the last act is almost entirely concerned with death and loss. Almost entirely, for in a very important way, the converse is true; for Emily's brief return to the scene she treasures from the past – her twelfth birthday, Tuesday 11 February 1899 – asserts for the smallest events of everyday life that value above all price: it is akin to Rockwell's soldier and his mother peeling potatoes in thanksgiving. Nowhere does Wilder get through to us more movingly than when George (Emily's husband) falls full-length at Emily's grave. Emily has just asked the Stage Manager, 'Do any human beings ever realise life while they live it? – every, every minute?': As George falls by her, she says to her mother-in-law in the next grave:

> They don't understand, do they?
> *Mrs Gibbs:*   No, dear. They don't understand.
>
> (p. 90)

The outward similarity between this and the conventional, sentimental deathbed scene is close. But there are marked differences, and the most important is the graveyard itself:

> *During the intermission the audience has seen the stagehands arranging the stage. On the right-hand side, a little right of the centre, ten or twelve ordinary chairs have been placed in three openly spaced rows facing the audience.*
> *These are graves in the cemetery . . .*
>
> *The dead do not turn their heads or their eyes to right or left, but they sit in quiet without stiffness. When they speak their tone is matter-of-fact, without sentimentality, and above all, without lugubriousness.*
>
> (p.74)

The setting and the direct address of the Stage Manager have a double effect. They deny dramatic realism, so that there is for the audience a sense of detachment; but, at the same time, they appeal to actual life – the life we know – so that the full impact of loss is felt. What Wilder manages to do, however, is to dramatise not loss in death (as the sentimentalists would) but loss in life, in what is left unrealised and untreasured in the ordinary things of the everyday world.

Although Wilder's touch is extraordinarily sure, there is the occasional moment of uncertainty. In Act 2, for example, there is a brilliant instance of a double break in illusion, and just after-wards the play hovers on the sentimental, a little in the fashion described by Brigid Brophy of *Peter Pan*.

Emily Webb and George Gibbs are to be married. The Stage Manager tells us directly about the event, breaking continuity in the way to which we have become accustomed. Then he announces that, like A and B in *Fulgens and Lucres*, he is going to take part in the play, and he comments upon the changing nature of the play, and about marriage in general:

> [*When all is ready the Stage Manager strolls to the centre of the stage, down front, and, musingly, addresses the audience.*]
>
> Stage
> Manager: . . . In this wedding I play the minister. That gives me the right to say a few more things about it.
>
> For a while, now, the play gets pretty serious.
>
> Y'see, some churches say that marriage is a sacrament. I don't quite know what that means, but I can guess. . . .
>
> This is a good wedding, but people are so put together that even at a good wedding there's a lot of confusion way down deep in people's minds and we thought that that ought to be in our play, too . . .
>
> (pp. 67–8)

The audience has now to suspend its disbelief of the Stage Manager in his role as commentator, and see him as minister and hear his 'sermon'. In this way the audience is 'taken into the play' as never before and just as it is to become 'pretty serious'.

As the congregation assembles an organ plays and then

Emily's mother arrives. As she goes to her place she turns back and speaks to the audience (so the stage direction):

> I don't know why on earth I should be crying. I suppose there's nothing to cry about. It came over me at breakfast this morning; there was Emily eating her breakfast as she's done for seventeen years and now she's going off to eat it in someone else's house. I suppose that's it.
>
> And Emily! She suddenly said: I can't eat another mouthful, and she put her head down on the table and *she* cried.   (pp. 68–9)

Now this *is* 'through the proscenium arch' and it comes close indeed to Peter Pan's appeal, only avoiding the same judgement because the audience does not have to respond actively and intervene in the play's action. Whereas the Stage Manager's shift in role to performer is skilfully achieved, Mrs Webb's change from performer to commentator is awkward and her assessment – 'The whole world's wrong, that's what's the matter' – is not saved from being trite by being spoken 'In half-amused exasperation' (p. 69). What the Stage Manager says is not much more profound, but his function is clearly established, and the matter-of-fact content of much of what he says, from the opening film-like credits to his bidding the audience, 'You get a good rest, too. Good night' (p. 91), provides a sure context for his philosophising.

Immediately Mrs Webb hurries to her place in the 'church', lightly suggested by the arrangement of chairs and the projection of a lantern slide showing a stained-glass window, the bridegroom enters, *through the auditorium*, to be catcalled by three baseball players 'by the right proscenium pillar'. (Surely it should have been the left pillar – or by 'right' does Wilder mean stage left?) Then, completing a triangle of dramatic illusions, the Stage Manager 'pushes them off the stage' (p. 69).

This short sequence, from the getting ready of the stage for the wedding to the baseball players being sent off (a little over two pages) demands a considerable degree of sophistication of theatrical response from the audience, not unlike that required by Shakespeare in *Troilus and Cressida* (see *Popular Appeal in English Drama to 1850*, p. 64). What makes this possible is the music-hall (in America, vaudeville) tradition. Wilder relies upon that tradition for dramatic effect and, curiously, he may get American and English audiences to 'think through the skin – through feeling' more effectively than can Brecht, whose techniques appear similar but demand a kind of break in response which English and American audiences put to other purposes.

One more point might be added about this remarkable play. Wilder had shown in his novel *The Bridge of San Luis Rey* (1927) his interest in reworking a particular event from several different points of view. In *Our Town* he does deliberately what Shakespeare does accidentally in *Othello*; he uses a double time-scale. The Stage Manager keeps real time: the time of the play. The action takes place over fourteen years, but the earliest period, 1899, comes as a flashback within the latest, 1913. Acts I and II are set in 1901 and 1904 respectively. Like the setting, this dual time scheme, because it is conscious, has the effect of ensuring that the audience is always aware it is in a theatre.

> Stage   That's the end of the First Act, friends. You can go
> Manager: and smoke now, those that smoke.
>   (p. 49)

For all that, the result is theatrical. In denying 'stageyness', Wilder yet creates an intensely theatrical experience.

Wilder's next play is now known as *The Matchmaker*. It was originally called *The Merchant of Yonkers*, was slightly adapted to its present form as *The Matchmaker*, made into a film in 1958, and into a musical (*Hello, Dolly*) in 1964. Wilder, in his Preface, says he has read 'small theses in German comparing it with the great Austrian original on which it is based' (p. 13), and implies that this is the wrong way to go about studying it. Wilder does not seek to imitate the special kind of Viennese theatre that is Nestroy. In a way he is closer to the Oxenford original, *A Day Well Spent* (1835). The most interesting characteristic of *The Matchmaker* in the context of this study does not feature in Oxenford nor, so far as I can tell, in Nestroy (although several characters have soliloquies). Wilder says the play shakes off the nonsense of the nineteenth-century staging (p. 13), and that that can especially be seen in the use of direct address to the audience. Unlike *Our Town*, the direct address is not (in the main) in the hands of a commentator, but is spoken by characters of the play coming down to the footlights to address the audience. Dolly Levi addresses the camera directly from early on in the film version, but in the play it is the Merchant of Yonkers, Mr Vandergelder, who has the first such speech. The original and revised versions of the play show textual modifications, as would be expected, but the most interesting difference is the slightly greater insistence on direct address to the audience in the later version. It is almost as if Wilder had gathered confidence in the experiment after the first production (directed in 1938 by Max Reinhardt, incidentally, who had directed *Six Characters in Search of an Author* fourteen years earlier). The very first passage of direct address (p. 194 in the Penguin edition; p. 19 in the 1939 New York edition of *The Merchant of Yonkers*) is marked: 'The following speech is addressed to the audience' in *The Matchmaker*, but this direction is omitted from *The Merchant of Yonkers*. However, both versions direct Cornelius to come to the footlights and address the audience in simple naive sincerity in Act Two (pp. 224 and 74 respectively). His speech is interrupted in the original by Barnaby's line, 'Can I take off my shoes, Cornelius?', though there is no reaction from Cornelius. In the revision, Barnaby's line precedes Cornelius's speech. Both versions direct Malachi to address the audience in Act Three (pp. 251 and 127), but the original also directs him to come down to the footlights after the first couple of words ('You're surprised?').

The most significant changes come at the end of the play. Mrs Levi has a long speech first, 'addressing an imaginary Ephraim' (her deceased husband) and then the audience. The direction, 'addressing an imaginary Ephraim' is not included in the original version and there are considerable verbal differences, one in particular showing how Wilder was wary of sentimentality and how he endeavoured to avoid it. In the revised version Mrs Levi says: 'Money, I've always felt, money – pardon my expression – is like manure; it's not worth a thing unless it's spread about encouraging young things to grow' (p. 278). The original has: 'Oh, my friends, – fellow-fools, fellow monsters, – I want to live in a world where there is just enough money for us to enjoy ourselves in moderation, and just enough freedom for us to play the fool in moderation' (pp. 173–4). The 'manure' image completely undercuts the sentimentality inherent in 'encouraging young things to grow', and is in accord with the muting found elsewhere in the speech, e.g. 'the six or seven human pleasures that are our right in the world' become 'four or five' in the revision.

At the end of the revised version, Miss Van Huysen addresses
the audience, and she is followed by Dolly. Then Barnaby is
'reluctantly pushed forward to the footlights', 'to tell us what the
moral of the play is', just like his almost namesake in *Nice
Wanton*. In the original there is only one speech direct to the
audience, instead of the three of the revision, and Dolly's, 'There
isn't any more coffee; there isn't any more gingerbread, and there
isn't any more play – but there is one more thing we have to do
. . . Barnaby, come here . . .' (p. 281) is much more sentimental
in the original: 'There isn't any more coffee; there isn't any more
gingerbread. But with a little encouragement, and – Heaven
helping us! – continued freedom, we'll all come down the
Hudson River again in search of a change.' The company then
joins hands in a semi-circle in *The Merchant of Yonkers* and sings
'Old Father Hudson'. Not, perhaps, quite as excruciating as
Leo's curtain speech in Clifford Odets's *Paradise Lost* (1935),[36]
but nevertheless a false note which Wilder was quick to excise.

The Skin of Our Teeth also begins, as Wilder points out (p.13),
'by making fun of old-fashioned playwriting', but there is more
to the play than that and more to it than seeing 'two times at once'
as Wilder puts it. If Wilder was not saying he was making fun of
old-fashioned playwriting, one would be tempted to suggest that
he was adopting Brechtian techniques in much the same way that
Our Town may be said to have been influenced by Pirandello and
The Living Newspaper. *The Skin of Our Teeth* had its first
performance in New Haven, Connecticut, on 15 October 1942
(directed by Elia Kazan). Brecht's *Mother Courage*, though
written in 1938–9, was only performed for the first time on 19
April 1941, in Zurich, and Wilder's play is at least as remarkable a
development of the epic technique of Piscator, Bronnen and
Brecht, as it is a parody and re-discovery of 'old-fashioned
playwriting'.

It is fairly easy to trace how Wilder began, like Fielding in
Shamela, by mocking a tradition in *Our Town* and *The Matchmaker*, by re-using the old forms (as Shaw had done in, for
example, *The Devil's Disciple*), and then developing a new form
in which 'legitimate' and 'illegitimate' modes were freshly
related. *The Skin of Our Teeth* begins with news announcements,
a step on from the opening of *Our Town*; it juxtaposes different
periods (an Ice Age complete with tame dinosaur and mammoth
who slip in with the telegraph boy to warm themselves by the

fire; the invention of the wheel and the alphabet; and the contemporary America of A & P store and Pennsylvania Station); there is no shortage of direct address to the audience; and the set instead of being sketchy, as in *Our Town*, falls apart from time to time. There is even a juxtaposition of the real time of the play and that of the play-world, as in *Our Town*, in Sabina's direct address to the audience in which she wishes it were 11 p.m. for she doesn't wish to be dragged through yet another performance (p. 105). Later, in a way that could be called Wilderian as much as Brechtian, Sabina speaks in her own person as the actress, Miss Somerset, and is rebuked from within the play by another character (Mr Antrobus), and from outside it by the Stage Manager:

Sabina:	. . . Oh, *I* see what this part of the play means now! This means refugees.
	[*She starts to cross to the proscenium*]
	Oh, I don't like it. I don't like it.
	[*She leans against the proscenium and bursts into tears*]
Antrobus:	Miss Somerset!
Voice of Stage Manager:	Miss Somerset!
Sabina:	[*energetically, to the audience*] Ladies and gentlemen! Don't take this play serious. The world's not coming to an end.

The refugees turn out to include Homer and Moses. Each speaks a few words of his own work, printed in Greek and Hebrew in the text (that for Moses – 'In the beginning was the Word . . .' being printed upside down in the Penguin edition). There is a sense of extravaganza and this is heightened in Act Three when it is announced by Antrobus that seven of the actors have been taken ill. Hasty recruitment among dressers, the wardrobe and the theatre ushers fills in the gaps but:

Antrobus:	. . . Now this scene takes place near the end of the act. And I'm sorry to say we'll need a short rehearsal, just a short run-through. And as some of it takes place in the auditorium, we'll have to keep the curtain up. Those of you who wish can go out

in the lobby and smoke some more. The rest of
you can listen to us, or . . . or just talk quietly
among yourselves.

(p. 158)

– but he tries to explain nevertheless, just as Bötticher does in
Puss-in-Boots. The play ends as it began:

Sabina: . . . Six o'clock and the master not home yet. Pray
God nothing serious has happened to him crossing
the Hudson River. But I wouldn't be surprised. The
whole world's at sixes and sevens, and why the
house hasn't fallen down about our ears long ago is a
miracle to me. [*She comes to the footlights*] This is
where you came in. We have to go on for ages and
ages yet. You go home.
The end of the play isn't written yet.
Mr and Mrs Antrobus! Their heads are full of plans
and they're as confident as the first day they began –
and they told me to tell you: good night.

(p. 178)

The lines up to the stage direction (*She comes to the footlights*) are
selected from the opening of Sabina's first speech (p. 99).

Wilder's use (no mere repetition or parodying) of tradition is
varied and skilful. Like a Fielding rehearsal play, or even a
Planché extravaganza, something serious is at issue. Unlike
Brecht produced in English, Wilder works with, not against the
vaudeville and music-hall traditions and the result is good theatre
which gets across its author's deep concerns. His own comment
on pp. 13–14 of the Penguin edition is a very fair and pointed
assessment of the play's affectiveness, especially at a time of
crisis.

There is much that those who would present Brecht in English
can learn from Wilder. It is strange that, despite a production in
London in 1945 directed by Sir Laurence Olivier, it has not had
greater impact on English theatre than has been the case. Perhaps
it came a little too early. Possibly a time of crisis and not of
victory was needed.

It would not be pertinent here to discuss all theatrical developments in America that have influenced English drama, but

perhaps two of the most significant might be mentioned in passing. First, Arthur Miller's adaptation for *Death of a Salesman* (1949) of Ibsen-like social concern to the kind of stage setting used for *Our Town* or the Living Newspaper, *One-Third of a Nation* (1938). And secondly, the development (or rather, freezing) of Stanislavski's teaching into 'The Method'. This integration of the individual's life and his acting, sometimes effectively but often falsely, can unwittingly deny the very theatricality of the drama in performance. I have a sneaking sympathy with the English actor who, reputedly, answered the American Method-director's urgent questions: 'Where have you come from? What is your motivation?' with, 'The wings. Money.'

On 10 April 1957, John Osborne's *The Entertainer* had its first night. Sir Laurence Olivier played Archie Rice, Dorothy Tutin played Jean, and Phoebe was acted by Brenda da Banzie. The director was Tony Richardson. Ten years later John Osborne dealt severely with the suggestion made in *The Penguin Dictionary of the Theatre* (edited by J. R. Taylor) that the play was Brecht-inspired. The entry reads:

> *The Entertainer* (1957), despite the advocacy of Sir Laurence Olivier, failed to integrate the realistic style of the body of the work with the Brecht-inspired, non-realistic, music-hall framework.

John Osborne writing in *The Times Saturday Review* (14 October 1967) said that the *Penguin Dictionary* was 'full of know-all shots in the dark' such as this assertion, for at the time 'Brecht was little more than a name to me. I had, however, been going to the music hall before the compiler was born.'

It is not difficult to see how the compiler could have imagined that Osborne knew a certain amount about Brecht, at least in the year before *The Entertainer* was first performed, for 1956 (the year of *Look Back in Anger*) was an important year for Brecht productions in London. The Berliner Ensemble visited London in the late summer and performed *Mother Courage, The Caucasian Chalk Circle* and *Pauken und Trompeten* (the starting point of which is Farquhar's *The Recruiting Officer*). The Royal Court Theatre (where *Look Back in Anger* and *The Entertainer* were both first performed) had put on *The Threepenny Opera* in February

1956 and *The Good Woman of Setzuan* later in that year, and,
according to John Willett,[37] John Osborne played the Water
Carrier in the latter play. The Royal Academy of Dramatic Art
presented *The Caucasian Chalk Circle* and Unity Theatre gave
The Exception and the Rule. The significance of these Brecht
productions was the more important because until 1956 only
three of his plays had been seen in London (in 1933, 1936 and
1938).[38] But whatever apparent Brechtian influence there is in
The Entertainer (and on the face of it, looking only at the play,
there *seems* to be an influence), John Osborne is completely right,
I believe, in asserting that, over and above its subject, *the*
influence is the music hall. It also seems to me that the author of
The Penguin Dictionary is completely wrong in suggesting that
there is a failure to integrate styles. Osborne, happily, like
Wilder, has written in the traditions he knew and for an audience
capable of responding to those traditions. To look at *The
Entertainer* and expect to find Brecht brings misinterpretation and
undervaluation. Look at the play as an exciting theatrical
experience that gets across what its author has to say, and it is
easy to see a brilliant use of conventional fourth-wall-removed
drama combined with the music-hall tradition. Indeed, rather
than to Brecht, it is to Planché and Fielding that one might look
back for such conscious presentation of the stage on-stage, and to
Fielding in particular for its concern with the society of its time.

The Entertainer* works in the way *Our Town* and *The Skin of
Our Teeth* work. Our response to one mode leaves us wide open
to emotions and feelings expressed in the other mode. Members
of an audience responding to a run-down music-hall act with a
certain detachment, prepared to smile their educated English
heads off (as Archie Rice suggests before his story of the negress
in the bar), find that *their* roles have been switched and that they
must respond to what otherwise they would be wary of (just like
the audience to the 'cemetery of chairs' in *Our Town*). Archie's
story of the negress epitomises the technique of the whole play.
He is going to tell us his most moving experience. Any respectable English audience will then firmly gird its collective loins
about it to ensure that it gives way to no emotion at all. But
Osborne is always one step ahead.[39]

The speech alternates between moments of feeling – even
sentimentality – read or heard in isolation, but juxtaposed with
undercutting deflation. The conventional comedian's patter

takes us slightly off-guard, because this is one of the domestic
scenes. Archie tells the audience about 'some negress', and the
'some', especially applied to a black woman, is dismissive,
almost contemptuous. '*Now you're going to smile at this*, you're
going to smile your educated English heads off' (the italics are
Osborne's) – and of course then we won't smile. Sentimentality
follows – you've never sat lonely and half slewed in *some* bar (my
italics – that 'some' again); Jean may not have done, but (at least
in 1956) many of Osborne's audience had. The next sentence
perfectly balances the sentimentality of the first half with
throwaway deflation – partially in 'that old fat negress', and then
completely in 'Jesus or something like that':

> But if ever I saw any hope or strength in the human race, it was
> in the face of that old fat negress getting up to sing about Jesus
> or something like that.

The next sentence pictures her totally and with utter simplicity; it
is something of this that just prevents Archie's deflating reference
to himself lapsing into self-pity: 'She was poor and lonely and
oppressed like nobody you've ever known. Or me, for that
matter.' Archie's speech continues in this manner and the total
effect is to convey a sense of that loss of feeling which has im-
poverished us as a people. Like Shaw, Osborne in *The Entertainer*
can criticise his audience without so offending them that they
don't listen. This he does through his use of the music-hall *idea*
(rather than the music-hall subject), those whispers of the past
that Billy knew. 'I'm dead behind these eyes' says Archie (p. 72),
picking up Osborne's stage direction of p. 59, as it were), but
dead 'just like the whole inert, shoddy lot out there', referring to
the audience listening, in its other role as music-hall audience.

After Mick's death, the two worlds of domestic life and music
hall begin to merge. The audience which, till then, had subcon-
sciously known its role, is now unwittingly caught between
those roles. Frank's blues in Number Nine – is it an act – about
Mick? Number Eleven is a stage announcement: Billy Rice is
dead. The funeral cortège passes – but with 'snatches of old
songs, wisps of tunes, the stumble of a banjo' (p. 83), in the
background. Which world is the audience in, domestic or music-
hall? Then the final scene, firmly back in the halls at first – but the
unfinished story, the man with his hook in the wings, the shift to

the bare stage, Phoebe's appearance with his coat, and Archie's faltering attempts to sing? For the audience both roles have coalesced and the effect is powerful. But Osborne has not done. He has Archie come down to the footlights and from the conventional 'thank you', turns the whole relationship upside down: 'You've been a good audience. Very good. A very *good* audience. Let me know where you're working tomorrow night – and I'll come and see YOU' (p. 89). It is a touch of genius, but it would not work unless the audience's two roles had been carefully defined in the first two acts (like the alternating moods of Archie's speech about the negress), and then skilfully brought together in the third act. Osborne provides the perfect means for doing this, but it requires in production all the techniques of conventional and music-hall theatres, and an actor to play Archie Rice who can hold an audience in an emotion-filled part but also take full note of Osborne's direction that whatever he says is 'almost always very carefully "thrown away". Apparently absent-minded, it is a comedian's technique, it absolves him seeming committed to anyone or anything' (p. 34).

Central to this chapter has been Tieck's play, *Puss-in-Boots*, so it is appropriate to conclude with a play that has successfully used similar techniques more recently. Tom Stoppard followed up the success of his 'behind the scenes' drama, *Rosencrantz and Guildenstern Are Dead* (1966), by a play that presents critics who become involved in what is presented before them: *The Real Inspector Hound* (1968).[40] The audience appears to be confronted by its own reflection in a huge mirror – or at least, rising from the back of the stage there appears to be an auditorium with 'pale smudges of faces'. As the play progresses, Stoppard directs that these 'can be progressively faded out' until only two seats remain visible. These are occupied by Moon, who is later joined by Birdboot, two 'drama critics'. Between the critics and the true audience is an acting area with as realistic a set as possible, on which will be played a conventional murder mystery. The dialogue is splendidly amusing and parodies drawing-room detective-drama clichés of the 1930s to perfection:

Cynthia: . . . fetch the Major down.
Mrs Drudge: I think I hear him coming downstairs now [*as she leaves*].
              [*She does: the sound of a wheelchair approaching*

> *down several flights of stairs with landings in be-*
> *tween. It arrives bearing Magnus at about 15 m. p. h.*
> *knocking Simon over violently.*]

Cynthia:	Simon!
Magnus:	[*roaring*] Never had a chance! Ran under the wheels!
Cynthia:	Darling, are you all right?
Magnus:	I have witnesses!
Cynthia:	Oh, Simon – say something!
Simon:	[*Sitting up suddenly*] I'm most frightfully sorry.
Magnus:	[*shouting yet*] How long have you been a pedestrian?
Simon:	Ever since I could walk.
Cynthia:	Can you walk now . . . ?
	[*Simon rises and walks*]
	Thank God! Magnus, this is Simon Gascoyne.
Magnus:	What's he doing here?
Cynthia:	He just turned up. (p. 23)

Stoppard does not quite make the same demand as a play submitted to Richmond Theatre in the late 1930s. This required that a murder be committed by a heavy roller running down hill and over the victim in full view of the audience. It was not performed.[41] The tone of the play-within-the-play is very much that of the thirties and early forties. The setting is that of Agatha Christie's *Murder at the Vicarage* (1930) or *Peril at End House* (dramatised 1949 and 1940 respectively), though Maurice Charney regards it as a parody of 'a hopelessly banal Victorian murder mystery'.[42] The play shows similarities to Tieck's *Puss-in-Boots*, with the critics at both plays exposed as sham intellectuals. Its structure is very close to that of a Jonson play with induction and intermeans – although one is in danger of being just as portentous as Moon and Birdboot in pointing this out:

Induction:	pp. 9–12.
Play-within-play:	Act I, pp. 13–26.
Intermean:	pp. 26–8.
Play-within-play:	Act II, p. 28–top of p. 35.
Intermean:	pp. 35–6.
Play-within-play:	Act III should begin at p. 36, but Moon answers the 'stage' telephone; it is for

Birdfoot – his wife complaining about his association with one of the characters, Felicity – who then enters and takes him for Simon, killed in 'Act II'.
Act I curtain repeated, p. 42.
Play and Frame: pp. 42–8.

The obvious difference is the way in which the frame and play-within-the-play coalesce, like *Fulgens and Lucres* (with Birdboot protesting at Moon becoming involved (p. 36), just as A protests when B determines to join the play), or like *The Entertainer*. The setting is similar to that for Act II, Scene 2 of Richard Brome's *The Antipodes* (1637), where the Doctor and Peregrine sit on one side of the stage and Letoy and his guests 'sit at the other end of the stage', masked so that they will not be recognised by Peregrine. A play-within-the-play then takes place between two groups of on-stage spectators, the audience providing a third group of spectators. Or one could even compare the setting with Bernini's 'extraordinary theatrical performance which occurred in Rome in the year 1637' when a double auditorium effect was achieved.[43] But this is to play into Stoppard's hands. *The Real Inspector Hound* is a farce, and it is good entertainment. To that extent it is not using these devices for the reasons Jonson or Brome, or Randolph or Tieck used them. There is certainly no attack on the audience, no attempt to educate the audience. Nor is the parody of the detective play of the thirties the basis for something more serious, as in Fielding or Wilder. But the play surely has a point. Not everyday can a dramatist get away with satirising the critics – the *Observer* critic's review, reprinted in part on the backcover of the published edition, might have been written by Birdboot:

> He has stayed faithful to his talent, which is comedy. *Inspector Hound* is deliberately smaller, lighter and more shamelessly unimproving than its predecessor. It's an object of pure, virtuoso craft and display, as luxuriously self-sufficient as a netsuke or Fabergé Easter egg.

But the real point of the satire of the critics is not the take-off of their review style, nor exposing their rivalries, but, surely, re-vamping Tieck's play, almost unnoticed.

4 The Contemporary Scene

In 1944, when drama of the *théâtre de boulevard* in London was in something of a rut and music hall was a declining art, S. L. Bethell wrote:

> It is to the despised popular theatre that we must look for a revival of the drama, since only there do the rudiments survive of an appropriate psychological situation.[1]

That was a bold statement at the time but within a dozen years, Bethell was shown to be right. On 3 August 1955 Beckett's *Waiting for Godot* was given its first English performance. It would be otiose to go over again the relationship of the play to the illegitimate drama – to Charlot, tramp acts, the boot routine, cross-talk technique, the references to the audience ('that bog') – just as it would be to detail the dramatic complexities and intellectual profundities which make *Waiting for Godot* so very much more than a mere vaudeville routine.[2] Nearly two years later, *Endgame* was first performed in English, and I tried in the Kathleen Robinson Lecture (1963) to suggest how aspects of that play are related to the popular comic tradition, particularly the representation of a music-hall comedian composing and trying-out a monologue. In that same lecture the popular dramatic origins of *The Birthday Party* (1957), *The Dumb Waiter* (1960) and *The Caretaker* (1960) were also discussed.[3] Earlier in this study, the relationship of *All that Fall* (1957) to radio comedy has been mentioned and the use made of the music-hall tradition in *The Entertainer* (1957) has been analysed. No less than four of the plays mentioned here were first performed in England in 1957. Quite suddenly the two traditions were once again united after a divorce that had lasted for about a hundred years.

By no means every contemporary play makes use of the popular dramatic tradition, nor is it essential that it should; but it is not unreasonable to suggest that the often exciting theatre of the past couple of decades or so owes much to its use of the popular tradition. It is not that cross-talk acts or monologues comparable in mode with those of music hall have been used – those are but outward signs – but that the audience has once again become a part of the theatrical experience. The music-hall audience even at its less than best was alive to the event, and considerable demands were made upon the imagination of each member of that audience. Fantasy, innuendo, the creation of actuality all took place in the mind. The audience was directly addressed, conversed with, cajoled, even insulted; it was never forgotten. Furthermore, it 'completed' the acts and songs in a very direct manner.

Overhearing a drama in a darkened auditorium, the players assuming there is no audience out there, but responsive even to the silence, can also be exciting. It would be a great pity if this relatively new tradition were completely lost. There is much to commend it, provided it does not monopolise the legitimate stage. How ironical that ending one monopoly, that of the Patent Theatres, should have led to another – that of the well-made audience! The past twenty or so years have seen many plays and productions which have acknowledged the existence of the audience. This may lead to gimmicks, like the opening of the Royal Shakespeare Company's *Taming of the Shrew* in 1978, in which a seemingly unruly member of the audience got involved in the play but turned out to be Christopher Sly; but even these are indicative of a fresh (if ancient) way of relating play to audience. And what may seem at first a gimmick may prove, as when the houselights went up early as Gloucester struggled off blinded in that same company's *King Lear* of a decade earlier, a creative insight into the relationship of play and audience. The blinded Gloucester had to struggle off, as it were, through an audience intent on interval refreshments.

We are now fortunate in having a theatre which can play to a particularly responsive audience, an audience educated as Jonson might have wished. Responsiveness is not a matter of applause or laughter or bated breath, welcome though they all are, but of that use of the imagination that enables plays such as *Landscape* and *Silence* to be completed in performance. If this is true of the contemporary drama, it is also true of the production today of earlier drama – Shakespeare, Marlowe, Jonson, Tourner, Webster, Ford, the Restoration dramatists, and even such little-known plays as O'Keeffe's *Wild Oats* (1779 – though it has been revived between then and now). The Royal Shakespeare Company's practice of presenting contemporary plays as well as those of Shakespeare and his time has been but one example of the way in which there has been beneficial cross-fertilisation between drama of the past and present.

The influence of the popular tradition is not without its dangers, however. It is easy to succumb to vulgarisation – as that word has come to be used – and the need which performers have (especially in the popular arts) to project themselves in their own stage person, rather than through the parts they play, can tempt those in the legitimate theatre to self-indulgence. Once one begins to take note of the audience as part of the performance, it is a short step to using the audience to gratify other ends than those of the work being produced for the benefit of that audience. The involvement of the audience in those modern versions of the dramatised sermon, street and fringe theatre political polemic, can be on a par with Peter Pan's plea to the audience to save Tinker Bell. It is vital to the theatre to remember its dramatic heritage, but it must bear in mind that part of that heritage is a dissociation from the sermon and the church. The 'burden of meaning' of a play may only rightly overwhelm an audience if it does so by dramatic and theatrical means. In the last two chapters I propose to discuss the use of the popular tradition in a number of recent plays in order to show how firmly that tradition has been re-integrated into the legitimate theatre; and then I shall consider some of the implications of that drama which endeavours to involve the audience for social or political purposes.

Dramatically and politically, and indeed in terms of his talent, John Arden can be seen as the English Brecht. His career in the theatre has not been without incident, and the outsider might suspect that he gets an even less than fair deal from his theatrical friends than from the non-theatrical Establishment (especially if one includes in the latter, the state school system, which has been a keen setter – and even performer – of *Serjeant Musgrave's Dance*, 1959). *Live Like Pigs* (1958) is the kind of play that must present a difficult dilemma for any company committed to using the theatre to effect social change. In the Introductory Note, Arden explains that he intended the play to be:

> not so much a social document as a study of differing ways of life brought sharply into conflict and both losing their own

particular virtues under the stress of intolerance and mis-understanding.[4]

Arden was 'accused by the Left of attacking the Welfare State' and yet the play was hailed as a defence of anarchy and amorality. That Arden had something to say is apparent from such attacks. Had he been concerned simply to make dramatic capital out of social conflict – to exploit the sentiment rather than to analyse the ethic (to adapt T. S. Eliot[5]) – all might have been well, or he would at worst have been attacked on only one flank. His approach is unsentimental. As he puts it in his Introductory Note, 'Today, quite simply, there are too many buildings in Britain, and there is just no room for nomads' (p. 10). As a result, he approves outright of neither family; he chose them because they illustrate his theme 'in a fairly extreme form'.

The expectation an audience might have of a John Arden work is that it will respond – even 'answer' – some particular political need. *Live Like Pigs* offers no such comfort. It might well be disappointing to an audience oriented to the political left because it does not dramatise issues in an oversimplified manner in order to provide a rallying point for a coterie. Instead it dramatises human inadequacies and prejudices that are shared very broadly. For that reason it might well be most effective with a fairly con-ventional, middle-class audience, prepared to find the play funny (which 'in a large part' Arden intends, p. 101), but willing to be disturbed. The question then to be asked is, 'Does disturbing the audience to this modest extent have any effect?' This can only be answered, I think, by asking another question of a play more clearly committed to a particular line, 'Does it prompt any action if it is only seen by those committed to roughly the same point of view?' No one could give a positive 'Yes' to the first question, but there might well be a longer-term effect, if no more than a nudge in the 'right' direction, whereas the second question might be answered by saying, 'About as much as does whistling in the dark'. A mark of Arden's touch in this play is his Housing Official. Far from his being a conventional ogre or a bureaucrat, he means well and, puzzled at the way the Sawneys treat the house and him ('I'll give yer one half minute to get off of this ground', he is told, p. 109), can only murmur:

I don't know. I don't know. A lovely house, I'd call it. I've not got a house like this, you know. *I* have to live in furnished lodgings, and like it.   (p. 107)

This is hardly the stuff of street drama designed to rouse a housing estate to a rent strike!

The only weakness of the play, apart form the occasional over-writing,[6] is the uncertain use of the ballads. Discussion of this aspect may usefully be preceded by noting Arden's use of techniques which break the continuity of theatrical illusion in two other plays of about the period of *Live Like Pigs*. *The Waters of Babylon* (1957), which begins as a satire on the Premium Bond system (p. 10), ends in a manner reminiscent of *A Nice Wanton* (1550). Krank, before he dies, breaks into verse and, like Barnabas, feels the need to give the audience advice:

> *Krank:*   I said I was not going to die;
> Truth? I am afraid, I think it was a lie.
> So, only a few minutes to live,
> I must see can I not give
> Some clearer conclusion to this play
> To order your lives the neatest way,
> For when after the voters have gone home.
> Mr Loap and lady, there is no bomb.
> Let the Bolshevik tyrants arrive:
> Conviviality shall thrive
> And the ceaseless peace no doubt ensue.
>
> (p. 96)

He continues for a further twenty-two lines before he dies and then there is, if not a prayer for her majesty, a quasi-liturgical exchange:

> *Barbara:*   Deceit upon his tongue. Quicksilver in his mind.
> *Teresa:*   No money in his pocket. Shouting in his house.
> *Bathsheba:*   Songs in his throat. Lightning and thunder in his bed.
>
> (p. 97)

That is followed, just as in *Nice Wanton*, by a song (to the tune of 'The Ash Grove', sung as a four-part round by seven of the characters). This similarity is doubtless coincidental (and I am not suggesting anything else) but it forms an appropriate coda to a moral satire, rather after the manner of *Nice Wanton*. It is the similarity of the artistic solution that is interesting. Here Arden manages the popular tradition effectively.

The Happy Haven (1960), written in collaboration with Margaretta D'Arcy, has a number of characteristics that ensure that the audience realises it is in a theatre, and some of them stem directly from popular drama. The masks used are specifically stated by Arden to be of the *commedia dell'arte* type. There is a Dog which the audience, as well as the performers, have to imagine – it is not a delusion (compare *Harvey*, 1944, with the invisible rabbit; see p. 165, n. 35). In the original production at Bristol University, an open stage 'following roughly the Elizabethan model' was used, with a recess and a small upper stage. This was part of an attempt to open out the conventions of the drama. Finally, there are instances of direct address to the audience.

The play begins with Dr Copperthwaite on the upper stage addressing the audience directly (as indicated by the stage direction), and like Wilder's Stage Manager, welcoming the audience.

> *Doctor:* Ah-hum. Good evening, ladies and gentlemen. First, let me say how glad I am to see you here and to extend a cordial welcome to the Happy Haven. We are, as you know, as yet only a small institution and our grant from the revenues of the National Health Service is alas not as generous as it might be – but, well, I dare say you'll know the old proverb – Time mends all. I'd like you to meet some of the old people who are in our care. As the phrase is, the evening of their lives – well, I've more to say about that later – . . .
>
> (p. 195)

Golightly has a long monologue at the beginning of I.3 and at the end of II.3. Mrs Letouzel talks to Golightly and the audience alternately:

> *Letouzel:* . . . Mr Golightly, what you need is a *friend*: a loving, loyal, and vigilant friend.

[*To the audience*] I have said too much.

[*To Golightly*] I should not have told you.

[*To audience*] I should not have told him. Business is business. Business isn't passion. Passion and rage: to me, that *must* be business. I have let myself go. I think I am an idiot. But let's look for advantage.

[*To Golightly*] I'll accept it: I've told you. I'd better tell you more. Tell you the lot. Come on.

(pp. 228–9)

The last two scenes of the play are both introduced by the Doctor addressing the audience directly, explaining the action, and, even though he is in a tearing hurry, sparing just sixty seconds to tell the audience who the distinguished visitors are. The use of an Elizabethan-style stage (particularly the upper stage) is helpful to such a technique, and the masks may serve to detach the audience a little from the subject, which treats old age without sentimentality. Arden's use of popular techniques is here well suited to his subject and there is an assuredness in the way they are handled. However, the introductory note to *Live Like Pigs* itself suggests less certain control (the italics are mine):

The singing of the ballads should be *in some way integrated* into the action or else cut out. At the Court they were unsuccessful because the singer was put on the stage between the scenes and quickly taken off again so that *no one was really clear* whether he was in the play or out of it.   (p. 102)

The problem is not one of production, however, but one of Arden's own making. The opening song works perfectly. The preliminary direction states that 'The first stanza of all should cut very violently into the hushed hum-and-shuffle that normally comes between the lowering of the house lights and the rise of the curtain' (p. 104). Arden has carefully judged the occasion, like Medwall in *Fulgens and Lucres*, and a voice of the timbre of A. L. Lloyd's (who sang at the first production) is perfect for this task.

The songs are placed 'at the beginning of each (*or nearly each*) scene' – the italics are again mine. Tucked away in parenthesis is one immediate problem. An expectation is built up of 'an introductory statement' (as Arden calls the songs) before each scene and that expectation is tricked to no very clear purpose. He also says that 'The same singer need not sing each stanza if it is considered that a better effect would be produced by varying the voices' (p. 104). The problem posed by these intentions and advices is apparent at the end of the first scene and the beginning of the second (p. 110). Sailor ends the first scene by singing, within the scene, an eight-line stanza of a ballad: 'Oh when I was a strong young man / I wandered on the sea . . .'. The second scene is preceded by two four-line stanzas. Who is to sing them? Someone pushed on for the purpose? Is Sailor to continue? Or Rachel or Rosie, who have the first part of the scene (to whom the song is appropriate)?

> To every woman is a man
> Or two or three or four:
> And she has not got a man
> Must fight a terrible war.

The difficulties scarcely need spelling out. If Sailor continues, the shift in scene is awkward (from interior evening to exterior morning); if a ballad singer enters this contrasts oddly with Sailor's singing; if *one* of the women sings it suggests 'an introductory statement' more appropriate to that woman. Possibly the best solution is to have Rosie and Rachel each sing a verse, especially as one enters slightly after the other. But there is still a problem, for the second stanza picks up the 'mermaids' mentioned in Sailor's song in the preceding scene, and confusion, rather than statement, is likely.

Some of the stanzas work very well, for example those before Scene 3 (to be given to Col?), Scene 4 (the Sailor, singing drunkenly?), and possibly Scene 5 (possibly Col again, as Doreen comes out?). However, the two verses before Scene 6 ('The Doctor's trade's a very good trade'), which have a fine gnomic quality about them, are very puzzling in the theatre. It is almost as if the song has been inserted because it is so attractive rather than relevant and, as a place had to be found for it, associated with Scene 6 because a doctor appears in that scene. There is little to suggest what kind of statement is being made so far as the doctor's role in the scene is concerned – she is far more the disapproving official than is the man from the Council – and so powerful a song is thus rather misleading.

It is a pity that the songs of *Live Like Pigs* are not more dramatically relevant. Arden asks for them to be integrated 'in some way', and hence it is to be assumed that he is not seeking an effect of complete detachment. But if he were, *some* are closely related to their scenes, and others are capable of effecting detachment, though not always to an obvious purpose. The use of this technique is not firmly controlled, therefore. Despite that, such is the strength of the play that it stands up well, with or without the songs. Perhaps even at this late stage they might be revised to advantage.

Edward Albee's first play was *The Zoo Story* (1958), that is, as he explains in a Preface, his first play except a three-act sex farce written when he was twelve, set 'aboard an ocean liner, the characters of which were, for the most part, English gentry, and the title of which was, for some reason that escapes me now, *Aliqueen*'.[7] *The Zoo Story* is not now Albee's most famous play, and it is very obviously not an English play. It is well worth analysis here, however, because its effect is wholly dependent upon music-hall (or rather, vaudeville) performer/audience relationships. It may also suggest, if very lightly, something shared in common by American and English drama. *The Zoo Story* is, briefly, about a man, Jerry, who has been to the zoo, and who insists on telling another man, Peter (whom he meets in Central Park, New York), about that experience. Peter resents the intrusion and fears being dispossessed of *his* bench. At the end of the play, Jerry impales himself on a knife held by Peter and dies. He never gets very far in telling Peter about the zoo, but he does tell him another story.

ALL RIGHT. [*As if reading from a huge billboard*] THE STORY OF JERRY AND THE DOG! [*Natural again*] What I am going to tell you has something to do with how sometimes it's necessary to go a long distance out of the way in order to come back a short distance correctly; or, maybe I only think that it has something to do with that. But, it's why I went to the zoo today, and why I walked north . . . northerly, rather . . . until I came here. All right. The dog, I think I told you, is a black monster of a beast: an oversized head, tiny, tiny ears, and eyes . . . bloodshot, infected, maybe; and a body you can see the ribs through the skin. The dog is black, all black; all black except for the blood-shot eyes, and . . . yes . . . and an open sore on its . . . *right* forepaw; that is red, too . . .   (p. 30)

This story is lengthy – over six pages of solid text. Peter reacts
but does not say anything. The effect is not unlike a long music-
hall monologue – or, in the light of Albee's family background
(his grandfather ran a vast vaudeville booking agency), a long
vaudeville tale or a 'stump speech'. This is the more marked
because of the way the story is phrased, particularly the moment
when Jerry buys some meat to mix with rat poison to kill the
fierce beast:

> When I bought the hamburger I asked the man not to bother
> with the roll, all I wanted was the meat. I expected some
> reaction from him, like: we don't sell no hamburgers without
> rolls; or, wha' d' ya wanna do, eat it out' a ya han's? But no; he
> smiled benignly, wrapped up the hamburger in waxed paper,
> and said: A bite for ya pussy-cat? I wanted to say: No, not
> really; it's part of a plan to poison a dog I know. But, you can't
> say 'a dog I know' without sounding funny; so I said, a little
> too loud I'm afraid, and too formally: YES, A BITE FOR MY PUSSY-
> CAT.   (p. 32)

What makes *The Zoo Story* particularly interesting is the way that
Albee uses a comic-monologue technique to describe what is
often vicious and cruel. Thus, after the dog has eaten the poison
pattie, it becomes ill and the landlady upset:

> AND IT CAME TO PASS THAT THE BEAST WAS DEATHLY ILL. I knew
> this because he no longer attended me, and because the land-
> lady sobered up. She stopped me in the hall the same evening
> of the attempted murder and confided the information that
> God had struck her puppy-dog a surely fatal blow.
>
> (pp. 32–3)

Not only is the centrepiece of the play a monologue (very
unusual in realistic drama) but the tone, though not its content, is
appropriate to the monologue. An audience is not quite sure how
to respond. The description is funny, the mode akin to one that
does not deal with life-and-death matters; but what is being said
is even more serious than the attempted killing of a none-too-
pleasant dog. Consequently, through the conjunction of realistic

and vaudeville techniques, the audience is 'caught between emotions', embarrassed. This is very important if the violent death of Jerry at the end of the play is not to seem a melodramatic absurdity. Peter has to be made to see (and the audience to *feel*) the effect of refusing to be involved, of refusing relationships. He must therefore be forced into committing an act which stems from that refusal, and which is in itself of a kind alien to him. For Albee the problem is to make that death dramatically logical and telling. This requires him to ensure that the audience accepts the end as logical, though excessive, and cares about Jerry enough to be upset by his death.

The play starts with Jerry imposing himself on the mild, inoffensive Peter. An audience is likely to reject Jerry at this point because it would see itself as in Peter's position. The monologue serves not only to catch the audience between emotions, but enables Jerry to win the audience's sympathy, not just through what he says, but because the monologue technique itself wins an audience to the teller. After the story, Jerry attempts to dislodge Peter from the public park-bench that Peter regards as his own. They quarrel violently, but the audience does not know whose side to take. Jerry is a bully and Peter is laying claim to what is patently not his. The audience does not know whether to be amused at the absurdity of the situation or exasperated by its pettiness. Three extracts will indicate the progress of events.

Jerry: Listen to me Peter. I want this bench. You go sit on the bench over there, and if you're good I'll tell you the rest of the story.

Peter: [*flustered*] But . . . whatever for? What *is* the matter with you? Besides, I see no reason why I should give up this bench. I sit on this bench almost every Sunday afternoon, in good weather. It's secluded here; there's never anyone sitting here, so I have it all to myself.

Jerry: [*softly*] Get off this bench, Peter; I want it.

Peter: [*almost whining*] No.

Peter: POLICE! I warn you, I'll have you arrested. POLICE! [*Pause*] I said POLICE! [*Pause*] I feel ridiculous.

Jerry: You look ridiculous: a grown man screaming for the police on a bright Sunday afternoon in the park with nobody harming you. If a policeman *did* fill his quota and come sludging over this way he'd probably take you as a nut.

Peter: [*with disgust and impotence*] Great God, I just came here to read, and now you want me to give up the bench. You're mad.

Jerry: Fight for it, then. Defend yourself; defend your bench.
Peter: You've *pushed* me to it. Get up and fight.
Jerry: Like a man?
Peter: [*still angry*] Yes, like a man, if you insist on mocking me even further.

(pp. 41, 43 and 45)

The tension felt by the audience through being caught between conflicting responses finds its natural, and dramatically logical, outlet in the killing. But in a curious way the audience has become party *to Peter's 'act'*, even though that act (defensively holding the knife Jerry insisted Peter took) leads to a catastrophe actually instigated by Jerry, for Jerry rushes on to the very knife he has given to Peter.

The social and political lessons underlying Albee's short play are many, but the dramatic lesson is not the least interesting. By combining realistic and popular dramatic techniques, Albee manipulates an audience into confronting its own reluctance to become emotionally involved in the concerns of others. Because of the reactions of others, inaction can be more dangerous than action and just as violent.

Pinter's use of popular dramatic techniques stood out clearly in some of his early plays. *The Dumb Waiter* is a good example of the use of music-hall (or film–comedy-team) routines. Later plays have used such techniques with great subtlety, but most of his work relies to some extent upon the juxtaposition of both modes of drama. As this relationship has not gone unnoticed, it might be more fruitful to turn to someone else. Peter Nichols makes great use of popular dramatic techniques, but, unlike the later Pinter, these are placed very prominently in his drama. His latest play, *Privates on Parade*, first performed by the Royal Shakespeare Company on 23 February 1977, is akin in structure and its use of the popular tradition to *The Entertainer*. It is drawn, like much of Nichols's work, from his own experience and, as he said in an interview published in the *Guardian* (22 February 1977), 'It uses song and dance and all those concert party tricks that I touched on in *Forget-me-not Lane*.'[8] There is a formal distinction between the stage and 'real' worlds, indicated by the use of a front-cloth for the former and the full-stage for the latter. Two non-speaking Chinese characters work in both worlds, some-times moving props and furniture in one, and acting as barmen, servants, or 'firing rapid bursts of stengun fire into the audience' (p. 101). His own description of how the two worlds are related could be applied as well to *The Entertainer*: 'You're never quite sure when you're on stage and when you're "real life". As it goes on the distinction becomes very blurred, just like in film musicals.' This can be seen, for example, in I.9, which begins with a song full of sexual *double entendres*, sung by characters with their faces lit only by hand torches; moves into a bedroom set with Sylvia and Steve in bed, fully lit; and ends as it began, with a further half-dozen torchlit verses of 'Black Velvet'.[9] The supposed funeral of Reg (I.11) bears some similarity in the juxtaposition of the two dramatic worlds, to Billy's funeral in *The Entertainer*.

The major difference in structure is the considerable use of direct address. Steve, Terri, Reg and Giles all speak directly to the audience. Steve's speeches (his letters home), set the scene (pp. 26, 42, and 69), although the last (p. 104) is a kind of winding-up of the story. Terri's are explications of his own character – how he has come to be as he is (pp. 31 and 37–8). Reg, appropriately as someone involved in the intrigue in Malaya, has speeches to the audience which are concerned with the plot of the play (pp. 26, 51, 57, and 77); and Giles, as befits his character, pontificates in a way that is almost a parody of Brechtian drama (pp. 72 and 101–2). These and other speeches are often simul-taneously related to what is occurring on-stage. As Giles speaks after the shooting (pp. 101–2), the casualties are tended and Charles kisses the dead Len farewell. At the end of II.5, Terri and Giles give their reactions to leaving Singapore antiphonally, one from each side of the stage (pp. 88–9). Sylvia ensures that Steve's last letter, spoken to the audience, contains the information that she is pregnant (pp. 104–5), and Terri's speech at the end of I.6 overlaps the opening of I.7, and as we take in the scene as Terri finishes what he has to say, he exits with an *entrechât* into the wings. Nothing could be better calculated to break the con-tinuity!

Privates on Parade shows that the form established by Osborne in *The Entertainer* is capable of continued use and further development twenty years later. Osborne's ending is much stronger than Nichols's. Nichols draws on his experience in Combined Services Entertainments in Malaya, and the play is rather like that episode in his life: incidental. Reg, dressed like a Chinese as the last stage direction indicates (p. 109), with his finger on his lips indicating silence, is nothing like as telling as Archie offering to come and see us at work. For a dramatist who can say so much in his plays (in *A Day in the Death of Joe Egg*, 1967, and the two plays yet to be discussed here), the effect is inscrutable.

By an odd coincidence *It Ain't Half Hot, Mum*, a television comedy series on a similar theme, began to be broadcast as Nichols was writing the play. As he explained in his *Guardian* interview, Nichols was understandably dismayed. There are similarities, but in the theatre the dual role of the audience is used to far greater effect (as in *The Entertainer*) than is possible with television. Apart from the audience serving as the 'audience-within-the-play' for the revue sketches, it also represents the 'race of mercenary savages who'll fight for the British against their fellow-Asians' (p. 95) into which the Chinese fire their stenguns (p. 101).

One, and possibly two, things are confused by Nichols in bringing together the two worlds of popular and overheard drama. In his *Guardian* interview Peter Nichols says the play 'is written in the language of 1948 with the understanding of 1948. It's absolutely a study of life at that time.' Steve, it is true, is very much a product of thirty years ago. His lack of sexual knowledge and his inhibitions are very well drawn. Terri's language, however, *seems* much closer to the time when the play was written. It is as if his lines have been up-dated by the addition of those that the *Carry On* film-makers thought they couldn't *quite* get by the censor – Terri's 'Merci blow-through', for example (p. 31). Some of the show material is certainly of the period, however:

> *Len:* Sorry I was not here on time.
> *Terri:* Never mind, Sergeant Len Bonny, Royal Electrical and Mechanical Engineers, tell me, where've you been?

Len: I've been buying my wife a dress.
Terri: A dress? That's nice. What kind of a dress?
Len: A Biblical dress.
Terri: A Biblical dress? What's that when it's at home?
Len: You know – Low and Behold!
Terri: [*with gestures to explain*] Low – and behold?
Len: I shall find it hard to look her in the face.
Terri: You'll find it hard to look – I refuse to listen to another solitary word.

(p. 16)

This is similar to the following exchange from a 1939–45 *Happidrome* recording:

Lovejoy: Well, if the girls run short of coupons for stockings, they'll have to bring the long dresses back again.
Ramsbottom: Whatever for Guv'nor?
Lovejoy: So that the bow-legged girls can come out of retirement. There's one thing about bow legs. They're few and far between.
Ramsbottom: I was out with a girl last night and she was wearing a Biblical Dress.
Lovejoy: I know, low and behold.
Ramsbottom: And don't you like the new military styles?
Lovejoy: Oh aye, they remind me of me army days, they're like Mills bombs. If the pin comes out it's a case of every man for himself.

However, though there was a theatrically gay world in the late 1940s (and it might have been gayer than I knew), Terri's world smacks of the 1970s, not the 1940s. It is not that this mixture of periods is of itself wrong, but not enough is made of the difference.

The second confusion is more serious. An audience cannot know how seriously to take the absurd figure of Reg – Sylvia's bruises, the room that must be whitewashed to cover up bloodstains (p. 67), the gunrunning, murder, his reputed madness, and finally his appearing dressed up like someone out of *Chu Chin Chow*. These elements cannot be disentangled and the resulting confusion indicates the kind of problem that a dramatist faces in using both dramatic modes.

One final point might be made about *Privates on Parade*. In his *Guardian* interview Peter Nichols referred to something he attributed to Stanley Reynolds: 'What all those BBC series about schools, battleships, hospitals are really about is the BBC itself. People at the BBC are all living in an institution and they're all fascinated by the workings of it.' *Privates on Parade* follows in the tradition of those plays which are fascinated by the theatre and how it works. There is nothing wrong in that, but, apart from some place names, it is strange that a play about Malaya during the Emergency should be so little concerned with the problems of the place in which the play is set. For example, the Malays who, in my modest service in Singapore a year or two before Nichols's, figured significantly, are ignored.

Peter Nichols had been extremely inventive in his earlier use of the popular dramatic tradition, especially in *The National Health, or Nurse Norton's Affair* (1969) and *Forget-me-not Lane* (1971). All three plays were directed in their first productions by Michael Blakemore, incidentally, and *The National Health* was first given at the National Theatre.

The National Health rightly has an alternative title, and with more point than many eighteenth-century plays. Like Hauptmann's *Rats* (1911)[10] and Strauss's opera, *Ariadne auf Naxos* (1912; revised 1916), two plays (and operas), distinctive in genre, are performed simultaneously. One play is set in a run-down National Health hospital. The scene is well suggested by the opening description: 'This daylight creeps through Victorian Gothic windows high in the rear wall. Above eight feet, the walls are pea-green, below this white' (p. 9). The other play is set in the fanciful world of TV medical drama – the cosy homeliness of Dr Finlay combined with the everyday miracle surgery of *Emergency Ward 10*. These exist in the novel that Barnet reads aloud from the side of the stage.

Barnet: Her bedside alarm gave raucous tongue and Staff Nurse Cleo Norton awoke in mid-afternoon suddenly, bewilderingly, and some moments passed before she could realise she was in her room at the nurses' residential hostel.
[*Staff wakes in the bed and mimes to the narrative*]
Her tousled hair and the rumpled sheets were

evidence enough of a fitful sleep. If evidence she needed! She flounced over in bed, flung back the sheets petulantly and swung her lithe coffee-coloured legs round till her feet touched the pretty coconut mat she brought from Jamaica all those years ago.

Staff: What's the matter with you anyway, Cleo Norton?
Barnet: – she demanded of herself, half angrily. But the mad ecstatic leap of her heart had already told her.
Staff: Neil!
Barnet: In the submarine strangeness of the night ward, young Doctor Neil Boyd's fingers had fleetingly touched hers. And his usually stern features had crumpled into a yearning smile. Their eyes had met and ricocheted away.
Staff: This won't do.
Barnet: She chastised herself ruefully.

(p. 26)

The other world also centres on Barnet. This is an intriguing mixture of depressing reality – the hospital world – and the music-hall turn. He first appears in 1.3, pushing a wheel chair. He begins (according to the stage directions) by talking with cheerful vulgarity to the patients, but as he comes downstage he faces the audience, addresses them directly, although the patients also react to his music-hall comedian's patter. Whilst he speaks, Flagg is being 'fed like a baby' by Nurse Sweet.

No, it's wicked to laugh. I said to this old man in the next ward, I said, 'Dad, you better watch your step', he said, 'Why?' I said, 'They're bringing in a case of syphilis'. He said, 'Well, it'll make a change from Lucozade'.

[*Laughter and applause from patients*]
Sweet: I didn't hear that remark.
Barnet: Whoops, sorry, nurse, I never saw you come on.
[*He ogles the audience and goes upstage with the chair.*]

(p. 23)

At the end of the scene, Barnet helps Nurse Sweet to walk Rees without success; Rees wets himself and is put back to bed, and then Barnet again moves out of his role within the play and addresses the audience directly:

Mackie:	Why are you keeping him alive? Like a baby?
Sweet:	[*packing Rees into bed*] Now, now –
Mackie:	You know he'll never walk again –
Sweet:	Mister Mackie, save it for a more suitable occasion.
Mackie:	We know, his wife knows –
	[*Barnet returns, gives pyjamas to Rees. Foster begins singing Gaumont-British theme*]
	But no, you keep the farce going –
	[*He gives up, coughing*]
Sweet:	Tuck up nice and warm and think of something nice.
Barnet:	[*to audience*] Why don't you all think of something nice?

(p. 25)

The 'nice thoughts' that follow are those mentioned already, enacted by the coloured Staff Nurse, Cleo Norton, as she awakes in mid-afternoon. The hollow, comforting world of fictionalised medical drama is also dramatised by a parody of *Dr Finlay's Casebook*, a once-popular television programme, full of pawky Scottish humour, in which the good-hearted but old-fashioned senior partner comes into conflict with the good-hearted but less-experienced, up-to-date junior partner. The pattern is a familiar one and has now moved south into the veterinary world of *All Creatures Great and Small*, where we are at least saved some of the worst excesses of comic accent. Nichols makes a particular point of the Scottish accent:

Neil:	You wanted to see me, father?
Boyd:	Och, there you are, Neil. Come in, come in.
	[*Boyd's Scots accent is heavier in this scene*]
Neil:	If it's about the informality of my ward-rounds, you can save your breath to cool your porridge. I believe I am the patients' servant not the other way round. I'm not going to have a lot of ceremony –
Boyd:	Now, now, dinna fash yesel. It's noo that. We agree to differ on the question of how to treat our fellows.
Neil:	Aye. You, the firm believer, seem to regard the weak and infirm as inferiors. I, the sceptic, behave to them as

> my equals.
> Boyd: Happily, the Almighty, in His infinite wisdom, has
>   not denied us the use of our common sense.

Their names presumably parody those of the conductor, Boyd
Neel.

The point at issue in Barnet's 'dream play' is whether Boyd's son,
Neil (who does not appear in the realistic play), should marry
Staff Nurse Norton instead of the 'wee Mary MacPhee'. Even
Neil's dead mother's memory is invoked, in the best traditions of
soap opera:

> Boyd: You can't hurt me. I'm here to fight. But you can hurt
>   your mother.
> Neil: Mother's dead.
> Boyd: Aye, she's dead. And almost her last wish was that you
>   two should marry, that Mary should be one of the
>   family. And now ye say ye're taking a wee coloured
>   girl to wife and . . . Mary is to be left on the shelf. At
>   thirty. Have you thought of that, son? While you're so
>   busy with your noble sentiments? Have you given a
>   wee thought to puir bonnie Mary at the age of thirty?
>   Have ye?   (p. 35)

The contrast with activity of hospital life, as it can be, if not as it
always is, follows at once: '*A steady groundbass of snores; incoherent
speech* [of] *patients sleeping or trying to; after some time, one of the
sleepers farts very violently, then groans with relief*' (p. 35).

An even sharper contrast comes later in the same scene. Barnet
enters in a travelling spot, pushing a trolley in precisely the
manner of a music-hall comic on an empty stage. The spot
isolates him from the 'reality' of the ward and this is intensified
by his entering into an argument with the technician managing
the spot. After that ironic by-play he turns to the audience with,
'No, but seriously' – always a comic's introduction to the
opposite. He shows the audience what he's carrying on his
trolley – not quite the apparatus for Dr Kildare: 'Wash bowl,
sponges, nail brush and file. Safety razor, scissors, tweezer.
Cotton-wool, carbolic soap.' And, quite matter of course,
'Shroud'. The comic routine (even to Barnet goosing himself as
he tells us that such apparatus neatly laid out like a tea service

'really brings me on'), introduces not just the inevitable fact of
life – death – but the preparation of the corpse. Nichols takes the
contrast even further by asking the audience what is the purpose
of the cotton-wool, just as might Max Miller or Tommy Trinder
in a music-hall routine:

> Now the cotton-wool. Can anyone tell me what I do with
> that? [*Reacts to same woman in audience*] You're right, madam,
> absolutely right. Been making that answer all your life and for
> the first time it's accurate, not just vulgar. Yes. We have to
> close the apertures, the points that might evacuate bodily
> fluids. Miss one out, they'll raise Cain in the mortuary. Lug-
> holes, cake-holes, nose-holes, any other holes, all right
> madam thank you very much indeed! [*More ogling the woman*]
> pp. 40–1)

As Barnet goes through his routine, nurses are erecting screens.
They remove the trolley, an oriental nurse is patted on the rump
in the process and gives a 'shocked magician's-assistant smile to
audience'. Barnet leaves – with the stand-up comic's exit line,
'Thank you very much indeed' – the screens are removed, and
Rees, the old man whom we saw helped to bed, has gone. His
bed is empty. Barnet's routine has, like a magician's patter,
covered a vanishing trick, but this time there is no return of the
body.

The first act has ten scenes and the second has nine, and
throughout most of the play the two worlds of squalid reality and
fictional wonderland are kept apart. Until II.5, *Nurse Norton's
Affair* has been presented only in Act I, Scenes 4, 6 and 9, and in
II.3. By then three of the patients have died (Lucas, Rees and
Mackie), the second and third to the accompaniment of a comic
routine from Barnet. The Chaplain, at the end of his visit in II.4,
fails to awaken Foster. With brave understatement he calls a
nurse: 'Nurse! Sister! I'm afraid the patient doesn't seem too
well . . .' (p. 90). In the following scene, both realistic and
fictional worlds are presented at once, the latter as if it were a
television programme. Attempts to revive Foster are bungled –
'Typical balls up,' Barnet tells the audience, 'No spanner for the
oxygen cylinder.' At the same time he tries vainly to prevent the
other patients from seeing what is happening to Foster by
manipulating screen. However, they prefer to concentrate on the

fictional world in which, through the marvels of modern surgery, coupled with the skilled dedication of fine men and women, transcending prejudice of every kind, the kidney of a beautiful coloured woman is transplanted by Boyd Senior into Boyd Junior. Though Foster dies, at least we and the patients can take comfort in the success of the televised transplant of the soap opera.

Except for II.5, then, the two worlds are kept apart, but Barnet appears in each, as commentator and member of the nursing staff in the National Health hospital, and as reader of the story which is dramatised as *Nurse Norton's Affair* (though he does not appear in I.6, and II.3, so well has the scene been set by Nichols). The play has not two but three points of focus. By having Barnet play a triple role, something much more complex than a simple, satirical juxtaposition of stories is effected. Nichols's control of the humour is masterly. Barnet's routines have the prime virtue of being funny, even though, without falling into Tieck's critics' demand for 'good taste', a comedy of cadavers could easily be offensive. Nichols avoids this, without concealing any of the realities, by a humour that is very much like that described by Vivian Mercier:

> *Whereas macabre humour in the last analysis is inseparable from terror and serves as a defence mechanism against the fear of death, grotesque humour is equally inseparable from awe and serves as a defence mechanism against the holy dread with which we face the mysteries of reproduction.* Oversimplifying, I might say that these two types of humour help us *to accept death and to belittle life.*[11]

Both types of humour seem to be at play in Nichols's plays, the first being particularly forceful in *The National Health*.

One very difficult problem that Nichols has to overcome is the conclusion of a tripartite story. In a sense, the high point of the play is II.5 – the scene showing simultaneously the kidney transplant and death of Foster. The play *could* end there, as a number of five–act Renaissance tragedies could end with Act IV. But Nichols, rightly, like Webster in *The Duchess of Malfi* (1614) goes on and, like Webster in his Act V, gives in Act II. 6–9 a coda that draws together the themes and their implications. All the scenes but the last are set in the National Health hospital. Barnet still has a few lines for the audience, but he is subdued and much of what little he says is devoted to explanation of how a patient (Ken), who had been discharged in I.2, has returned after another motorcycle smash and is alive but now an idiot. He has caused two coaches to collide, killing or maiming sixty mongols and old-age pensioners. Though he addresses the audience from the familiar spot of light, there is no badinage with the travelling spot operator and very little with the audience. There have been four deaths and Flagg and Loach are discharged to uncertain futures. The little hope remaining is that Ken is being cared for by Ash – a former teacher dismissed for homosexuality – and Tyler, whose legs have been amputated, but keeps determinedly cheerful. Nichols then tempts us, as O'Casey did in *Juno and the Paycock*, with the world of unreality. His final scene is 'a real pantomime transformation' in which we see the double wedding of Boyd and Nurse McPhee, and Neil and Nurse Norton – complete with kilts, Union Jacks, and the Chaplain (now, a Bishop of course). On comes Barnet, blacked-up, to give his and the play's last line: 'It's a funny old world we live in and you're lucky to get out of it alive.' They all dance and the curtain descends, but only to rise so that the dancers can take their bows, and leave, as a silent tableau, the patients 'frozen in their attitudes' (p. 109).

The juxtaposition of the realistic and fanciful; of life, death and imagined reality; of outrageous comedy and uncomfortable truths; of legitimate and illegitimate; is brilliantly managed. Although one can see why Nichols should have had his greatest success with *Forget-me-not Lane*, this is his most uncompromising play (which cannot win a work ready popular success), and a work very much in the tradition of the bitter satires of the Jacobean period in tone, technique and deaths. *The Revenger's Tragedy* springs to mind.

In his *Guardian* interview, Peter Nichols said he got his own back, gently, on his father in *Forget-me-not Lane*. Its starting point, he said, was his father 'with his trousers rolled up and a handkerchief on his head for a masonic ritual' (see pp. 54–5). The play carries the description, 'Humorous, serious and dramatic selections'. The description suggests a concert party routine and there is not only a Mr Magic and Miss 1940 but, as a kind of master of ceremonies, Frank, the central figure of the play. The play uses an elaborate variation of Ibsen's technique of retrospective exposition. We are shown three stages in the development of a family: between 1940–8 approximately; 1965; and the present day (1971). As with Ibsen, the effect of the past on the present is dramatised, though not in a wholly realistic vein. There are many individual moments that are presented realistically, but, in addition to frequent speeches direct to the audience (by Frank especially, but also by Ursula, Amy and Charles), there is an enormous amount of slipping from one period into another. This is managed with great facility by Nichols, though careful totting-up of the ages does suggest that not only Richard II and Bolingbroke aged at different rates. Thus, Charles is 50 on p. 14 and 75 on p. 75; Amy in the former scene is 40 (p. 16) and in the latter, '55 or so' (p. 78). Ursula is 38 'present day' (p. 103), which would mean that she was 14 in 1947, but she is thirteen when Frank is fourteen (p. 33), in about 1942 (and Ivor shows pin-up pictures of 1943, when she is said to be fourteen, p. 36). This is no more noticed in performance than the different rates of ageing in *Richard II* and, whether intentional or accidental, helps ensure that the time slips are not seen as factual, but as expressions of the memory subject to the vagaries or remembrance of things past. Thus, Ursula corrects one error in Frank's recall of the past, breaking continuity in the process:

Frank:	Why don't you take some interest in his music? Isn't that one of your common interests?
Charles:	You hold your tongue, Sonny Jim.
Frank:	Sonny Jim? I'm nearly forty. A middle-aged man with three whopping kids.
Ursula:	No, at this time you were nearly thirty and Matthew hadn't been born.

(p. 89)

What is more fascinating is the way that Nichols not only slips from one period to another, back and forth, but will overlay two different periods and sometimes even three.[12] Pinpointing the precise dates, or even being sure which decade characters are in, is not, in fact, particularly important. Nichols manages to keep the various periods going simultaneously with great skill and without ever confusing the audience as they follow the pattern of events. Much of the credit for this must go to his choosing the 'illegitimate format' of the concert party, which has the effect of the play-within-the-play, the audience being more convinced of the truth of what it sees and hears.

Peter Nichols has used the techniques of popular drama – direct address, concert party, army show and television soap opera – more frequently and variously than any other contemporary writer, and with great success. What is so very interesting is that what seemed so novel, when Wilder wrote, or when *The Entertainer* appeared (the more so because knowledge of the traditions behind these plays seemed rather limited), has become established in its own right. There is no question of Nichols simply imitating. He is *using* traditions, traditions long established, and which have been reformed relatively recently. Thus *Privates on Parade* makes much greater use of direct address by characters involved in the 'real' rather than the stage world than does *The Entertainer*. I happen to think Osborne's play the better of the two, but there is no doubting the dramatic and theatrical skills displayed in *Privates on Parade*. *Forget-me-not Lane* bears some similarities to Arthur Miller's *Death of a Salesman* (1949) and both plays (Miller's the more closely) develop Ibsen's technique of retrospective exposition.[13] Both plays also use *décor simultané* (as does II.5 of *The National Health*). Again it is interesting to see how what seemed a novelty in 1949 (despite its being so ancient a technique), has become a 'normal' form of staging. Nichols offers in these three plays 'realistic' drama of contemporary or near-contemporary events, without being bound by realistic conventions. By using popular comedic techniques in such drama, he is able to draw on all the theatrical resources he requires instead of being restricted to those of the realistic-legitimate tradition. That he can deal with the most intimate and ultimate of experiences – the laying-out of a corpse – through a music-hall comedian's patter, suggests how greatly emancipated the drama has become from the restrictions of what, in its own day, was itself a considerable achievement: the drama of realism. The full recovery of the technique open to Marlowe, Shakespeare, Jonson, Tourneur, Middleton and Webster has, fortunately, come at a time when there are many dramatists capable of using such techniques, and directors and actors who can present their work. The one constant that has never been absent from English theatre is the capacity of audiences to respond to such complex theatre, and audiences now have their reward.

5 Offending the Audience

Trevor Griffiths's play, *Comedians* (1975) makes much use of direct-address techniques, as its date and title suggests. It shows four stand-up comics and a duo act putting into effect what they have been taught at night school. They present their acts at a north of England club under the eye of their teacher, a disillusioned music-hall star, the Lancashire Lad of Yesteryear (played in the first production by a genuine music-hall comedian, Jimmy Jewel).[1] Two of the comedians are Irish and one is Jewish; the members of the cross-talk act come from Blackley, near Manchester; the fifth act, Price's, begins with mime, has a patter that leaves the concert secretary 'probably shocked', which seems hardly possible, and concludes with four bars of 'The Red Flag' played on a Grock-like miniature violin, 'very simple and direct'. Act I is a warm-up and final briefing, held at the night school centre. The second act takes place in the club, between sessions of bingo, and the last act is a post-mortem. There is added tension for the prospective professional comedians (and the audience) in that a talent spotter, Bert Challenor, with whom their coach (Eddie Waters) does not see eye to eye, has come to assess their acts. In the event, he books two of the five, but more to the point is his contempt for the final act which he describes as repulsive and aggressively unfunny.[2] We are inclined to assume at first that we should reject Challenor's assessment. In the first act, Waters has given a succinct account of how he sees the art of the comic:

> *Waters:* A joke that feeds on ignorance starves its audience. We have the choice. We can say something or we can say nothing. Not everything true is funny, and not everything funny is true. Most comics *feed* prejudice and fear and blinkered vision, but the best ones, the best ones . . . illuminate them, make them clearer to see, easier to deal with. We've got to make people laugh till they cry. Cry. Till they find their pain and

128

their beauty. Comedy is medicine. Not coloured
sweeties to rot their teeth with.

(p. 23)

When Challenor arrives, he gives *his* assessment:

Challenor: . . . A couple of . . . hints. Don't try to be deep.
Keep it simple. I'm not looking for philosophers,
I'm looking for comics. I'm looking for someone
who sees what the people want and knows how
to give it them. It's the people pay the bills,
remember, yours, mine . . . Mr Waters's. We're
servants, that's all. They demand, we supply.
Any good comedian can lead an audience by the
nose. But only in the direction they're going.
And that direction is, quite simply . . . escape.
We're not missionaries, we're suppliers of
laughter.

(p. 33)

When the others have all left, Price asks Waters what he thought
of his act, the act the club secretary and the talent scout found so
embarrassing. To Waters, 'It was terrifying'. Price, angrily
bursts out with, 'I didn't sell you out, Eddie' (p. 63). He
maintains that he tried to be *himself* talking, but Waters accuses
him of throwing out love, care and concern:

Waters: [*eventually*] It was ugly. It was drowning in hate.
You can't change today into tomorrow on that basis.
You forget a thing called . . . the truth.

(p. 65)[3]

Their argument ends ambivalently, each describing his concept
of truth. Waters found it at Buchenwald. It was not that the place
was horrifying, that was to be expected; what so shocked him
was that he also found it sexually stimulating. Price finds truth in
another clown, Grock:

Not like Chaplin, all coy and covered in kids. This book said
he weren't even funny. He was just very truthful, everything
he did. (p. 67)

Waters's concept of truth for the comic has been outlined in the
first act:

> *Waters:*   . . . a true joke, a comedian's joke, has to do more
> than release tension, it has to *liberate* the will and the
> desire, it has to *change the situation*. [*Pause*] There's
> very little won't take a joke. But when a joke bases
> itself upon a distortion – [*At Price, deliberately*] a
> 'stereotype' perhaps – and gives the lie to the truth so
> as to win a laugh and stay in favour, we've moved
> away from a comic art and into the world of 'enter-
> tainment' and slick success.
>
> (p. 20)

There is no simple resolution to the play, nor should there be.
Griffiths brings it to a neat conclusion by having Waters laugh at
a Hindu joke that enables the Indian to handle for others the
carcases of beasts sacred to him. What Griffiths does is dramatise
the relationship of the comedian's self to his act through Price and
Waters, together with the function in the act of the 'true joke'. At
the same time, he shows how these comedians see change being
effected. It is pointed, moving and dramatic. It also sharply
distinguishes two approaches particularly relevant to those who
would see change effected through drama. To Price the audience
'was all ice out there'. He loved it; hating his audience, *he* felt
expressed: 'I stand in no line. I refuse my consent' (pp. 67–8). To
Waters, who stopped being funny after his experience at
Buchenwald, Price's act was ugly, drowning in hate: 'You can't
change today into tomorrow on that basis' (p. 65). To Waters,
love, care and concern are an essential part of the relationships of
performer and audience, and the performer Price affects to
admire so much, Grock, would surely have agreed with Waters.
Apart from his being 'a little crazed on everything English . . . I
can't do anything but praise them', Grock was, he said, 'innately
incapable of understanding how one nation can hate another or
bear a grudge against another'.[4]

For a long time, drama has been considered an agent through
which change can be effected. It was an underlying motivation
for the religious cycles in the Middle Ages; the writers of the
moralities saw themselves as dramatising stories that would
change men's ways and even their religion; Bale would not have

wasted time on entertaining the mob. In the early years of the Soviet Union, drama was used to persuade people – nomadic tribesmen, for example – to accept the new order. The Living Newspaper was similarly motivated, if not by the US Government, at least by many who wrote, produced and acted in it. The English documentary film was concerned to effect social change. Whereas control of what was performed in the latter days of the Lord Chamberlain's censorship concentrated on the kind of language an audience might hear, though this was not its sole activity (*Smith of the Shamrock Guards: The 'Ragged' Officer*, 1903,[5] is an interesting and little-known exception), in the days of the Tudors it was concerned with weightier matters, stemming from a fear that the drama might subvert men's minds from the 'true' religion and from obedience to the state. The mystery cycles did not die out because they could not compete with the new drama. In the first place the new drama was London-based and the greater extant cycles existed in cities far way – Chester, York, Wakefield, for example; and secondly, they were expressly forbidden by the Privy Council because they were popular and associated with 'the old faith', still strong in the north. Walpole's ministry in the eighteenth century feared the effect of drama. Much nearer to our own day, television authorities everywhere have refused to screen the telefilm, *The War Game* (1966), which Peter Watkins made for the BBC, showing the effect of an atomic bomb falling on an English town. Ironically, a film version is readily available, and, what is more, from a quasi-government agency, the British Film Institute.

Not all these restrictions are of a piece. However much one might disagree, it is possible to see why Elizabeth I's ministers feared stirring up religious controversy, especially at a time when the hobgoblins of heresy loomed large in people's minds. Walpole may have acted more out of personal resentment than for reasons of state. The banning of *The War Game* is particularly puzzling. Is it feared that it will prevent atomic war? Perhaps efforts should be made to insist upon the film being shown everywhere instead of preventing its projection.

Those who believe in censorship must believe that literature, drama and films can be influential, though they do not always behave as if that were so. Paradoxically, most of those who believe literature, drama and film to be effective do not believe in censorship (unless, perhaps, it be of views opposed to their own). In what ways these art forms do affect people has been a matter of study and increasing concern, especially since the development of the mass media – but that goes far beyond the limits of this book. What is relevant here is the attempt to use popular dramatic techniqes to effect changes in society or in attitudes.

Although there are rare occasions when a play might have brought about a direct social improvement – Winston Churchill seeing Galsworthy's *Justice* (1910) for example – this is rare indeed. Peter Brook once wrote (in connection with *US*, 1966, and its film follow-up, the ironically-named *Tell Me Lies*, 1968):

> It is said that *The Marriage of Figaro* launched the French Revolution, but I don't believe it. I don't believe that plays and films and works of art work this way. Goya's *Horrors of War* and Picasso's *Guernica* have always seemed the great models, yet they achieved no practical results.[6]

Brook is surely right, and his experience of *US* must have provided good practical experience to back his argument. Nevertheless, theatre and film people attempt from time to time to show otherwise. So far – which is not forever – it seems as if theatre can rarely if ever effect specific, direct, immediate change. Did *Cathy Come Home* cause more houses to be built? Did even *A Day in the Death of Joe Egg* effect any immediate practical response? No – alas, no. It *might* be that the theatre can become directly effective, as Peter Handke has suggested, by adopting a new approach to life:

> when the [Berliner] Kommune theatricalize real life by 'terrorising' it and quite rightly make fun of it, not only making fun of it but, in the reaction provoked, making it recognizable in all its inherent dangerousness, in its lack of awareness, its false nature, its false idyllicism, and in its terror. In this way, theatre is becoming directly effective. There is now Street Theatre, Lecture-hall Theatre, Church Theatre (more effective than 1,000 Masses), Department Store Theatre, etc.: the only one that doesn't exist anymore is Theatre Theatre – at least not as a means of immediately changing prevailing conditions: it is itself a prevailing condition.[7]

Yet, in England at least, fringe groups, though they may enliven the 'general theatrical scene', though they may feed the mainstream theatre with new ideas, tend to be very much a coterie theatre, 'private', enclosed, like much of the theatre of the 1630s. It is important to stress 'tend', because local allegiances are built up, but it seems of the nature of such theatre, or rather of its personnel, that there is either a lack of long-term commitment or an inability to recognise that audiences make theatre. It is a theatre which seems considerably more removed from the dreams and actualities of life of most of the population than is mainstream theatre (which sets out to serve both, if with varying degrees of honesty). The intentions of the fringe groups *seem* irreproachable, but their disenchantment with the Britain they live in, no doubt because of the hollowness and hypocrisy of the Socialist dream as it has been practised, leads to a latter-day, Jacobean-style melancholia, painful and self-perpetuating.[8] They are the Prices to the Waters of mainstream serious theatre. But it is not my concern to criticise such theatre, still less to forecast its future. What is relevant here is the use it makes of a particular popular dramatic technique.

The oldest of all popular dramatic techniques is direct address. As often as not it is the medium of storytelling and through it the performer builds a relationship with the audience. That relationship is fundamentally amicable, even loving. We have an affection for the Vice, for Falstaff, for Richard III even, however evil they may be. The clown, the stand-up comic, has no evil dramatic intent, so that inhibition is not present. That does not mean to say that a clown will aways treat his audience with deference. Frankie Howerd's 'now shut your gobs' is not the most genteel of requests. Max Miller's 'shuddup, shuddup' was, perhaps, rather less insulting, but he would tell a woman with a loud laugh, 'I'm bad enough, you don't have to bother lady', or check rudely on the memories of his audiences:

> I went in the back way, through the kitchen through the dining room, into the drawing room an' there's a fellow standin' there – not a stitch on (L). Can you imagine that lady! (L). How's your memory girl? (L).

But this is all clearly in fun. Lenny Bruce or Mort Sahl could insult an audience to the point of disorientation:

The theoretical aim is to purge the spectators, through their own laughter, of all their shoddy, narrow, materialistic notions. The comic catharsis is meant to be moral and political, but it usually goes beyond ethical norms to a feeling of weightless, euphoric wish fulfilment.[9]

There is nothing especially new in this. Jonson has the children imitate different members of the audience in the Induction to *Cynthia's Revels*, and in *Every Man out of His Humour* has Asper pick out a particular kind of critical gallant from the audience:

> And, MITIS, note me, if in all this front,
> You can espy a gallant of this marke,
> Who (to be thought one of the iudicious)
> Sits with his armes thus wreath'd, his hat pull'd here,
> Cryes meaw, and nods, then shakes his empty head,
> Will shew more seuerall motions in his face
> Than the new *London*, *Rome*, or *Niniueh*,
> And (now and then) breakes a drie bisquet iest,
> Which that it may more easily be chew'd
> He steeps in his owne laughter.[10]

Webster is more generally insulting in his Induction to Marston's *The Malcontent*:

> *Sly:*   . . . What do you thinke might come into a mans
>   head now, seeing all this company?
> *Cundale:*   I know not sir.
> *Sly:*   I have an excellent thought: if some fiftie of the
>   Grecians that were cramd in the horse belly had
>   eaten garlike, do you not thinke the Trojans might
>   have smelt out their knavery?
> *Cundale:*   Very likely.[11]

And, as a final example, Jonson ends his mock contract with the spectators before *Bartholomew Fair* by saying that though the Fair is not being kept in its proper place but in a theatre, the place is as dirty as Smithfield 'and as stinking every whit'. There is, then, nothing very new in insulting the audience, but in these examples the play element is strong. George Bernard Shaw was even more skilful in that he attacked his audiences by inverting the comic norms. Instead of the 'odd man out' – the Jaques or Malvolio – being mocked and excluded because he could not or would not conform to the conventions supported in the play world *and by the audience*, he made his hero the exceptional character and required the rest of society – and therefore the audience – to change. By implication, the audience – Ibsen's compact liberal majority – was wrong. But even if it did advance, it would only be to the position such a hero as Dr Stockman would have reached a decade earlier in Ibsen's world.

It may be that exasperation with audiences as much as with the inability to effect change has led to the urge by some contemporary dramatists and companies to intensify insults to the audience. Peter Ansorge in his account of the fringe theatre in England,[12] comments on plays which attack the audience. Thus, *Come Together* (a typically adolescent-style double-entendre title) was 'the optimistic heading of London's first underground jamboree', held at the Royal Court in 1969. It brought together about twenty groups but 'seemed for the most part to have little new to offer apart from a series of highly surrealist and frequently adolescent audience-baiting games' (pp. 38–9). The intention of *The Journey* (1969-70) was, he said, 'to embarrass the audience' (p. 44);[13] or:

> Works like Howard Brenton's *Fruit,* Pip Simmons' *Do It!* and *England's Ireland* were conceived on Living Newspaper lines more intent upon shocking or offending audiences with immediate issues than creating solid and lasting works of art. (p. 76)

Of course, 'creating works of art' may not be the prime intention of such drama, but how justified and how effective is drama that aims to offend audiences? Writing of Snoo Wilson's work, Ansorge said that his plays created the kind of reactions amongst audiences 'normally reserved for the more bizarre techniques of urban guerilla warfare' (p. 13). Nor is Ansorge alone in describing this attitude of fringe performers to their audiences. James Roose-Evans wrote that 'For four or five hours the audience is likely to be battered, bored, stimulated, provoked, assaulted' by The Living Theatre, the aim being, as its director explained, to 'make the spectator feel pain at a public ceremony' in the hope that he would never want to commit violence again [14] – the 'have-you-stopped-beating-your-wife' syndrome. Priests, MPs and actors share a privilege in being unanswerable in the pulpit, the House or on the stage. But are their rights 'to offend the public' identical? Certainly the actor, if he misuses that privilege, does not have an MP's protection and he might find that he has incited a response unintended by the author or his theatre company. One of the most intriguing responses by an audience refusing to be abused was drawn to my attention by Professor John Brushwood.[15] Pirandello's *Cada cual a su manera*, described by the author as being in two or three acts, 'depending on the attitude of the audience', has, in fact, only two acts. The actors have to ensure that the performance is disrupted so that the theatre can be cleared before a third act can be presented. Thus, actors pretending to be members of the audience, loudly criticise the play, argue with the stage-actors, and a lady in the orchestra stalls (also an actress) is so insulted by those on-stage that she is forced to leave the theatre.

However, Germán de Campo went especially to the Teatro Fábergas with a party of friends, determined to call Pirandello's bluff. 'Pirandello', he said, 'becomes boring with his yen for pulling the audience's leg. Let's pull his for a change.' He therefore intervened, and, in a stentorian voice, proceeded to put down the actors. The first act, in consequence, ended in confusion and the actors appealed to the police and a representative of the city council to restore order. However, de Campo was not to be gainsaid:

'Your intention amazes me, gentlemen', argued Germán, holding up his programme. 'It is apparent to me that you know nothing of Pirandello or of his works. I have been to Rome, I have seen them presented there, and the audience always takes part in the performance. This is their great cultural value for the masses.' Turning to the representative of the city council, he concluded: 'Look at the programme: "in two or three acts *depending on the attitude of the audience*", so the audience is authorised to adopt some attitude. And such authorisation is granted jointly by the author, the theatre proprietors, and the city council.'

The representative assented and the incident closed with the solemn declaration by the authorities that Germán had the right – common to all spectators – to 'adopt an attitude'.

Naturally, the altercation continued in the second act (the last Pirandello had written for the play). When the act concluded, an actor stepped in front of the proscenium arch and announced that, in view of the audience's unruly behaviour, 'the performance is suspended'.

'You lie!', roared Germán. 'The only disturbance generated here was that provoked by the actors in order to suspend the performance. It is a cheap trick to save you doing the work necessary to perform the third act.'

The bewilderment of the 'director' reached its maximum and, not knowing what attitude he should adopt, he chose the worst: he continued in his role: 'I have said that in view of the disturbance generated among the spectators . . .'

He was unable to finish, so intense was Germán's indignation.

'Do you think you can make us believe that Parra and his accomplices are innocent members of the audience? We have been seeing them on the stage since we were infants! Now we demand that you continue with the third act because we have paid to see the whole play.'

The whole audience then made the demand its own: 'The third act! The third act!'

The actor, with no third act to offer, and without Pirandello there to get him out of the mess, was obliged to order the lights to be extinguished. And so the audience left, furious because it had been cheated of the play's supposed third act.

The development of the direct address into abuse and assault of the audience by the performer has now been formalised in a drama, Peter Handke's *Offending the Audience* (1966), first performed in England in 1970.[16] Nicholas Hern describes the play as a practical joke that 'only really works on unsuspecting people' and 'does not bear repetition to those that know it'.[17] He makes a very interesting comparison with the masque, especially in the light of what has been said about Jonson in *Popular Appeal in English Drama to 1850* (p. 94). He equates the 'role of the audience in Handke's play with that of the audience of a court masque or a Happening' (p. 38). According to Handke himself, as quoted by Hern, the intention is that members of the audience should become not only better playgoers, but *better able to cope with life*:

The play has not been written so that the usual audience should make way for a different audience, but that the usual audience should become a different audience. The play can serve to make the spectator pleasantly or unpleasantly aware of his presence, to make him aware of himself. It can make him aware that he is there, that he is present, that he exists. . . . It can make him attentive, keen of hearing, clear-sighted, and not only as a playgoer.   (p. 43)

Four actors make statements of varying lengths; the audience is told it will hear nothing it has not heard before; the audience itself is described; it is told that the actors are only themselves (which is not in itself true, nor is it even true within the play, for they also describe themselves as the mouthpieces of the author); that the possibilities of the theatre will not be exploited; that there is no drama; but that the members of the audience should try to sense themselves; and that before they go they will be insulted:

We will insult you because insulting you is also one way of speaking to you. By insulting you, we can be straight with you. We can switch you on. We can eliminate the free play. We can tear down a wall. We can observe you.   (p. 35)

Thirteen sections of insult follow, concluding with a courteous farewell:

You who embrace life. You who detest life. You who have no feeling about life. You ladies and gents you, you celebrities of public and cultural life you, you who are present you, you brothers and sisters you, you comrades you, you worthy listeners you, you fellow humans you.
You were welcome here. We thank you. Good night.

(p. 38)

The curtain falls and rises again to recorded 'Roaring applause and wild whistling', the actors remaining stock-still, until the audience begins to leave, when the curtain finally descends.

There is a joke element about this play which distinguishes it from the work of, say, The Living Theatre, but that must undermine Handke's intention of reforming his audience and enabling it better to cope with life. Like any practical joke, there is an element, often a considerable element, of self-indulgence on the part of the joker; but if this is a joke, it is, in the best 'pataphysical sense, 'a serious hoax'.[18] But can Handke's intention be realised? It is very much to be doubted. The play is like an academic exercise for use in the training of actors, and the sort of piece that might itself have been the product of a class exercise in 'creative' writing. Nicholas Hern describes it as a prologue to, amongst other things, Handke's subsequent plays (p. 45), and that suggests that the hoax is a more serious exercise for Handke than anyone else.

To set about abusing an audience through the medium of direct address may also be said to take the theatre back to its roots. The denunciatory sermon, in which a minister hurls abuse at his congregation, is an ancient device. It is even regularised in the Book of Common Prayer in the form of an Exhortation read by the minister when members of his flock 'are negligent to come to the Holy Communion', and in the 'Commination, or denouncing of God's anger and judgements against Sinners'.[19] Whatever aims Handke might intend, his fulminations can hardly have the force, and certainly will not fulfil the function, of a Commination addressed to a confessing congregation, which is party to a contract freely entered into. Despite the interest that such dramatists and producers have in role-playing, therefore (and in particular, the roles they cast for their audiences), they err at the outset in their understanding of the audience's role. A Commination rebukes people for not doing what they undertook to do, but an audience that is reviled in the theatre has not mistaken its role, so is unjustly so treated; it is the actors who, on the dramatist's behalf, are presumptuous in exceeding the privilege of their position.

Nevertheless, it is easy to see how dramatists, producers and performers, with a concern for what is going on around them, should be anxious to get across their concern directly to their audience, even if it means breaking their 'contract' with the audience. One of the outstanding attempts of this kind in the past decade or two was the Royal Shakespeare Company's production, US.[20] In 1968 the script, together with an illustrated description of the creative and rehearsal process which 'transmitted this raw material into a new kind of performance' (p. 21) and notes on source material, was published as The Book of US. Three things must be said at the outset. First and foremost, there is no doubt of the sincerity of the company's intentions. As George Farmer, Chairman of the Governing Board of the RSC told the Lord Chamberlain, who wished the production stopped, 'the degree of personal endeavour which was going into the performance removed it from an easy propaganda posture' (p. 145).

Second, Peter Brook says in his introduction, '*US* made no claims' nor, he says, does publishing details about the company's work constitute a claim. He describes the book as a progress report, 'not to be used except as a reference' (which is underlined, p. 9). These non-claims are not easy to interpret. *US* could not but make claims as a piece of theatre, and it was undoubtedly making claims upon its audiences; indeed, its claims were enormous. If it didn't claim to be theatre having 'a voice that could be listened to seriously' (for which Albert Hunt under-standably argues, p. 17), what was it all about? As Arnold Wesker pointed out in an 'Open Letter to the Team' written immediately after the first performance, 'You have assumed an awful responsibility' (p. 205). There is surely sleight of hand in this introduction: take *US* – us? – desperately seriously – but we make no claims – no claims to be taken seriously?

It is easier to accept that no claim is being advanced in pub-lishing details of the process of how *US* came to be, and certainly no claim is implicit in publishing responses to the production. But the proviso that the book be only used 'as a reference' is puzzling. It may mean that the script is not to be performed by others, because it was created out of the very guts of the original team and only that experience entitles others to offer a per-formance. That would surely be wholly acceptable. But it may mean, 'we have published this but you are not allowed to argue with what we have done'; this no one need accept. What is even more puzzling is the justification offered that 'it arose from experimental laboratory work'. But the experiment in the laboratory was brought before the public as a deliberate, planned confrontation, in which the actors, as the audience's representa-tives, 'trained and prepared to go farther than the spectator' (p. 10), would explore the contradiction of the horror of Vietnam and 'the normal life' led by the spectators. Laboratory work is private and its progress reports are for the cognoscenti; but once the drug – the stimulant – is on the market, then claims *are* being made, and one cannot hide behind the formula that it is only 'experimental laboratory work'.

What seems to be claimed in the introduction to US by Peter Brook is (a) that no claims are made at all, and (b) that the actor is trained and prepared to go farther than the spectator. But in what is the actor trained and prepared to go farther? In acting, of course, for that is his job; but also, it would seem, in the pursuit of truth, in moral piety and in righteousness, so enabling him to lead the spectator 'down a path the spectator knows to be his own' (p. 10). What is being claimed as a sort of no-claim bonus for the actor is a priestly function, and this comes out rather interestingly in what Brook said to the actors the morning after their first night. Rehearsals for US had been a way of life, but now Brook would not be seeing the actors every day. Whereas Grotowski, 'in his small Polish provincial town, in that Communist/Catholic country' could 'make it monastic', Brook, in London, was 'not prepared to give fifteen hours a day for the next ten years', nor even for the length of the show's run, to living with the actors: 'I am not prepared to surrender all the outside world', he said (p. 150). And why should he, or the actors? Unless, of course, they were claiming to be (as they were in this show) other than they were. Can commitment be so shut off and on by the performers whilst demanding continuous commitment of an audience?[21] Inevitably, that cannot but lead to confusion on the stage and in the auditorium. D. A. N. Jones's comment in the *New Statesman* (printed in *The Book of US*, it must be pointed out), rather cruelly illustrates that confusion of roles:

> The end of Act Two also alienates in the wrong way. They stand there, miming contempt or stoicism or something, and watch you go out – apparently pleased that you don't know whether it's the end or not.   (p. 189)

The third comment to be made is that this was far from the new kind of performance it claimed to be. The tradition of direct appeal is very old, but even if this were ignored as irrelevant (Brook claims 'whatever has been handed down to us, has been cheapened out of recognition', p. 9), it had been reintroduced in a telling manner by T. S. Eliot in *Murder in the Cathedral* some thirty years before. US. Of course, Eliot was not claiming for his actors greater moral piety and furthermore his play was intended for a specifically 'church' audience concerned with a peculiarly anti-clerical event and its religious implications. But the 1930s provided a closer source for *US*, as Charles Marowitz realised:

> Many reviewers, in my opinion, have been subtly intimidated by the urgency of this subject and the unfamiliarity of the treatment which both you and I know is nothing more than Living Newspaper technique brought up to date. This has angered me and many like me who would like criticism to stare down the po-faced intensities of productions like *US* which with the best intentions in the world, produce superficial flurries on incendiary subjects that can be justified neither on artistic nor ideological grounds.   (p. 196)

It is surprising that, despite Marowitz having pointed out how *US* was following the Living Newspaper tradition, two years later the claim should still be made that a new kind of performance was being created. It is especially ironic in that one of the banned American Living Newspaper productions dealt specifically with 'imperialist intervention' – Italy's invasion and conquest of Ethiopia in 1935[22] – and that an English Living Newspaper production of 1938, *Busmen*, should have included prominent political figures of the time.

According to the title-page of the version in *One Act Play Magazine*, *Busmen* was written by John Allen but, in the manner of *US* nearly thirty years later, it is also stated that it was written and produced by members of the company under the general direction of John Allen (p. 252). Reading it through again, one is struck by how much it has in common with *US* – or rather, how much *US* has in common with *Busmen*. One of the interesting features of *Busmen* is its conclusion. In Scene 22 the tramwaymen are shown deciding not to support the busmen. There is a slow black out and then, against a background of cries of 'Strike!', 'Again!', 'Strike, strike, strike!', a busman, Fred, 'comes to the front of the stage and addresses the audience',

> *Fred:*   Well, folks, you've just heard *Waiting for Lefty* [by Clifford Odets, 1935] by the Unity Theatre club, and that shows us how the cabmen went on strike in America, and how their problems weren't much different to ours . . .

There are cheers as he persuades those listening – the audience – to continue the busmen's strike, and he concludes by starting some community singing with 'that good old favourite, "Daisy"'. They sing, with the audience joining in, to show the Transport Board Headquarters that they're 'not downhearted'.[23] At that very moment, news is brought that the Union Executive has decided to call off the strike. It is a remarkable adaptation of a technique that goes back to *A Nice Wanton*.[24] The final scene, 24, shows the outcome of this deflation: the proposal, which proves abortive, to start a rival union. The one great distinction between *Busmen* and *US* is that the former was the work of a struggling minority group, whilst *US* was produced by a very wealthy and powerful arm of the establishment: the Royal Shakespeare Company.

There is no doubt about the sincerity of those involved,[25] but the ambivalence one detects from time to time, and the claiming whilst not claiming a highly privileged role – 'a company with an international reputation making a statement about Vietnam in one of its two great theatres' (an important element in Brook's strategy – p. 14) with actors protected by the personae adopted whilst making the audience victims of, as Charles Marowitz put it, 'an aggressive More-Committed-than-Thou approach to life' (p. 195) – highlight the delicacy of the task.

US attempted (using Living Newspaper techniques, coupled with contemporary actor-training methods)[26] to enable 'current atrocities' to be as worthy of attention as the 'civilised after-dinner fare' of the past (p. 9). *The Book of US* contains many fascinating insights into how the production was evolved. Take, for example, the sequence in which seven American servicemen describe their reactions to the war. The juxtaposition of the scene is discussed (p. 66) and the way it was to be presented (p. 68). It was first rehearsed 'as a piece of naturalistic theatre'. As rehearsals progressed the actors built up the characters and created atmosphere, but then these elements were pared down so that 'no more than the essence of each statement remained'. Then, 'The actors were lined up at a bar and told to speak their words straight out at the audience, as if they were being inter-viewed, or as if they were on trial', the trial of shot-down American airmen being proposed by Ho Chi Minh about that time. Actor-control seems to be undermined by that bald statement: 'The actors were lined up at a bar and told . . .'.

It is in the presentation of 'the facts' that serious problems arose. The company was not so naive as to imagine that the facts were unequivocal. Early in their thinking on the project, well before rehearsals began, it was borne in upon the production team that 'to stand on a stage and simply demand American withdrawal seemed both impertinent and inadequate' (p. 14). [27] Facts are difficult creatures at the best of times, hard to be sure of, especially in political matters, and not easy to manage in the theatre. It is one thing to assert 'A theatre that is alive must be willing to confront audiences with important, challenging facts', but a bit awkward when as examples of these one is given 'Churchill's *alleged* involvement in the death of Sikorski' or the '*mystery*' of President Kennedy's assassination (my italics). And consider:

> we were aware that it was impossible to do justice to all the complexities of the situation in the context of the panoramic sweep we were attempting. What we said had to be simple. We believed that the simplification was justified here. A theatre is alive . . .   (p. 51)

What this amounts to is asserting that what *we* believe, what *we* feel, what *we* simplify, is tantamount to the facts, the basis for bringing the audience to 'the moment of truth'. The same sort of short-cut is referred to later: 'The aim was not to reveal the complete diplomatic truth of the war, but to give, in a brief scene, an image of the network of double-talk and contradiction which characterises diplomacy on both sides' (p. 112). That diplomatic double-talk needs exposure no one will doubt, and that it is meat for drama is certainly possible; but if an *impression* of fact is to be given, one cannot but wonder at the double-talk of an aim that is not to reveal the complete truth. [28]

There was some disagreement as to whether the play was 'Theatre of Fact' (see p. 197). The theatre critic of the *Sunday Telegraph* complained it was not Theatre of Fact but Theatre of Advocacy (p. 188). Bryan Magee, a philosopher, argued that it was not documentary theatre but art because it transfigured fact, 'and for that matter half-truths, propaganda and downright lies', into 'the theatre of compassionate involvement' (p. 193). In his introduction, Peter Brook makes it plain that the company was not interested in Theatre of Fact but in the theatre of confrontation.

Writ small, theatre of confrontation is the old technique of direct address, especially when that mode is the prime form, not something which forms part of a larger work (as in Gloucester's address in *Richard III*, I.i, or Launce's in *The Two Gentlemen of Verona*, II.iii and IV.iv). The stand-up comic confronts and must win over his audience. A music-hall performer, especially one not at the top of the bill was very much in the position of one 'confronting' a crown, even a mob, until he had won them over into being a responsive audience – and he had very little time in which to do that. What the normally contemplative Aldwych audience was offered was a similar technique, but the content was to be a script based on the actors' response to material the production team offered them (the 'facts'), shaped by a playwright (p. 17). The response? As Brook told the company on the morning following the first night, they had offered themselves to the audience (note the sacrificial image) and 'were rewarded by the quality of the audience's silence' (p. 150). Was that quite the full interpretation?

The Book of US has a revealing sentence describing how the audience was to be treated. It refers to the song called 'The Leech'. Richard Peaslee, who composed the music, 'complained mildly to Adrian Mitchell that all the songs he'd written so far had been anti-American'. Mitchell went away to write an anti-Vietcong song which he called 'The Leech'.

> He solemnly insisted that the song was a criticism of VC violence – though it didn't read that way to anybody else in the team. Peaslee composed a great martial tune, and the song became an inspiring call to arms – except, of course, that like many of the songs it progressed towards an assault on the audience in the last verse.   (p. 63)

Roger Howard, in 'Declaration of Intent to Write Propaganda' – in the theatre – later analysed the technique which seems to be used here:

> The theatre of ideas should never, however, reject word-as-sound altogether but only when it is used independent of a meaning capable of constituting a social position, only when distinct, in other words from an ideological standpoint. In

fact, the forcing of an audience to accept ideological points is greatly aided by the dialectic being expressed in forms that expand consciousness . . .[29]

Although Howard was not referring specifically to *US* but writing generally, the RSC's technique of 'forcing' the audience to accept its point of view shows Howard's theory in practice.

Arnold Wesker, unaware of this reasoning behind the production – 'of course . . . it progressed towards an assault on the audience' – referred to the lack of reaction by the audience at the end of the show to the burning of the butterflies (which might have been real or might have been artificial, p. 184[30]):

> One last point – for the moment at least – going back to the burning of the butterfly. If Peter [Brook] did want people to cry out 'don't' then, one: the actor must take a longer pause before applying the flame so that people have time to absorb the knowledge that he's actually going to do it; and two: he must alter the entire shape of the production in order to condition us to protest. You cannot hammer at an audience for three hours, demanding it look at you, listen to you, think about you then in the last minute expect it to react. You don't jeer at people you've paralyzed because they can't walk.
>
> (p. 205)

Wesker is surely more percipient than is Brook in his introduction. Brook claims that *US* wasn't drama but a kind of seduction, using fun-language to woo and annoy the spectator. This 'wooing' was, Brook explained, a form of preparation like those phases in the bullring when the bull is taunted prior to the kill. Wooing as rape; seduction as killing! The revealing giveaway comes in what follows: 'We aimed not at a kill, but at what the bullfighters call the moment of truth' (p. 10). But who experiences 'the moment of truth'? The bull – or the bull-fighter? And who is it intended should be killed in the bull-ring? The bull – or the bullfighter? The 'moment of truth' was to be experienced by Mr Brook and company; the audience was the victim, to be assaulted and killed. And, in its silence, it acted its role to perfection.

How effective was the play? In a theatrical sense it was undoubtedly tremendously powerful – as powerful, one is tempted to say, as a first-rate melodrama for a nineteenth-century audience. Those who conceived and produced *US* did not imagine it would have the effect that Galsworthy's *Justice* had on solitary confinement. It is probable that Vietnam was seen afresh in a way that went beyond the televised horrors, but it may be that, simply by attending, people felt they had done what they could about Vietnam, as if by proxy. It almost certainly enabled producers, writers and actors of the Royal Shakespeare Company to feel for a while not 'captured by the Establishment',[31] even though, with the National, they are the theatrical Establishment, and putting the authority of the RSC to use was itself part of Brook's strategy. Indeed the kind of counter which only the really powerful can play was considered when there was fear that the Lord Chamberlain might prevent a performance at the Aldwych:

> at Stratford, we *were* licensees and our own landlords. I shall not forget for a long time Peter Hall sitting in the pub at lunchtime before the run-through, weighing up whether, if we put on an unlicensed performance of *US* at Stratford-upon-Avon instead of the Aldwych, the authorities would risk the ridicule of taking our license away, and thus preventing the Stratford Shakespeare season.   (Michael Kustow, p. 146)

One has to be powerful to think in such terms. Such was hardly an option open to the Unity in 1938. Writing in April 1968, Peter Brook evidently felt that though the intensity of impact might seem a good thing, 'because we want our theatre to be powerful and immediate', it could not go deep: 'when the trigger is so light, when the ejaculation comes so soon, when the first reaction is so strong, it is not possible to go very deep. The shutters fall fast' (p. 11). Peter Ansorge, writing of *The George Jackson Black and White Minstrel Show* (1973) by Pip Simmons, seems to be taking this a step further.

> For Simmons himself seems to be half in love with his fantasies of power, race and revolution. There is a fascination with theatrical shock efforts which seem only to confirm the underlying feeling of cynicism and moral nihilism. Anything goes, it seems, in overcoming the apathy of liberal audiences even if it means leaving audiences without any sense of 'moral

and political direction' at the end of an evening.

(p. 35)

Two things are misunderstood in drama which tries to be powerful and immediate by confrontation, by assaulting the audience (quite apart from whether actors should regard themselves as the moral superiors of their audiences). First of all, an actor should not deceive the audience by pretending to be acting but, at root, appearing *in propria persona*. It is quite remarkable that so very distinguished a director as Peter Brook could begin his introduction to *The Book of US* by expressing the nausea he feels at times at the artificiality of the theatre! Of course the theatre is artificial! That is its very nature. It is basic to theatre that it reaches truth *through* its artificiality, not by trying to pretend that it is 'real'. The origin of *US* lay not only in The Living Newspaper but also in J. M. Barrie's *Peter Pan*, in that moment when the members of the audience are asked to show they believe in fairies in order to save Tinker Bell. Peter Pan's bursting through the proscenium is no different from the confusion of the role of the actors and actresses in *US* and such-like productions. This, perhaps, is the moment to remind readers who have forgotten precisely what Barrie wrote in *Peter Pan*:

> Peter: Why, Tink, you have drunk my medicine! [*She flutters strangely about the room, answering him now in a very thin tinkle*] It was poisoned and you drank it to save my life! Tink, dear Tink, are you dying?

A longish and excruciatingly embarrassing 'stage direction' follows, at the end of which Peter Pan is on his knees and saying:

> Her light is growing faint, and if it goes out, that means she is dead! Her voice is so low I can scarcely tell what she is saying. She says – she says she could get well again if children believed in fairies! [*He rises and throws out his arms he knows not to whom, perhaps to the boys and girls of whom he is not one*] Do you believe in fairies? Say quick that you believe! If you believe, clap your hands!

Barrie's next two comments are revealing of a degree of tongue-in-cheek not probably shared by Peter Brook. Many clap, he says, *'some don't, a few hiss . . . But Tink is saved.'* Then after thanks from Peter to those who clapped, he is off to rescue Wendy. Act IV concludes with the second revealing comment: *'Tink is already as merry and impudent as a grig, with not a thought for those who have saved her . . .'*[32] With not a thought for those who have responded? A true characterisation doubtless – but then characterisation has just been sacrificed by Peter's plea. Tinker Bell is one of us, like the characters of *US*. Has the audience been fooled? Is Barrie quietly amused? And Brook? Surely not!

Music-hall performers, who *seem* to appear as themselves, manage a separation of stage persona and self. If direct address is to be used, perhaps a lesson might still be learned from listening to Max Miller recordings (with audience), paying particular attention to the audience–performer relationship.

Secondly, it is a fantasy to imagine that drama can lead to immediate change in law, wars or attitudes. I find it odd that this should still need to be said. If one does not like artificiality and wants to effect change in society, then get out of the theatre. What the theatre, and the allied art of cinema, have done has been to play a very significant part in changing our apprehension of reality. From the coming of realism and for almost a hundred years, the theatre and the film have shown us what, *seemingly*, the world is like. When both have been fanciful (as in musicals), audiences have realised they have been fanciful, but when they have been shown a Chalk-Garden, Waterloo-Road-like world, audiences have been tempted to assume that that is what life is like. Peter Nichols dramatises it to perfection in *The National Health*, II.5. Nowhere is this more apparent than in the conventions governing film editing from the 1930s to 1950s. Cutting carefully noted time lapse (by dissolves and fades) and cause and effect (by the juxtaposition of shots). The world was a rational world and film editing reflected that. This was hardly what the originators of realism had in mind. By showing the world as it really was, they hoped to effect change, and over the years, though specific changes were not brought about immediately, social changes did come, and drama can claim a share in changing attitudes if only by sometimes showing 'how things really are'. Had this not firmly been believed practical, it is very unlikely that ameliorist dramatists would have continued so long to be dedicated to the realistic drama of social concern. But neither the world, nor behaviour within it, is governed by rational laws.

Freud, Einstein, Heisenberg and Gödel present us with a very different understanding of a world motivated irrationally, subject to relative time, governed by uncertainty. Drama since the late 1950s has reflected *that*, and film may now be edited for mass consumption without recourse to the laws of a supposedly rational world. But for nearly a hundred years many millions of people have had their apprehension of reality moulded by realistic films and plays. Now a generation is growing up, born in the 1950s and 1960s, in which popular drama, film and television show an irrational world, and the traditional conflict between generations is heightened by these two different ways of interpreting the world that has been dramatised for us. Peter Brook asks in his introduction to *US*, 'What is living theatre?' and replies:

> We have no answer today. Whatever we know, is not it. Whatever we have seen, is not it. Whatever is labelled theatre, isn't. Whatever is defined as theatre, misses the point. Whatever has been handed down to us, has been cheapened out of recognition. Whoever claims to know what theatre was or could be, doesn't. We are now before a long period of perpetual revolution, in which we must search, attempt to build, pull down and search again.   (p. 9)

I don't believe this, and in using the kind of traditions he does, I don't think Brook worked as if he did. I am much more taken with a statement by Peter Schumann, director of the Bread and Puppet Theatre:

> you can't simply shock an audience, that will only disgust them. We don't necessarily have to revolutionize the theatre. It may be that the best theatre – if it comes – will develop from the most traditional forms. A theatre is good when it makes sense to people.[33]

The determination to use popular dramatic techniques as a means of shocking an audience – the direct address, the bursting through the proscenium arch (real or metaphorical) – is to pervert the use of one of the most valuable traditions available in theatre.[34] It may be that our most distinguished actors and directors, in mainstream, fringe and underground movements, really believe with Grotowski that there is 'a long English tradition in avoiding seriousness in theatrical art',[35] equate run-of-the-mill *théâtre de boulevard* plays with all English theatrical art, and forget the wealth of traditions open to the dramatist and the theatre in Britain. The future of drama, as George Bernard Shaw said, lies in its past, and many recent plays have shown that our varied dramatic traditions are capable of dramatising even the most painful and sacrosanct of subjects, and without abusing the audience:

Now the cotton-wool. Can anyone tell me what I do with that? [*Reacts to the same woman in audience*] You're right, madam, absolutely right. Been making that answer all your life and for the first time it's accurate, not just vulgar. Yes. We have to close the apertures, the points that might evacuate bodily fluids. Miss one out, they'll raise Cain in the mortuary. Lug-holes, cake-holes, nose-holes, any other holes, all right madam thank you very much indeed! [*more ogling the woman*]

Appendix I: Continental and English Drama of the 19th and Early 20th Centuries

ENGLAND	ENGLAND	FRANCE
Legitimate	*Illegitimate*	
	1802 'melodrame'	
1809 Old Price Riots		
1814 Shelley, *The Cenci*		
1817 Gas lighting		
		1820 Scribe: well-
	1829 *Black-Ey'd*	–60 made play
	Susan	1830 Hugo, *Hernani*
1840 *Money*		
1841 *London Assurance*		
1843 Theatre Monopoly ends		
		1851 *Italian Straw Hat*
		1852 *La Dame aux*
	1854 New Canterbury	*camélias*
	Music Hall	1855 Augier, *Marriage of Olympia* rejects prostitute's rehabilitation
1859 *On the Origin of Species*		
1860 *Colleen Bawn*		1860
1865 *Arrah-na-Pogue*	1862 *Lady Audley's*	–1907 Sardoodledom
1867 *Caste*	*Secret*	
1871 *Pygmalion & Galatea*		
The Bells		1873 Zola, Preface to
	1875 Gilbert &	*Thérèse Raquin*
1878 Irving at Lyceum	–96 Sullivan	
	1881 Savoy lit by	
1884 Tennyson, *Becket*	electricity	
		1887 Antoine
		–96 Théâtre Libre
1889 *Doll's House* performed		
1892 *Widowers' Houses* performed		
1893 *Second Mrs Tanqueray*	1893 *Gaiety Girl*	
1894 *Mrs Warren's Profession* written	(George Edwardes)	
1894 Poel's Elizabethan		
–1905 Stage Society	**IRELAND**	
1897 *The Liars*		1896 Jarry, *Ubu Roi*
The Devil's Disciple	1889 Yeats, *Countess*	
1904 Royal Court as	*Cathleen* perf.	1901 Brieux, *Damaged*
–7 experimental theatre	1902 *Shadow of the*	*Goods* (Preface
	Glen	by G. B. Shaw)
1907 Miss Horniman's	1907 *Playboy of the*	
–21 Gaiety Theatre	*Western World*	
(Manchester Realists)		
1907 Granville–Barker, *Waste*		
1909 Galsworthy, *Strife*		
1910 Galsworthy, *Justice*		
	1924 *Juno and the Paycock*	

SCANDINAVIA	RUSSIA	GERMANY & AUSTRIA
		1797 Tieck, *Puss-in-Boots*
		1821 *Der Freischütz*
	1837 Lobachevsky, 'Imaginary Geometry'	1836 Büchner, *Woyzeck*
	1840s Chernishevsky, theories of realism	1842 Nestroy, *Einen Jux will er sich machen*
Ibsen:		
1850 *Catiline*		1850 Wagner, *Lohengrin*
	1860 Ostrovsky, *Storm*	
1863 *Pretenders*	1864 Dostoievsky, *Notes from Underground*	
1866 *Brand*		
1867 *Peer Gynt*		
		1876 Bayreuth established
1877 *Pillars of Society*		
1879 *A Doll's House*		
1881 *Ghosts*		
1882 *An Enemy of the People*		
1884 *The Wild Duck*		
1886 *Rosmersholm*		
Strindberg:		
1887 *The Father*		
1888 *Miss Julie*	1888 Tolstoi, *Powers of Darkness*	1889 Hauptmann *Before Dawn*
		1891 Wedekind, *Spring's Awakening*
		1892 Hauptmann, *Weavers*
		1894 Hauptmann, *Hannele*
		1895 Wedekind, *Lulu Plays* −1904
	1898 Moscow Art Theatre	1899 Freud, *Interpretation of Dreams*
	1901 *Three Sisters*	
1902 *Dream Play*	1902 *Lower Depths*	
	1904 *Cherry Orchard*	1905 Einstein, *Special Theory of Relativity*
1907 *Ghost Sonata*		

	UNITED STATES	
	1916 *Bound East for Cardiff*	
	1920 *Emperor Jones*	1927 Heisenberg, *Principle of Uncertainty*
	1922 *The Hairy Ape*	
		1931 Gödel's *Theorem*

Appendix II: A Select List of Recordings of Music–Hall Acts

With one or two special exceptions, this list does not include details of recordings of music–hall songs. A list of such recordings is given in my *Songs of the British Music Hall* (p. 240). The list of acts provided here indicates the principal sources of performances referred to in the text. Only representative recordings are given, especially for such music–hall stars as George Robey and Sandy Powell, for some of these performers made a very large number of recordings. Where possible, recordings before audiences are given. Most of the recordings, including some of the long-playing records, are no longer readily available, of course.

LONG-PLAYING RECORDINGS

The Golden Age of Music Hall (includes Leno, Robey, Roberts and Little Tich)	Delta TQD 3030
Top of the Bill: Famous Stars of the Music Hall (includes Little Tich and Leno)	Fidelio ATL 4010
Vintage Variety (includes *ITMA*, Will Hay, *Variety Bandbox*, *Over the Garden Wall*, *Take it From Here*)	BBC Records 134M
Fifty Years of Radio Comedy (includes Sandy Powell, Max Miller, Arthur Askey and Richard Murdoch, Murgatroyd and Winterbottom, Revnell and West, Robb Wilton, Frankie Howerd and a number of extracts from such shows as *ITMA*, *Bandwaggon* and *Hancock's Half Hour*)	BBC Records 138M
Great Radio Comedians (includes Elsie and Doris Waters, Stainless Stephen, Jewell and Warris, Al Read, Gillie Potter and Cyril Fletcher)	BBC Records 151M
Memories of ITMA (extracts from ten broadcasts, 1941–8)	Oriole MG 20032

SINGLE ACTS (MAINLY ON 78s)

Arthur Askey and Richard Murdoch: The Proposal	HMV C3173
	(Re-recorded on BBC 138M)
Jeanne de Casalis: Mrs Feather	Decca F3273
Gracie Fields: Complete act recorded at Holborn Empire, 11 October 1933. (Issued in the kind of album then normally reserved for symphonies and concertos.)	HMV C7450-1-2
Sid Field: Sid Field Plays Golf	Columbia DB2163
Flanagan and Allen: Diggin H'OI'les	Columbia DO1479
The New M.P.	Columbia DO840
Underneath the Arches (their most famous song)	Columbia DB2725
Joyce Grenfell: Useful and Acceptable Gifts	HMV B8930
Nursery School/Joyful Noise	HMV 7EG8787
Grock: Grock dans son sketch de Music Hall (in album with notes)	Odéon 222.017-020
Happidrome: Let Me Tell You (Grand Theatre Blackpool)	Columbia FB2679
Frankie Howerd: English as She is Spoken (with the bandleader, Billy Cotton)	Columbia DB2694
Jewel and Warriss: Extract from *Up the Pole*	BBC 151M
Little Tich: The Weather/The Waiter	Pathé 5339
Max Miller: In the Theatre (Holborn Empire)	HMV BD615-6-7
In the Theatre Again (Holborn Empire)	HMV BD646-7-8
In the Theatre (Finsbury Park Empire)	HMV BD770-1-2
With the Forces	HMV BD883-4-5
Entertains War Workers (in Factory Canteen)	HMV BD980-1
In the Theatre (Finsbury Park Empire)	HMV BD1022-3
At the Met[ropolitan], Edgware Road	Pye GG0195
That's Nice Maxi. (A very sad recording of Max Miller near the end of his career, working hard for laughs at the Black Lion Public House, Patcham.)	Pye PLP1084
Murgatroyd and Winterbottom: About Cruises/ Art	Parlophone A6585
Clothes/Seaside	Parlophone F800
Music/Grub	Parlophone R2039
Sandy Powell: On the Dole	Broadcast 647
Sandy, The Doctor	Broadcast 728
A Night on the Embankment	Rex 8256
George Robey: And Very Nice Too/More in Sorrow than in Anger	Columbia 3006

I Stopped, I Looked, I Listened (from *The Bing Boys*)	Columbia L1034
Archibald, Certainly Not	Columbia 2985
Burt Sheppard: A Political Meeting (recorded 27 January 1899)	Berliner 1050
Harry Tate: Motoring. (Recorded several times, e.g. Gramophone and Type-writer Co GC 1322; Columbia 320 and DOX 194)	
Fishing	Regal–Zonophone MR1483
Selling a Car	Columbia 870
Fortifying the House (*with Violet Lorraine*)	Columbia 504
John Tilley: The Scoutmaster (includes the 'Shell' act)	Columbia DX648
The Anti-Arson Squad	Columbia DO1145
Army Estimates	Imperial 2741
London Transport Board	Columbia DX569
Tommy Trinder: Stage Show (The Embassy, Peterborough)	Columbia FB2552-3

Appendix III: A Chronological List of Plays and Acts Discussed

As some of the plays and acts discussed are not well known, a chronological list may prove a useful reference guide. It should be noted that not every play can be precisely dated and acts, though recorded at a specific time, were repeated over many years. They have therefore been related to decades rather than years. Not all plays are referred to here but one or two other significant dates are included, as in Appendix I.

1497	Medwall: *Fulgens and Lucres*
1550	*A Nice Wanton*
1559	Jonson: *Every Man Out of His Humour*
1602	Bidermann: *Cenodoxus*
	Percy: *Aphrodysial*
1604	Marston: *The Malcontent*
1605	Jonson *et al*: *Eastward Ho!*
1608	Day: *Humour out of Breath*
1636	Corneille: *The Theatrical Illusion*
1655	Quinault: *La comédie sans comédie*
1797	Tieck: *Puss-in-Boots*
1820	'The Steam Packet'
1856	Carroll: 'The Three Voices'
(1859	Darwin: *On the Origin of Species*)
1864	Dostoievsky: *Notes from Underground*
1867	Robertson: *Caste*
1877	Ibsen: *The Pillars of Society*
1885	Gilbert & Sullivan *The Mikado*
1888	Strindberg: *Miss Julie*
1892	Anstey: 'Frankly Canaille'
1893	Roberts: 'Not a Word!'
1895	James: *Guy Domville*
(1899	Freud: *The Interpretation of Dreams*)
1900	*Sleeping Beauty*
1900s	Little Tich
	George Robey

157

1900s	Burt Sheppard
	Harry Tate
	Mark Sheridan
1904	Barrie: *Peter Pan*
(1905	Einstein: *The Special Theory of Relativity*)
1911	Hauptmann: *The Rats*
1912	Strauss: *Ariadne auf Naxos*
1921	Pirandello: *Six Characters in Search of an Author*
1922	Eliot: *The Waste Land*
1924	O'Casey: *Juno and the Paycock*
1928	O'Neill: *Strange Interlude*
1930s	John Tilley
1930s	Flanagan and Allen
and 40s	Max Miller
1931	Wilder: *The Happy Journey to Trenton and Camden*
1935	Eliot: *Murder in the Cathedral*
	Odets: *Paradise Lost*
1938	Wilder: *Our Town*
	The Matchmaker
	Allen: *Busmen*
1939	*Bandwaggon*
1940s	*ITMA*
	Sandy Powell
	Tommy Trinder
	Sid Field
	Joyce Grenfell
	Happidrome
1942	Wilder: *The Skin of our Teeth*
1944	Miller: *Death of a Salesman*
1945	Rice: *Dream Girl*
1950s	Frankie Howerd
and 60s	Tony Hancock
	Harry Worth
1955	Beckett: *Waiting for Godot*
1956	Osborne: *Look Back in Anger*
1957	Arden: *The Waters of Babylon*
	Beckett: *All that Fall*
	Endgame
	Osborne: *The Entertainer*
	Simpson: *A Resounding Tinkle*
1958	Albee: *Zoo Story*
	Arden: *Live Like Pigs*
1959	Pinter: *Last to Go*
1960	Arden: *Happy Haven*
	Pinter: *The Caretaker*
1963	Pinter: *The Lover*
	Oh What a Lovely War!

1966   Grass: *The Plebeians Rehearse the Uprising*
        Handke: *Offending the Audience*
1966   Stoppard: *Rosencrantz and Guildenstern Are Dead*
        US
1968   Pinter: *Landscape*
        Stoppard: *The Real Inspector Hound*
1969   Nichols: *The National Health*
        Pinter: *Silence*
1970   Stoppard: *Where Are They Now?*
1971   Nichols: *Forget-me-not Lane*
1975   Griffiths: *Comedians*
1977   Nichols: *Privates on Parade*

Notes

NOTE TO THE PREFACE

1. J. R. Planché, *Recollections and Reflections* (1872) II, 69.

NOTES TO CHAPTER ONE: INTRODUCTION

1. There is a good account of a riotous would-be audience for *The Christmas Prince* by Griffin Higgs in the Revels Accounts for 1607–8, St John's College, Oxford. When the section called 'Periander' was performed, those in the hall were 'very quiet and attentive'. However, those outside who had been unable to get in made such a hideous noise and raised such a tumult, breaking windows about the College and throwing stones into the hall, that the College officers (having first been dared to appear) rushed out with about a dozen whifflers (attendants armed with staffs), 'well armed and swords drawne' and chased off some 400–500 people attempting to get in to see the performance. The ring-leaders were arrested and committed to the Porter's Lodge, 'where they lay Close Prisoners till the play was done, and then they were brought forth, and punished and so sente home' – *The Christmas Prince* (Malone Society, Oxford, 1922) pp. 285–6. Such behaviour was not restricted to England. Royall Tyler, in *The Contrast* (1787), has his 'stage Yankee', Jonathan, describe an unwitting visit to a playhouse in the New World to see 'The School for Scandalization'. This was preceded by hissing 'like so many mad cats' and an insistent thumping and stamping 'like our Peleg threshing wheat' (III.i).

2. Reprinted in *Victorian Dramatic Criticism*, ed. George Rowell, pp. 173–81, esp. 178. See also Charles Lamb's essay, 'On the Custom of Hissing at the Theatre', *The Reflector*, 1811 (in *The Works of Charles and Mary Lamb*, ed. E. V. Lucas, I, 87–92). This was prompted by the reception of his farce, *Mr H.* (1806). As Lucas notes, 'Lamb omits to say that he joined in the hissing of the farce' (I, 411). The long-standing nature of such ill-mannered behaviour by audiences is vividly dramatised by Shadwell in Act IV of *A True Widow* (1678), a part of which is conveniently to be read in A. M. Nagler, *A Source Book in Theatrical History*, pp. 212–13.

3. *The Revels History of Drama in English*, vol. VI: *1750–1880*, ed. Clifford Leech and T. W. Craik, pp. 22–3.

4. *The Pamphleteer*, 1814, III, 6, 513.

5. Leo Hughes, *The Drama's Patrons: a Study of the Eighteenth-Century London Audience*, p. 52 (and see pp. 63–4). Later in his study, Professor Hughes sounds an important warning against assuming that the considerable range of prices in theatres at that time can be directly related to those financially most likely to afford them, and he warns against assuming 'that the relatively high cost of admission to any part of the house barred all but the most affluent' (p. 170). He amusingly supports his case in part from Pepys's diary

for 1 January 1668.

6. *The Victorian Theatre: a Pictorial Survey*, p. 68; Planché, *Recollections and Reflections*, I, 127.
7. Austin Brereton, *The Life of Henry Irving*, I, 225.
8. *The Complete Plays of Henry James*, ed. Leon Edel, pp. 474–80. There is a short French film of about 1904 called *The Twins at the Theatre* which, despite its absurd slapstick, may in one section give a pretty fair simulation of a lively gallery audience. The twins' activities are comically exaggerated (e.g. wringing out the tears from their handkerchiefs with which they have dabbed their eyes so that the bald heads below them are drenched) but when early on they are vigorously told to desist by other galleryites we see what a disturbance was very probably like. The film is conveniently to be seen as part of Noël Burch's film *Correction Please* (1979).
9. Allardyce Nicoll, *Stuart Masques and the Renaissance Stage*, pp. 133–4.
10. A. M. Nagler, *A Source Book in Theatrical History*, pp. 89 and 272.
11. Anthony D. Barlow, 'Lighting Control and Concepts of Theatre Activity', *Educational Theatre Journal*, 25 (1973) 140–1. At the beginning of his article, Barlow rightly points out: 'central to our archetypal image of a theatre today is the concept of an audience area darkened and a performance area well lit' (p. 135).
12. See Applebee's contribution, 'Stage Lighting' in *The Oxford Companion to the Theatre*, ed. Phyllis Hartnoll (2nd edn, 1957) pp. 466–8. The date of 1849 was derived from the *Theatrical Journal*, 13 December 1849, which Applebee quotes.
13. Reproduced in Rowell (ed.), *Victorian Dramatic Criticism*, p. 171.
14. Terence Rees, *Theatre Lighting in the Age of Gas*. In *Theatre Lighting before Electricity*, Frederick Penzel refers to the fact that the chandelier in the auditorium could be dimmed 'although not darkened, due to pilot lights, which had to remain lit' (p. 53), and he notes that 'With the house darkened, the direction and intensity of their principal light source was now changed, and actors had to withdraw behind the proscenium' (p. 54), but he dates neither occurrence.
15. Nagler, *Source Book in Theatrical History*, p. 585. Nagler describes this preface as 'perhaps the most articulate manifesto of naturalistic stagecraft' (p. 583). It is noteworthy that naturalist staging and a darkened auditorium go hand in hand. Although Strindberg was still seeking a darkened auditorium in 1893, it was by then common in England.
16. A. D. Barlow, 'Lighting Control and Concepts of Theatre Activity', p. 142.
17. It was in the 1840s that Chernishevsky evolved theories of realism that were profoundly to affect art and also ensure for him twenty-one years of exile in Siberia. The Tsarist government saw, as have later such governments, that man can bear only a very little reality on the stage if oppressive régimes are to survive. Zola's preface to *Thérèse Raquin* (1873) should be particularly noted. *Documents of Modern Literary Realism*, ed. G. J. Becker, provides a good introduction to the subject and Damian Grant's *Realism* in the Critical Idiom series is a useful corrective (especially p. 14). See also *The Modern Tradition*, ed. Richard Ellman and C. Feidelson.
18. *Henry Irving: the Actor and his World*, p. 311.

19. *New Theatres for Old*, with a new Preface by the author, p. 148.
20. The principle of multiconscious response is S. L. Bethell's. He sums up the first chapter of *Shakespeare and the Popular Dramatic Tradition* by saying:

> I believe I am justified in asserting that there *is* a popular dramatic tradition, and that its dominant characteristic is the audience's ability to respond simultaneously and unconsciously on more than one plane of attention at the same time. I shall call this the principle of multi-consciousness.   (p. 29)

He argued that the reactions of an Elizabethan audience and those of a music-hall audience, or for a Marx Brothers or Harold Lloyd film, were akin to one another (e.g. pp. 28, 30, 38). This is also my starting point, and my debt to S. L. Bethell is much deeper than specific references can indicate. (His major concern was, of course, with Shakespeare.) So important – so truly seminal – a study is *Shakespeare and the Popular Dramatic Tradition* that it was selected as the principal work to be reprinted in volume 8 of *Literary Taste, Culture, and Mass Communication: Theatre and Song*, ed. Peter Davison, Rolf Meyersohn and Edward Shils (Cambridge, 1978) 14 vols.

NOTES TO CHAPTER TWO: THE MUSIC-HALL TRADITION
 1. Reprinted in *The Sacred Wood*, 1928 edn, p. 70. Hugh Kenner quotes this passage in the *Invisible Poet*, p. 173. He then cites a number of passages from articles describing English music hall, which Eliot wrote as London correspondent of *The Dial* in 1920–2. The last is the obituary for Marie Lloyd, regarding which see Peter Davison, *Songs of the British Music Hall*, pp. 99-101.
 2. Histories of the music hall are often nostalgic and inaccurate. The earliest standard history (difficult and costly to obtain) is C. Douglas Stuart and A. J. Park, *The Variety Stage* (London, 1895), and the origins of the halls are well described in *The Early Doors* by Harold Scott. Christopher Pulling's *They Were Singing* is warmly recommended. It is sociologically oriented and has as an appendix a useful, short history. Raymond Mander and Joe Mitchenson give a good visual impression of the halls in *British Music Hall*. J. S. Bratton, *The Victorian Popular Ballad*, and Martha Vicinus, *The Industrial Muse*, provide much general and detailed information and analysis. Some fifty songs are reproduced and analysed in Peter Davison, *Songs of the British Music Hall*. A splendid source book of facts about the halls and taverns is *London Theatres and Music Halls, 1850–1950* by Diana Howard. M. Willson Disher's *Winkles and Champagne* and Clarkson Rose's *Red Plush and Grease Paint* are affectionate but rooted in reality, and *Sweet Saturday Night* by Colin MacInnes tempers analysis with a sense of what has been lost. The north of England scene is described by G. J. Mellor in *The Northern Music Hall*. David Cheshire's *Music Hall in Britain* provides a good illustrated survey and also gives some account of finance and legal aspects of the halls; among the illustrations are a number of plans of music halls. *British Music Hall: an Illustrated Who's Who from 1850 to the Present Day* by Roy Busby provides a wealth of information in an area where fact and

myth are hard to disentangle. Laurence Senelick contributed a short, illustrated survey, 'A Brief Life and Times of the Victorian Music-Hall' to *Harvard Library Bulletin*, 19 (1971) 375–98. Most of the books mentioned have bibliographies.

3. For a fuller account see my *Henry V in the Context of the Popular Dramatic Tradition;* for *Conceited Pedlar* see *Popular Appeal in English Drama*, p. 122.

4. *Quips upon Questions*, B2ʳ.

5. A very telling photograph of Robson singing 'Villikins' in 1853 is reproduced in *Victorian and Edwardian Entertainment from Old Photographs* by Raymond Mander and Joe Mitchenson (no. 12).

6. Compiled from Diana Howard, *London Theatres and Music Halls, 1850–1950.*

7. Harold Manning, 'Holder's and Day's: Two Early Birmingham Music Halls', *Alta*, 2 (1969) 92–4. Holder's Rodney Inn and Concert Hall is also illustrated in David Cheshire, *Music Hall in Britain*, p. 18.

8. An even cheaper form of 'hall' was the 'penny gaff', and any full account of the development of entertainment of this kind must discuss the part played by the Gardens, such as Vauxhall and Ranelagh; the catch clubs and musical societies; penny gaffs and so on. Mayhew gives a vivid account of the penny gaff in his *London Labour and the London Poor* (1851), conveniently available in *Mayhew's London*, ed. Peter Quennell (London, 1969) pp. 86–90. For an account of early nineteenth-century entertainments in a provincial city, see Kathleen Barker, 'Bristol at Play 1801–53: a Typical Picture of the English Provinces?', *Western Popular Theatre*, ed. David Mayer and Kenneth Richards, pp. 91–103. An important part of the popular tradition was carried on until quite recently by such events as chapel and Band of Hope concerts, particularly in northern industrial areas.

9. M. R. Booth in Leech and Craik (eds), *The Revels History of Drama in English*, vol. VI, *1750–1880*, p. 20. The information is derived from R. Mander and J. Mitchenson, *British Music Hall*, who derived it from the *Era Almanack*, an annual published by the music-hall trade journal, *The Era*, between 1868 and 1919. Mander and Mitchenson name the halls, ten of which are described as 'small tavern halls'. They calculate – on the same basis – that there were 300 halls in the rest of the British Isles. David Cheshire refers to 57 theatres, 347 music halls, and 272 'smaller places consisting of public-house concert rooms, harmonic meeting places etc.' in London in 1878 – a total of 676. In addition, Surrey magistrates licensed 61 music halls and the City of London, six. These 471 theatres and music halls could accommodate 301,900 people (*Music Hall in Britain*, p. 32).

10. A detailed analysis of 'Villikins and his Dinah', with illustrations, words and music, will be found in Peter Davison, *Songs of the British Music Hall*, pp. 20–5.

11. In *Memories of London in the Forties* (1908), quoted by Christopher Pulling, *They Were Singing*, p. 173. The song is discussed in Peter Davison, *Songs of the British Music Hall*, pp. 12–15.

12. *Index Librorum Prohibitorum*, I, 136. Ashbee lists 47 titles, with some details, under the entry for *The Blowen Cabinet of Choice Songs. Fanny Hill's Bang-Up Reciter* is not mentioned by Ashbee. It was printed in 1835 and again in the following year by G. K. Edwards, 44 Wych Street, nr. St Clement's

Church, London, and re-issued in 1965 by P. R. Wells Publishing Co, London. The title-page assures the purchaser that the book contains 'Nothing but regular out and outers'. It was to Wych Street that The Drama was taken in Planché's *The Drama's Levée* (1838) to see burletta (see *Popular Appeal in English Drama to 1850*, p. 161). Another collection of such songs has recently been issued in facsimile as *Bawdy Songs of the Early Music Hall*, ed. George Speaight. It was adversely reviewed by J. S. Bratton in *Nineteenth Century Theatre Research*, 5 (1977) 55–6.

13. *Songs* (London, 1820) by Thomas Hudson, p. 14. 'The Steam Packet' is unusual in this series in being mainly patter; the tune for the song is 'The Nightingale'. Nine collections (all but that for 1820 being called *Comic songs*) were published from 1818 to 1828.

14. David Cheshire quotes a very interesting letter by T. Middlebrook, which lists what distinguishes a music hall from a theatre (*Music Hall in Britain*, pp. 34–5). That, for example, the details of plasterwork in the ceiling were called as evidence that a building was, in fact, a music hall and not a theatre, suggests how similar halls and theatres might be to any but an expert towards the end of the nineteenth century.

    For a very interesting account of the 'war against prostitution in the halls', from a point of view not too fully represented nowadays, see Guy Thorne, *The Great Acceptance: the Life Story of F. N. Charrington*. Charrington gave up his family inheritance in the large brewery of that name and ran the Tower Hamlets Mission from 1869. See especially pp. 116–21 re Lusby's Tavern and Music Hall (later The Paragon, where Marie Lloyd was booed off the stage). See also *Why We Attacked the Empire* by Mrs Ormiston Chant.

15. The whole song appears on pp. 40–5. Perhaps the satire of Mr Punch's introduction to the song would not be lost on us even today: 'Any ditty which accurately reflects the habits and amusements of the people is a valuable human document . . .' (p. 40).

16. *The Entertainer* (London, 1961) p. 32. The extracts from recordings (by Max Miller, Burt Sheppard, Tommy Trinder, Harry Tate, etc.), are from transcripts made by the author from recordings in his collection. Details of these recordings are given in Appendix III. As the recordings were made before the days of long-playing records, and some over eighty years ago, they are, in the main, difficult to find nowadays.

17. Quoted from *The Comic in Theory and Practice*, ed. J. J. Enck, E. T. Forter and A. Whitley, p. 27.

18. *Fifty Years of Spoof* (London, 1927) p. 140.

19. Interview with Ronald Hayman, *The Times*, Saturday Review (24 June 1972) p. 11.

20. W. Macqueen-Pope, *Queen of the Music Halls*, p. 88. It is told by Naomi Jacobs in *Our Marie* (London, 1936) pp. 82–3, and her version is drawn on by Martha Vicinus in *The Industrial Muse*, p. 264.

21. Bram Stoker, *Personal Reminiscences of Henry Irving*, p. 47.

22. Elkan and Dorotheen Allan have some pertinent comments to make about the need for an 'applaudience' for certain radio broadcasts, especially if a music-hall performer is involved (*Good Listening: a Survey of Broadcasting*, pp. 130–1). They are also very revealing, and amusing, about the intro-

duction of chorus girls into radio programmes, to give atmosphere to BBC radio variety, even though they could only be heard dancing (p. 132).
23. *The Victorian Popular Ballad*, p. 201. She shows how such songs were 'a complex of reference, verbal, conventional, and realistic, appealing to a series of responses which the audience *is trained and willing to supply* and the writer versed in provoking' (p. 200 [*my italics*]). Although the social contexts are a world apart, this relationship with the audience has much in common with the Jacobean masque. As Stanley Wells puts it in describing the masque: 'There was in fact another collaborator in the success of a masque. This was the audience. Masques were given for particular audiences, even for particular individuals; and the spectators were also literally participants in the action' (*Literature and Drama*, p. 62).
24. Reprinted in M. M. Booth, *English Plays of the Nineteenth Century*, v, 403.
25. *Prime Minister of Mirth*, p. 49.
26. The section from 'I went back home the other night' to 'he's come 'ere to use the phone', was used in the film *Triple Echo* (1972) to create a sense of listening to a wartime radio variety show.
27. *Looking Back on Life*, pp. 63–4.
28. 'Film Form, 1900–06', *Sight and Sound*, 47 (1978) 147–53, esp. p. 151.
29. I am grateful to Les Beaurline of the University of Virginia for suggesting this to me (23 March 1971) and for telling me of Professor Arthur Kirsch's term, 'self-conscious dramaturgy', which strikes me as a very accurate way of describing certain kinds of theatrical performance.
30. *The Yeoman of the Guard (1888)*, Act II (one-volume edition of *The Savoy Operas* (London, 1962) p. 429).
31. *'Can You Hear Me Mother?': Sandy Powell's Lifetime of Music Hall*, by Harry Stanley, pp. 62–3.
32. See, with section of the original script (10 October 1941), *Tommy Handley*, by Ted Kavanagh, p. 142. Kavanagh wrote the *ITMA* scripts. It became 'Can I do yer now, sir?' by 'sheer accident' according to the producer of the show, Francis Worsley (in his *ITMA*, p. 21).
33. *Good Listening*, p. 137.
34. The recording is flat and disappointing, perhaps because there was no audience. A rather different, printed version of the act is to be found in Kenneth Blain's sketch, *Golf*, published by Reynold & Co., London, about 1948 or 1949. (The sketch is not dated.) With it is a 'Humorous Medley for Four Characters' which adapts the words of 18 well-known songs to golf. Thus Harry Lauder's 'I Love a Lassie' becomes 'I took a brassie, a steel-shafted brassie', and the item concludes with all four in chorus singing 'Oh, There's Something about a Golfer' to the tune of 'Something about a Soldier'.
35. Sid Field, discovered late by London in 1943 at the age of 39, after years of work in the provinces, died quite young, in 1950, after only a few years of national success. He played not only in variety but with great success in Mary Chase's *Harvey* (1944). Jerry Desmond committed suicide in 1967.
36. Jeanne de Casalis, *Mrs Feather's Diary* (London, 1936). This adapts the technique to printed form.
37. This version is from a recording. It is to be found in a slightly different form in her *George – Don't Do That . . .* (London, 1977) with five other nursery-

school sketches.

38. Words, music, illustrations and commentary for both songs in Peter Davison, *Songs of the British Music Hall*, pp. 110–17. See also the Arthur Roberts's act in my 'Contemporary Drama and Popular Dramatic Forms', pp. 163–4. Mark Sheridan committed suicide in 1924.

39. *Winkles and Champagne*, p. 125.

40. *The English Inside Out*, pp. 180–1.

41. A good critique of the film, with a comparison of film and stage show, will be found in *Movie Comedy Teams*, by Leonard Maltin, pp. 245–51.

42. This kind of running gag is a hardy perennial of pantomime. It is doubtless very much older, but I vividly recall such a gag in the first pantomime I saw. The year was 1930 and the place Newcastle upon Tyne. The memory is vivid because I became so upset that I had to be removed, screaming.

43. *Rotha on Film*, pp. 100–1. The Living Newspaper is mentioned briefly below, pp. 142–3.

44. *Movie Comedy Teams*, pp. 115–16. S. L. Bethell gives further Marx Brothers examples in *Shakespeare and the Popular Dramatic Tradition*, p. 38.

45. Grierson first applied the term 'documentary' to the work of Robert Flaherty, in particular to his *Nanook of the North* (1922). Elizabeth Sussex in her excellent study, *The Rise and Fall of British Documentary: the Story of the Film Movement Founded by John Grierson*, concludes that 'talented as some of Grierson's original protégés undoubtedly were; it seems they were just not talented enough or sure enough to develop the thing they had begun. . . . Probably nothing that might be described as a movement in the arts has produced less major art than the British documentary movement' (pp. 210–11). However, whether Grierson and his protégés were primarily concerned (like MGM) with '*Ars gratia artis*' is very doubtful.

46. T. S. Eliot, *The Waste Land*, II, 139–49 (*The Complete Poems and Plays, 1909–1950*, p. 41).

47. S. L. Bethell said that Eliot 'exploits music-hall devices in the service of the highest aims' in *Murder in the Cathedral* (*Shakespeare and the Popular Dramatic Tradition*, p. 29).

48. Quotations are taken from the conveniently available *Three Plays* (St Martin's Library: London, 1957).

49. *All that Fall* (London, 1957) p. 33: 'the men's, or Fir as they call it now, from Vir Viris I suppose, the V becoming F, in accordance with Grimm's Law'. But according to Grimm's Law, as Beckett undoubtedly knows, P (as in 'pater') becomes F (as in 'father').

50. From *ITMA*, no. 59, 3 April 1942 (*The ITMA Years*, pp. 52–3). Script by Ted Kavanagh.

51. I am inclined to the view, after playing recordings of 1930s and 1940s music-hall acts to students on a number of occasions, that the responses of popular audiences in those decades were particularly fast, and certainly quicker than those of university and college students today. It may be that the content is too difficult on occasion – for example, when Flanagan and Allen base jokes on English grammar (though it is surprising that those went well in the music halls forty years ago), but it may be that dependence upon television (i.e. a visual medium) instead of radio has brought this about.

52. *The Caretaker* (rev. edn., 1962) pp. 14–15, 15–16, 31, 32, and 35–6. Arthur English has, in recent years, 'gone legit.' with considerable success.
53. Martin Esslin, *Pinter: a Study of his Plays* (2nd edn, 1973) p. 176.
54. Esslin, *Pinter*, p. 175, n. 1; from a letter to the director of the first German production of *Landscape*.
55. Harold Pinter, 'Writing for the Theatre', *Evergreen Review*, 33 (Aug/Sept, 1964) 80.
56. Esslin, *Pinter*, p. 226.
57. Ibid., pp. 204–5.
58. Ibid., p. 204; the italics are Esslin's. The pauses and silences of *Silence* are discussed from a different point of view by Richard Wilson in *Studying Drama: an Introduction: 'Silence'* (Open University, 1976).
59. Quotations from *Last to Go* are from the text published in *A Slight Ache and Others Plays* (London, 1961) pp. 127–30. This sketch was performed for the first time in the revue *Pieces of Eight*, on 3 September 1959 (not 1969 as stated by Esslin, *Pinter*, p. 190).
60. Quotations from *Landscape* and *Silence* are from the 1970 edition containing both plays. The Note appears on p. 8.
61. In *The Collection and The Lover* (London, 1963) p. 71.
62. Contrast H. Karasek's view, following a German production of the play, that *Silence* is a play that 'tries to wrap itself up in a minimum of stage effectiveness' (quoted by Rüdiger Imhof in 'Pinter's *Silence*: the Impossibility of Communication', *Modern Drama*, 17 (1974) pp. 450 and 457, and picked up by Richard Wilson in his Open University introduction, p. 30). This seems to me to interpret *Silence* as many people read a masque: without any awareness of the part played by the audience. Karasek's statement appeared originally in *Die Zeit* (16 January 1970) p. 16.

NOTES TO CHAPTER THREE: FROM TIECK TO BRECHT
1. *A History of English Drama, 1660–1900,* vol. V. *Late Nineteenth Century Drama, 1850–1900,* p. 73.
2. Shaw wrote an introduction to the English translation of *Three Plays by Brieux* (London, 1911). This collection includes *Damaged Goods*.
3. Compare *The Lady of Pleasure*, I.2 with *The School for Scandal*, II.1.
4. *Ionesco*, p. 23.
5. *The Field of Nonsense*, p. 6.
6. English edn (London, 1959) p. 76.
7. W. S. Gilbert, *Selected Operas*, second series (London, 1928) p. 175. There is nothing novel in the relativity of time in literature. Gilbert may well have had in mind *As You Like It*, III.ii.328–55, or Bolingbroke in *Richard II*, I.iii.261.
8. The play shared third prize with Ann Jellicoe's *The Sport of my Mad Mother* and the Australian play *The Shifting Heart* by Richard Beynon, in a competition organised by the *Observer*. Kenneth Tynan, in a review at the time (1957), thought Simpson's work was derived from 'the best Benchley lectures, the wildest Thurber cartoons, and the cream of the Goon shows. It has some affinities with revues of Robert Dhéry, and many more with the plays of M. Ionesco' (*Tynan on Theatre*, p. 63). J. R. Taylor linked the play 'with such humble native prototypes as *ITMA* and *The Goon Show*,

even without dragging in Lewis Carroll and the English nonsense tradition' – *Anger and After* (London, 1962) p. 58. The fact that the play, though full length, can be curtailed to fit various formats suggests it is primarily 'fun' (which is no discredit).

9. *A Resounding Tinkle*, Penguin New English Dramatists, no. 2 (Harmondsworth, 1960) pp. 123 and 125.

10. *Notes from Underground*, trans. Andrew R. MacAndrew (New York, 1961) pp. 117–18. It will be recalled that 'the Popish doctors' of Slawkenbergius's tale in *Tristram Shandy* maintained that God could make two and two add up to five – an idea taken up by Orwell in *1984*.

11. It is not suggested that Pinter had Carroll's poem in mind. What is more interesting is that both poem and play should present the force of circumstance in so critical a manner. The 'stories' are totally different.

12. Quotations are from the 1883 edition, pp. 87–117. For the additional stanzas as padding, see *The Diaries of Lewis Carroll*, ed. Roger Lancelyn Green, II, 418, for the entry of 19 May 1883. The 1883 edition has fourteen excellent drawings by Arthur B. Frost. When these were shown as slides with a partial dramatisation of the poem on 4 November 1976, at St David's University College, Lampeter, they particularly attracted the attention of Friedrich Dürrenmatt, then visiting the College.

13. Alfred Tennyson, *Poems*, 2 vols (London, 1845) II, 146–7.

14. *Waiting for Godot* (London, 1959) pp. 73–4.

15. Quotations are taken from the Edinburgh Bilingual Library edition (Edinburgh, 1974), edited and with an introduction by Gerald Gillespie. Perhaps it should be mentioned in passing that J. R. Planché's *Puss-in-Boots* (1838) is an 'Original, Comical, Magical, *Mew*-sical Fairy Burletta' in one act, and not in any way related to Tieck's play.

16. The text referred to is also in the Edinburgh Bilingual Library (Edinburgh, 1975), edited and translated by D. G. Dyer and Cecily Longrigg. D. G. Dyer refers in the introduction to the tripartite structure (pp. 19–21) and the use of comedy (pp. 21–3). At line 210 there is a reference to giving 'the finish to this play of his' (*Dabo peractum hanc fabulam*): 'his' being Cenodoxus; at lines 764–5, Hypocrisy uses theatre imagery: 'Virtue deserves its place / On such a stage' (*Hoc theatrum debuit / Habere virtus*). The use of asides is more telling, however. In II.3, for example, Cenodoxus, prompted by Self-Love, is asking his servant, Dama, for reports of the good things said about him. He must 'recount' these if he would 'count' on his food (and there is a pun in the Latin original, as Dyer points out, on '*edis*'/'*edes*'). Although they are not marked in this edition, Dama has at least three asides, two quite long: lines 571–9, 596–7, and 612–17. This last could easily be a short monologue.

17. Lionel Abel asks, 'What has happened in this play? A tragedy was predicted, but did not occur. And if it did not, this was because of the dramatic invention of King Basilio, who substituted for the play intended by fate one of his own invention. The tragedy fails. Basilio's play succeeds. Metatheatre has replaced tragedy' (*Metatheatre*, p. 72).

18. Pierre Corneille, *The Cid, Cinna, The Theatrical Illusion*, trans. John Cairncross (Harmondsworth, 1975); also the two plays both titled *La Comédie des comédiens* by Gougenot (1631) and Scudéry (1632), and

Quinault's *La comédie sans comédie* (1655).
19. I am greatly indebted to Dr Manfred Draudt of the University of
Vienna for answering many questions for me about Tieck and his interest
in Elizabethan drama. Basic sources are: Karl Goedeke, *Grundriss zur
Geschichte der Deutschen Dichtung* (Berlin, 1898) VI, 28–45; H. Lüdeke,
Ludwig Tieck und das alte englische Theater (Frankfurt a. Main, 1922); Robert
Minder, *Un poète romantique allemand: Ludwig Tieck* (Paris, 1936). The
information to the end of this paragraph has been drawn from that given to
me by Dr Draudt. Needless to say, any confusion or errors are my own.
20. Gerald Gillespie remarks: 'Tieck's mocking of the Berlin National Theatre
under Iffland and deft social and political thoughts precluded any immediate production of *Puss-in-Boots*' (p. 12); and, 'the play constituted an
attack mainly against the theatre public itself' (p. 17). When Tieck was at
Göttingen University, he would have been able to read Fielding's plays in
the edition of 1762. Professor Bernhard Fabian, who has made a study of
the purchase of English books by Göttingen University Library in the
eighteenth century (see *The Library*, VI, 1 (1979) 209–24), tells me that it can
be safely assumed that such books were bought immediately upon pub-
lication or, at the latest, within a year or two thereafter. Thus, the four-
volume edition of Fielding's *Works*, edited by Arthur Murphy in 1762, was
bought for five guineas from Thomas Osborne's catalogue for 1764.
(Information provided by Professor Fabian.) Volumes 1 and 2 of this
edition reprint Fielding's plays.
21. Gerald Gillespie notes that these characters 'represent the ruling critics and
taste of the day', Bötticher being Karl August Böttinger, author of a 'much
ridiculed theatrical treatise' (p. 132). Tieck hits off beautifully in Bötticher's
analysis of the cat's coat a critical approach still seriously applied today:

You've probably noticed that it's not one of the black cats? No, on the
contrary, he's almost entirely white and has only a few black spots. That
expresses his good nature quite splendidly. We see, as it were, the course
of the entire play, all the sentiments which it is supposed to excite,
already in his coat (p. 71).

22. See Gillespie's edition, pp. 12–13.
23. For a succinct analysis, with translated extracts from 'Conversations with
my Characters' (1915) and the essay, 'Illustrators, Actors, and Translators'
(1908), see the Open University's introduction to *Six Characters in Search of
an Author* by Peter Rink, pp. 8–9.
24. Gillespie, pp. 11–12. Felicity Firth accurately summarises the position: 'It is
impossible to say to what extent Futurism, the *grotesque* movement and
Pirandello's work acted upon each other. It is probably far more to the
point to see all three as different reactions to a general dissolution in
European thought and culture caused by the explosive doctrines of
Darwin, Einstein and Freud, who were all popularly interpreted as destroying the eternal values' (*Luigi Pirandello: Three Plays*, p. xx). She does
not mention Tieck.
25. See Rink's introduction to *Six Characters*, p. 5; he quotes Felicity Firth,
Luigi Pirandello: Three Plays, p. xxvi. It is amusing that Randolph should
have used a title three hundred years before Pirandello to do just what

Pirandello is described as doing: holding a mirror up to art.

26. *The Messingkauf Dialogues*, trans. John Willett, p. 102.
27. Ibid., pp. 58–9. Brecht also has the actor erroneously imagine that the Dramaturg wishes to revert to asides, and he has him incorrectly state that although the theatre has gone downhill, 'it has at least respected the forms. It never addressed the audience directly, for instance' (p. 52).
28. John Willett, *The Theatre of Bertolt Brecht* (1967 edn) p. 112.
29. John Willett, *Brecht on Theatre*, p. 11. The title and translation are Mr Willett's. There would have been a particularly sharp irony had he been rehearsing – or had Grass selected – *The Life of Galileo*.
30. Quotations are taken from the translation of the play by Ralph Manheim (Harmondsworth, 1972). This edition includes Grass's Address, given at the Adademy of Arts and Letters, Berlin; and a 'Documentary Report of the Workers' Uprising in Berlin on 17 June 1953', by Uta Gerhardt. Brecht was, in fact, rehearsing Erwin Strittmatter's contemporary play, *Katzgraben*, and not *Coriolan* at the time of the uprising (p. 33).
31. See Ewan MacColl, 'Grass Roots of Theatre Workshop', *Theatre Quarterly*, 3, 9 (1973) 58–68. Joan Littlewood arrived in Manchester in 1934 and joined Ewan MacColl, who was then working in street theatre. Shortly afterwards the Theatre of Action was formed.
32. By Theatre Workshop, Charles Chilton and the members of the original cast. Quotations are from the 1967 edition, pp. 34–5.
33. Thornton Wilder, *Our Town and Other Plays* (Harmondsworth, 1962) p. 14. Quotations from Wilder's plays are from this edition.
34. Three of his plays have been translated by Max Knight and Joseph Fabry as *Johann Nestroy: Three Comedies* (New York, 1967). There is a foreword by Thornton Wilder. A comparison of Nestroy's play and its source will be found in W. E. Yates, *Nestroy: Satire and Parody in Viennese Popular Comedy*, pp. 140–4. In *Play within a Play*, Robert J. Nelson referred to 'the fashionable Pirandellianism of Wilder's play', arguing that 'it could not be farther from the daring improvisations of the Italian master' (p. 2). Influences on Wilder are more varied, however. Nelson, despite his criticisms (e.g. the 'ambiguous use of the Stage Manager'), does think that '*Our Town* forces us to reconsider the very basis of dramatic illusion, to ask: What is a play?' (pp. 2–3). More than forty years after Wilder took Nestroy's play as his starting point, Tom Stoppard followed suit with *On the Razzle* (1981).
35. 'Sentimentality', *Sunday Times Magazine* (20 December 1964) pp. 38–9 and 41. The references are all to p. 39.
36. A few extracts will give a not too inaccurate impression:

> Everywhere men are rising from their sleep. Men, men, are understanding the bitter black total of their lives. Their whispers are growing to shouts! They become an ocean of understanding! *No man fights alone.* Oh, if you could only see with me the greatness of men. I tremble like a bride to see the time when they'll use it. . . . The world is beautiful. No fruit tree wears a lock and key. Men will sing at their work, men will love. Ohhh, darling, the world is in its morning . . . *and no man fights alone! (. . . Everyone in the room . . . is deeply moved by this vision of the future . . .)* Let us have air. . . . Open the windows. (*As he crosses to the*

windows a short fanfare is heard without.) *Six Plays* by Clifford Odets (New York, 1939) p. 230.

Though not addressed to the audience directly through the proscenium arch, this declamation has much in common with direct address, and, indeed, with the sermon and the stump oration. According to *The Literary History of the United States*, ed. Robert E. Spiller *et al.*, 3rd edn (New York, 1963), Odets 'professed to regard [*Paradise Lost*] as his most important work' (*History*, p. 1329).

37. John Willett, *The Theatre of Bertolt Brecht*, p. 222.
38. Full details are to be found in *Bertolt Brecht in Britain* (1977), compiled by Nicholas Jacobs and Prudence Ohlsen. They agree with Kenneth Tynan 'that it was primarily the directors as opposed to the writers who were most immediately affected' by the influence of Brecht, although that was to change later on. Only John Arden is regarded as 'deeply influenced by Brecht' (pp. 69–70).
39. References are to *The Entertainer* (London, 1961). Archie's speech is on pp. 70–1.
40. References are to the second edition (London, 1970).
41. Information from my mother, who read plays submitted to Richmond Theatre, London, just before the Second World War.
42. *Comedy High and Low*, p. 104. Charney gives a brief but pointed assessment of the play, noting the 'false portentousness' of Moon's proposed review and the way that the audience is not allowed to become involved in the farce (p. 105).
43. Ann Righter, *Shakespeare and the Idea of the Play*, pp. 206–7; she quotes from Richard Bernheimer, '*Theatrum Mundi*', *The Art Bulletin*, 38, pp. 225–47. See also Gordon Williams, 'Shakespeare, Kyd, and the Nature of Reality', *Trivium*, 12 (1977) 30, where Bernini's *Commedia dei due Covielli* (1637) is set in European and English traditions.

NOTES TO CHAPTER FOUR: THE CONTEMPORARY SCENE
1. *Shakespeare and the Popular Dramatic Tradition*, p. 28. Compare David I. Grossvogel, *Twentieth Century French Drama* (1961): 'When two segments of what had once been a single audience move further apart, writers of a "legitimate" drama that perpetually dies begin to take note of the ever regenerating popular forms' (p. 15). Grossvogel's book was originally published in 1958 as *The Self-Conscious Stage in Modern French Drama*.
2. Maurice Charney recalls that when Bert Lahr acted Estragon he played him for laughs in vaudeville style (*Comedy High and Low*, p. 109). This characteristic is essential to a thoroughly satisfying performance.
3. 'Contemporary Drama and Popular Dramatic Forms', pp. 165–70, 175–9, and 181–7.
4. John Arden, *Three Plays* (Harmondsworth, 1964) p. 101. References are to this edition. In the first production, at the Royal Court Theatre, Margaretta D'Arcy played Rosie; Wilfred Lawson – Sailor Sawney; Robert Shaw – Blackmouth; Francis Cuka – Daffodil; and; appropriately, in the light of things to come, the Police Sergeant was played by Stratford Johns. The play was directed by George Devine and Anthony Page. A. L. Lloyd set and sang the ballads.
5. In his 1931 essay on Thomas Heywood, Eliot wrote, 'it is usual for inferior

authors at any time to accept whatever morality is current, because they are interested not to analyse the ethics but to exploit the sentiment' (*Selected Essays*, p. 179).

6. For example, Rachel's 'How'd you like a real screaming sow to raven your paunch for you, hey?' (p. 109); and Daffodil's, 'I'm shaking like a west wind' (p. 125).

7. *The American Dream and The Zoo Story* (New York, 1963). *The Zoo Story* was first performed, in German, in Berlin on 28 September 1959, and four months later in America by the Provincetown Playhouse.

8. References to Peter Nichols's plays are to the 1970, 1971 and 1977 editions of *The National Health*, *Forget-me-not Lane* and *Privates on Parade*, respectively.

9. Steve's and Sylvia's first speeches are almost a parody of Staff Nurse Norton's response to Neil's proposal that they make love: 'I'll never do anything dirty before marriage' (p. 52 in each edition).

10. Hauptmann described *Rats* as 'A Berlin Tragi-Comedy'. The play has two stories, one tragic (that concerning Mrs John and her desire for a child), and the other comic (that centred on the old actor-manager, Hassenreuter). Both plots are dramatised in the 'legitimate' mode and are not blended together. At a time when unity of action was regarded as a main criterion, that seemed a fault. Thus, Ludwig Lewisohn, in his introduction to the play, complains that the elements are not 'firmly interwoven: they appear, at first sight, merely juxtaposed' (*Dramatic Works*, ed. L. Lewisohn (London, 1913) II, xi). Margaret Sinden does argue for a relationship between the two stories: 'we see one incident in the light of another: the comedy is darkened by the shadow of the tragedy, and the tragedy is broken by irony, by a sense of the ridiculous and the grotesque. . . . Or, again, the incidents are in themselves a blend of the comic and tragic' (*Gerhart Hauptmann: the Prose Plays*, p. 207). If *The Rats* is not entirely successful, it does nevertheless point forward in a very interesting way to the drama of forty years later. In Strauss's opera, Jourdain engages two companies and requires them to perform simultaneously. One gives a representation of the legend of the opera's title; the other is made up of *commedia dell'arte* performers: Zerbinetta, Brighella, Arlecchino, Scaramuccio and Truffaldin. There are similarities in technique between *The National Health* and Elmer Rice's *Dream Girl* (1945). Although Rice does not use the technique of direct appeal to anything like the extent that Nichols does, the relationship of the dramatised dream sections to the main narrative line anticipates Nichols's scheme.

11. Vivian Mercier, *The Irish Comic Tradition*, 48–9.

12. Charles has retired and Amy is telling Ursula how unsettled he is (p. 84). The year must be about 1965 for Charles is 75 (p. 75). Although Frank is only dreaming of Mr Magic and the Slave Girl and mentally stripping her, this is simultaneously acted out. Mr Magic is of the 1940s period, and earlier, after his attempted seduction of Frank, he has said, 'I'm part of your mental landscape for ever, duckie, whether you like it or – ' (p. 48). This brings together the 1940s and 1960s. However, Frank has introduced his father's retirement from the standpoint of the present. Thus an audience might see him as of the 'present day', Amy and Ursula as of 1965, and the

Slave Girl as of the 1940s. It is worth noting in this context that in January 1970, Tom Stoppard's *Where Are They Now?* was broadcast. This intercuts a school dinner of 1945 and an Old Boys' Dinner of 1969. As Stoppard says in a note to the 1973 edition (p. 61). 'Part of the idea is to move between the two *without using any of the familiar grammar or fading down and fading up*; the action is continuous' (my italics). For 'the sake of absolute clarity' Stoppard has had a line scored across the page of the printed text when the time shifts. Stoppard's *Artist Descending a Staircase* has an even more complex time scheme, but that was not performed until November 1972.

13. Miller uses retrospective exposition in its purest form. What has caused Biff to become as he is is only revealed at the end of the play. Biff and his father are simultaneously humiliated when Biff discovers the woman in Willy's room. Miller's technique of combining time present and time past does more than explain how the past has affected the present. It makes for great tension and that (as in *Forget-me-not Lane*) is so expressed through humour as well as pathos that the result is intensely dramatic. One can also see behind Miller's play, in addition to Ibsen's dramatic technique, something of the issues, the comedy and the tragedy of *The Wild Duck* (1884).

NOTES TO CHAPTER FIVE: OFFENDING THE AUDIENCE

1. Jimmy Jewel started his career at the age of ten with his father, a popular Yorkshire comedian, just after the First World War. From 1934 to 1967 he worked with his cousin, Ben Warriss, in a music-hall cross-talk act. They had a popular radio show, *Up the Pole*, in the 1950s with Jimmy as the put-upon partner (Roy Busby, *British Music Hall . . . Who's Who*). A section from their show is included in the BBC recording, *Great Radio Comedians* (151M). In this, Jimmy Jewel is being promoted as a boxer, and there is a description of a supposed fight with the champion, Randolph Turpin. As Ben Warriss describes what happens (and it all has to take place in the minds of the listeners and the studio audience), Jimmy Jewel comments on what is happening to him. The result is a neat juxtaposition of the absurd and a·real boxing contest:

> *Warriss:* Turpin leads with a left, a right to the jaw, and a left, and a right, left, right, left, right . . .
> *Jewel:* [*imitating army sergeant*] Squ-a-a-a-d halt! Le-e-eft turn! [*Mildly*] May I have this waltz? (L)
> *Warriss:* Oh don't be silly (L), James, Can't you hear the crowd is roaring? The crowd is roaring – they want blood!
> *Jewel:* [*somewhat plaintively*] Well, don't look at me! (L)

In the 1970s, Jimmy Jewel 'went legit.' with considerable success, although he still performs in music-hall revivals.

2. *Comedians* (London, 1976) p. 60. In an interview in *Theatre Quarterly*, 6, 22 (1976) 25–46, Griffiths said of *Comedians*: 'It's basically about two traditions – the social democratic and the revolutionary tradition. It's about a tradition in culture that, say, Richard Hoggart represents, which is the persuasive, the rational, the humane tradition – arguing, educating for good, trying to change through education, through example. Set against

that, there is a younger tradition, very violent, very angry, very disturbed, that says, "No, that isn't the way". . . . Basically, that is the confrontation. The play has been read as being about humour, as a play about comedians. At another level, it is probably that, too' (p. 42).

3. Compare: 'The humourist as understood by Pirandello must be compassionate; humour is almost pity' (Felicity Firth, *Luigi Pirandello: Three Plays*, p. xxv).

4. Grock, *Life's a Lark*, trans. by Madge Pemberton, ed. Eduard Behrens, pp. 210 and 274.

5. *Smith of the Shamrock Guards* was published by Greening & Co. (London, 1903). Its author is not named, the book being signed by 'Officer'. In a prologue and five acts, the author endeavours to expose 'ragging' in the army. In his introduction he gives a number of examples and some account of the Standford Case. Ragging was directed at those, such as merchants' or tradesmen's sons, who entered crack regiments and who, being 'socially unconnected', were deemed unfit by their 'brother' oficers to be in their company. If they did not resign of their own will, they were 'ragged' – bullied in ways 'ungentlemanly, brutal, and disgraceful' – until they did (p. 14). Letters from the Lord Chamberlain objecting to the play are printed and passages specifically arousing his ire are underlined. It is not a good play but it is a very interesting social document.

6. From an article in *The Times*, 17 February 1968, reproduced in *US: The Book of the Royal Shakespeare Theatre Production*, p. 209. Quotations from *US*, and comments thereon, are from this edition.

7. Peter Handke, 'Brecht, Play, Theatre, Agitation', trans. by Nicholas Hern, *Theatre Quarterly*, 1, 4 (1971) 90. The article originally appeared in *Theater Heute*, April 1968.

8. One cannot help but wonder whether this detachment from the lives of ordinary men and women, and a contempt for a bourgeoisie that seems to include most of the population – and pretty well all their audiences – coupled with artistic innovation in so public a medium as theatre, does not stem from a period in adolescence spent in a supremely élite world of learning, wit, youthful idealism, and play. It is remarkable how many gifted theatricals who work in this public medium and show such originality, but are seemingly alienated from those who would form their public, are products of Oxford and Cambridge, especially the latter. John Barton, Tony Bicat, Howard Brenton, David Frost, Peter Hall, David Hare, Jonathan Miller, Trevor Nunn and Peter Wood are amongst those from Cambridge. Oxford has produced Lindsay Anderson, Peter Brook, Peter Dews, William Gaskill and Kenneth Tynan. Expressing surprise that Snoo Wilson should have been to the University of East Anglia, Peter Ansorge described Cambridge as 'a rather surprising base . . . for an underground old boy network' (*Disrupting the Spectacle: Five Years of Experimental and Fringe Theatre in Britain*, p. 13).

9. So Maurice Charney of Lenny Bruce's act (which he likens to Peter Handke's play *Offending the Audience*), *Comedy High and Low*, p. 106.

10. Jonson, *Works*, ed. C. H. Herford and P. and E. M. Simpson, *Grex*, ll. 158–67.

11. *The Plays of John Marston*, ed. H. Harvey Wood, I, 144.

12. *Disrupting the Spectacle.* The book is the outcome of interviews conducted for *Plays and Players* from 1972. Peter Ansorge criticises and draws conclusions as well as describing and tracing origins.

13. A rather more gentle, not to say genteel, view of embarrassing the audience, which explained how the audience delighted in such experiences, was described by Francis Wyndham in *The Sunday Times Supplement*, 13 September 1964, pp. 38–40. Embarrassment is seen in terms of scenery collapsing and actors forgetting their lines, or, 'Perhaps the greatest ever embarrassment-success in the American theatre . . . *Who's Afraid of Virginia Woolf.*' But that was 1964.

14. *Experimental Theatre from Stanislavsky to Today*, p. 143.

15. I am most grateful to Professor John Brushwood, Roy A. Roberts Professor of Latin American Literature, University of Kansas, for drawing my attention to this account and for making a translation (from which I quote). The original is to be found in *Germán de Campo, una vida ejemplar*, by Juan Bastillo Oro (Mexico, 1930). It is reproduced in *Teatro: Boletin de Informacion e Historia*, no. 2 (Sept 1964). My warmest memory of this kind of performance is when a Birmingham audience refused to be passively assaulted and retaliated. In the fight that ensued, the actors were roughly handled. Somewhat ironically, bearing in mind what their intentions had been and their anti-authoritarian stance, they complained to the authorities. So far as I recall no further performances were given. The audience may also be attacked in the cinema. For some account of 'aggression' towards the film audience (which goes back at least half-a-century), see Noël Burch, *Theory of Film Practice*, trans. by Helen R. Lane (New York, 1973) ch. 8 'Structures of Aggression'.

16. References are to *Offending the Audience and Self-Accusation* (London, 1971). Ansorge gives a brief account in *Disrupting the Spectacle*, pp. 45–6.

17. *Peter Handke: Theatre and Anti-Theatre*, pp. 33–4.

18. It is the critic, Nicholas Hern, who describes it as a practical joke (and he refers particularly to the opening), not Handke. But Hern is right. The final courteous farewell disarms some of the sense of insult.

19. Not only does the minister have a duty to act in this manner, but he is addressing those who have deliberately contracted (through Confirmation) to behave in a way that should not require such admonishment. The theatre audience is party to no such agreement. As George Bernard Shaw, quoting Johnson, reminded his readers in his review of Henry James's *Guy Domville*, 'the drama's laws the drama's patrons give' (see above, pp. 5–6). Furthermore, though an actor may be no less moral than a minister of religion, the man (who may be evil and corrupt) is distinguished from his office of priest, as explained in Article of Religion XXVI: 'Of the Unworthiness of the Ministers, which hinders not the effect of the Sacrament'. *US* is, in this respect, as confused and primitive as *A Nice Wanton* (pre-1553), at the end of which Barnabas points the moral directly to the audience. But drama has come a long way since 1553 and no longer has a direct link with preaching.

20. The first performance was on 13 October 1966. Rehearsals had begun, ironically, on 4 July of that year. The film based on *US*, *Tell Me Lies*, opened in London in February 1968. The idea for the show was conceived

by Peter Brook (who was also the main driving force); the script and production were evolved corporately, though Charles Wood joined 'the team' as 'the main playwright' (*Book of US*, p. 14).

21. Compare the Bishop of Woolwich's categorisation of the play as liturgy: 'The whole thing reminded me more than anything else of Holy Week Liturgy. . . . It judged, but it did not pretend to save' (book of *US*, p. 198).

22. The banning of *Ethiopia* is described by Jane de Hart Mathews, *The Federal Theatre, 1935–1939: Plays, Relief, and Politics*, pp. 62–8. Hallie Flanagan gives her account in *Arena: the History of the Federal Theatre*, pp. 65–7; Elmer Rice gives his story, very briefly, in *Minority Report*, pp. 357–8. Three Living Newspaper scripts were published in *Federal Theatre Plays* (New York, 1938): *Triple-A Plowed Under*, *Power* and *Spirochete*. *Ethiopia* was printed in *Educational Theatre Journal*, 20 (1968) 15–31. See also: Arnold Goldman, 'Life and Death of the Living Newspaper Unit', *Theatre Quarterly*, 3, 9 (1973) 69–89; Arthur Arent, 'The Techniques of the Living Newspaper', *Theatre Quarterly*, 1, 4 (1971) 57–9. Joseph Losey was responsible for staging *Triple-A Plowed Under*.

23. Aug–Sept 1938, pp. 211–52. A brief note on *Busmen* is included in Malcolm Page, 'The Early Years at Unity', *Theatre Quarterley*, 1, 4 (1971) 60–6. O'Neill wanted audiences to join in choruses of *Lazarus Laughed* (1928).

24. The technique has been imaginatively adapted for the Welsh National Opera production of *The Magic Flute* (1979). As the *Guardian* review by Tom Sutcliffe described it, 'The frequent "morals" are sung out from the front edge of the stage, *with the house lights up*' (my italics; 23 January 1979). The producer was Goran Jarvefelt from Gelsenkirchen Opera House, Germany. Some of the audience failed to grasp what was intended, and at least one member of the orchestra thought a mistake had been made in the lighting arrangements – so have theatre-going conventions changed.

25. Herb Greer, an American playwright, writing under the title 'Players and Protesters' in the *Observer* (29 July 79), commented specifically upon the sincerity of what he called 'celebrity-agitators': 'And yet these *are* honourable people, they *are* sincere. Paradoxically that only makes it worse. Why? Because something else – something strange and a bit tragic – happens to certain stars when they take up political roles. The part plays the actor, so to speak, and the result can be a particularly ugly species of bigotry.'

26. The book gives a fascinating insight into improvisation and games, what happened, and how the individual actors responded. Grotowski came over especially to work with the actors for two weeks (pp. 132 ff).

27. Compare the responses of three members of the company (Michael Kustow, Bob Lloyd and Pauline Munro) to the appeal made to launch the Russell War Crimes Tribunal a fortnight before the first night when their 'sense of outrage had been raised to fever pitch . . . the same woefully inadequate prescriptions for action' were handed out (pp. 142–3).

28. Jean-Paul Sartre correctly interpreted *US* to mean also 'us', but went on to define 'us', somewhat narrowly for a countryman of some of those who fought at Dien Bien Phu, as the English and the Americans (p. 199).

29. *Culture and Agitation: Theatre Documents*, p. 9.

30. In an interview in *Theatre Quarterly*, 2, 5 (1972), Edward Bond remarked,

'anybody who would want to kill an animal as part of a ritual on the contemporary bourgeois stage strikes me as a bit cretinous'. The interviewer asked him, 'Even the burning of the butterfly at the end of *US*?', to which Bond replied: 'Did they burn a butterfly? They ought to have been kicked up the backside' (p. 12).

31. The danger for the outsider of being absorbed by the Establishment, the mainstream, the bourgeoisie, or, perhaps even worse, by 'the English', was neatly put by Pip Simmons, a fringe writer and producer: 'The English are very good at absorbing everything. I mean, they've absorbed us' (quoted by Peter Ansorge, *Disrupting the Spectacle*, p. 76). There is a delightful example of the ambivalence of the fringe's relationship with the institutional world earlier in Ansorge's book. Tony Bicat's film, *Skin Flicker* (1972), is described as 'this semi-underground (it has been backed by the BFI) English film . . .'! (p. 8). *The Alternative Theatre Handbook 1975– 1976* ('a descriptive guide to "theatre" companies who perform primarily in non-theatre places for non-theatre audiences'), compiled by Catherine Itzin, gave details of 133 fringe groups. Of these, 35 received no grant. Of the 98 which did, some received very small amounts – as little as £162 – but the total of grants *declared* by 70 of the groups amounted to £700,927; on average £10,000 per group. A further 54 grants of undisclosed amounts were received. The Pip Simmons group was given £25,000 in 1975. Although that was relatively generous, it was considerably less than the £35,000 granted to Moving Being (South Wales), and the £40,000-plus received by each of Theatremobile (Lancashire) and the Great Georges Community Arts Project (Liverpool). To these amounts must often be added grants for specific performances, in my limited experience being sums between £50 and £100 for a single event in a small place. It would seem that the total being spent by government and local authorities, etc., on alternative theatre in 1975 must have been of the order of £1,250,000. Some idea of the growth of subsidy from the Arts Council for such drama is suggested by figures given in *Theatre Quarterly*, 8, 32 (1979), drawing on Arts Council Annual Reports: 'in 1971/72 the Arts Council of Great Britain gave two socialist theatre groups a total of £10,363; by 1973/74 it was paying eleven groups £41,490; and in 1976/77 eighteen groups were receiving a total of £421,093. This does not include locally-financed groups, or groups in Wales and Scotland' (p. 27). Sandy Craig in 'The Bitten Hand: Patronage and Alternative Theatre' (in *Dreams and Deconstructions*, which he edited), states that in 1969/70 the Arts Council subsidy to alternative theatre was £15,000 but in 1978/79 'from the Drama Panel of the Arts Council alone, it was over £1.5 million. The total public subsidy in that year was in excess of £2 million . . . there are now around sixty full-time companies receiving subsidies' (p. 177). By early 1981 swingeing cuts had been introduced, however. A traditionalist attack on subsidised theatre can be found in *Theatre Inside Out*, by Kenneth Hurren, especially chapters 6 and 7 (pp. 49–78). A salutary comparison might be with the cost of military bands: popular but pricey.

32. *The Plays of J. M. Barrie*, ed. A. F. Wilson (rev. edn. 1942) pp. 557–8.

33. Quoted by James Roose-Evans, *Experimental Theatre from Stanislavsky to Today*, p. 121. A little later Roose-Evans graphically contrasts the creden-

tials of Peter Schumann's theatre group with those of Julian Beck's Living Theatre: 'Where the Living Theatre attacks the audience because the price of their ticket could have bought a meal for a child in Biafra, The Bread and Puppet Theatre never charge' (p. 124). For a vigorous argument for a theatre dedicated to the overthrow of capitalism and the class system, and for the establishment of socialism, see John McGrath's 'The Theory and Practice of Political Theatre', *Theatre Quarterly*, 9, 35 (1979) 43–54. See also David Edgar's account of the shortcomings of the socialist theatre, 'Ten Years of Political Theatre, 1968–1978', *Theatre Quarterly*, 8, 32 (1979) 25–33: and further comments on both articles by Steve Gooch and Michelene Wandor in *Theatre Quarterly*, 9, 36 (1980) 25–30.

34. For an impassioned but sane appeal for 'The actor as social scientist', see the section so entitled in Clive Barker's *Theatre Games: a New Approach to Drama Training* (London, 1977) pp. 211–17. Barker says, 'It angers me when the crucial importance of the actor's work is diminished, both inside and outside the theatre, by treating him as simply the mouthpiece of the dramatist's words, or the expressive instrument of the director's concept' (p. 211).

35. Michael Kustow records the shock when actors of the *US* company were made to face this surprising proposition. Even if the actors had never come across the work of the Wakefield Master (he did, after all, write for amateurs), and had never heard of Ben Jonson, or any of his contemporaries (Shakespeare presumably being excluded as primarily a businessman), they might at least have considered the work of Peter Hall and Peter Brook to be serious. Shaw and O'Casey would doubtless have to be excluded because they were Irish. One wonders whether an English actor burned at the stake in the sixteenth century for practising his art would regard the flames as frivolous.

Select Bibliography

This bibliography lists primary works, other than plays, and secondary works which have been referred to directly or indirectly. Texts of plays quoted are given in the notes and details are not repeated here unless reference has been made to their introductory matter. A separate list is provided of acts on record (Appendix II). Many of the plays and acts discussed are not well known (hence the fairly full quotations) and as a supplement to the sources given in the notes it was thought that a chronological list would be more useful to the reader than a separate bibliography. Quotations from Shakespeare, if not from specified editions, are from W. J. Craig's one-volume Oxford edition. Jonson is quoted from C. H. Herford and P. and E. M. Simpson's edition (Oxford, 1925–52).

Abel, Lionel, *Metatheatre: A New View of Dramatic Form* (New York, 1963).
Allan, Elkan and Dorotheen, *Good Listening: A Survey of Broadcasting* (London, 1948).
Ansorge, Peter, *Disrupting the Spectacle: Five Years of Experimental and Fringe Theatre in Britain* (London, 1975).
Anstey, F.A., *Mr Punch's Model Music-Hall Songs and Dramas* (London, 1892).
Arent, Arthur, 'The Techniques of the Living Newspaper', *Theatre Quarterly*, 1, 4 (1971) 57–9.
Armin, Robert, *Quips upon Questions* (London, 1600): reprinted in *The Collected Works of Robert Armin*, ed. John Feather (New York and London, 1972).
Ashbee, Henry Spencer (= *Pisanus Fraxi*), *Index Librorum Prohibitorum* (London, 1877) 3 vols; issued also as one volume in paperback as *Index of Forbidden Books* (London, 1969).
Barker, Kathleen, 'Bristol at Play 1801–53: a Typical Picture of the English Provinces?', *Western Popular Theatre*, ed. David Mayer and Kenneth Richards (London, 1977) pp. 91–103.
Barlow, Anthony D., 'Lighting Control and Concepts of Theatre Activity', *Educational Theatre Journal*, 25 (1973) 135–46.
Becker, G.J., *Documents of Modern Literary Realism* (Princeton, 1963).
Bethell, S.L., *Shakespeare and the Popular Dramatic Tradition* (London, 1944).
Binder, Pearl, *The English Inside Out* (London, 1961).
Bond, Edward, Interview, *Theatre Quarterly*, 2, 5 (1972) 4–14.
Bratton, J.S., *The Victorian Popular Ballad* (London, 1975).
Brecht, Bertolt, *The Messingkauf Dialogues*, trans. by John Willett (London, 1965).

Brereton, Austin, *The Life of Henry Irving* (London, 1908) 2 vols.
Brophy, Brigid, 'Sentimentality', *Sunday Times Magazine* (20 December 1964) pp. 38–9, 41.
Busby, Roy, *British Music Hall: An Illustrated Who's Who from 1850 to the Present Day* (London and New Hampshire, 1976).
Chant, Mrs Ormiston, *Why We Attacked the Empire* (London, 1895).
Charney, Maurice, *Comedy High and Low* (New York, 1978).
Cheshire, David, *Music Hall in Britain* (Newton Abbot, 1974).
Coe, Richard N., *Ionesco* (Edinburgh, 1961).
Craig, Sandy (ed.), *Dreams and Deconstructions: Alternative Theatre in Britain* (London, 1980).
Davison, P.H., 'Contemporary Drama and Popular Dramatic Forms', Kathleen Robinson Lecture, University of Sydney, 1963; printed in *Aspects of Drama and the Theatre*, Richard N. Coe *et al.* (Sydney, 1965).
——, *Songs of the British Music Hall . . . A Critical History of the Songs and their Times* (New York, 1971).
——, 'Governments Unpurposed Contributions to the Art of English Drama', *Trivium* 15 (1980) 47–54.
——, *Henry V in the Context of the Popular Dramatic Tradition* (Winchester, 1981).
Disher, M. Willson, *Winkles and Champagne* (London, 1938).
Edel, Leon (ed.), *The Complete Plays of Henry James* (London, 1949).
Edgar, David, 'Ten Years of Political Theatre, 1968–78', *Theatre Quarterly*, 8, 32 (1979) 25–33.
Eliot, T.S., *The Sacred Wood* (London, 1928).
——, *Selected Essays,* 3rd edn (London, 1941).
——, *The Complete Poems and Plays, 1909–1950* (New York, 1952).
Ellman, Richard and Feidelson, C., *The Modern Tradition* (New York, 1965).
Enck, J.J., Forter, E.T. and Whiteley, A. (eds), *The Comic in Theory and Practice* (New York, 1960).
Esslin, Martin, *Pinter: A Study of his Plays*, 2nd end (London, 1973).
Firth, Felicity, Introduction to *Luigi Pirandello: Three Plays* (Manchester, 1969).
Flanagan, Hallie, *Arena: The History of the Federal Theatre* (New York, 1940).
Gillespie, Gerald, Introduction to *Der gestiefelte Kater (Puss-in-Boots)* (Edinburgh, 1974).
Goldman, Arnold, 'Life and Death of the Living Newspaper Unit', *Theatre Quarterly*, 3, 9 (1973) 69–89.
Gooch, Steve, 'The Surveyor and the Construction Engineer', *Theatre Quarterly*, 9, 36 (1950) 25–27.
Gorelik, Mordecai, *New Theatres for Old*, with a new Preface by the author (New York, 1962).
Grant, Damian, *Realism* (London, 1970).
Green, Roger Lancelyn, *The Diaries of Lewis Carroll* (London, 1953) 2 vols.
Greer, Herb, 'Players and Protesters', *Observer*, 29 July 1979.
Griffiths, Trevor, 'Transforming the Husk of Capitalism' (Interview), *Theatre Quarterly*, 6, 22 (1976) 25–46.
Grock, *Life's a Lark*, trans. by Madge Pemberton, ed. Eduard Behrens (London, 1931).
Grossvogel, David I., *Twentieth-Century French Drama* (New York, 1961).

Handke, Peter, 'Brecht, Play, Theatre, Agitation', trans. by Nicholas Hern, *Theatre Quarterly*, 1, 4 (1971) 89–90.

Hartnoll, Phyllis (ed.), *The Oxford Companion to the Theatre*, 2nd edn (Oxford, 1957).

Hern, Nicholas, *Peter Handke: Theatre and Anti-Theatre* (London, 1971).

Howard, Diana, *London Theatres and Music Halls, 1850–1950* (London, 1970).

Howard, Roger, 'Declaration of Intent to Write Propaganda', *Culture and Agitation: Theatre Documents* (London, 1972) pp. 6–10.

Hudson, Thomas, *Comic Songs* (London, 1818–28) 9 vols.

Hughes, Leo, *The Drama's Patrons: A Study of the Eighteenth-Century London Audience* (Austin, 1971).

Hurren, Kenneth, *Theatre Inside Out* (London, 1977).

Imhof, Rüdiger, 'Pinter's *Silence*: the Impossibility of Communication', *Modern Drama*, 17 (1974) 449–60.

Irving, Laurence, *Henry Irving: The Actor and his World* (London, 1951).

Itzin, Catherine (ed.), *Alternative Theatre Handbook, 1975–76* (London, 1976).

Jacobs, Nicholas and Ohlsen, Prudence, *Bertolt Brecht in Britain* (London, 1977).

Jerome, Jerome K., *On the Stage – and Off: The Brief Career of a Would-be Actor* (London, 1885).

Kavanagh, Ted, *Tommy Handley* (London, 1949).

Kenner, Hugh, *The Invisible Poet* (London, 1959).

Lamb, Charles, 'On the Custom of Hissing at the Theatre', *The Reflector*, 1811; in *The Works of Charles and Mary Lamb*, ed. E. V. Lucas (London, 1903) I, 87–92.

Leech, Clifford and Craik, T.W. (eds), *The Revels History of Drama in English*, vol. VI: *1750–1880* (London, 1975).

MacColl, Ewan, 'Grass Roots of Theatre Workshop', *Theatre Quarterly*, 3, 9 (1973) 58–68.

McGrath, John, 'Better a Bad Night in Bootle . . .', *Theatre Quarterly*, 5, 19 (1975) 39–54.

——, 'The Theory and Practice of Political Theatre', *Theatre Quarterly*, 9, 35 (1979) 43–54.

MacInnes, Colin, *Sweet Saturday Night* (London, 1967).

Macqueen-Pope, W., *Queen of the Music Halls* (London, n.d.).

Maltin, Leonard, *Movie Comedy Teams* (New York, 1970).

Mander, Raymond and Mitchenson, Joe, *British Music Hall* (London, 1965).

——, *Victorian and Edwardian Entertainment from Old Photographs* (London, 1978).

Manning, Harold, 'Holder's and Day's: Two Early Birmingham Music Halls', *Alta*, 2 (1969) 92–4.

Mathews, Jane de Hart, *The Federal Theatre, 1935–1939: Plays, Relief, and Politics* (Princeton, N.J., 1967).

Mellor, G.J., *The Northern Music Hall* (Newcastle upon Tyne, 1970).

Mercier, Vivian, *The Irish Comic Tradition* (Oxford, 1962).

Nagler, A.M., *A Source Book in Theatrical History* (New York, 1959).

Nelson, Robert J., *Play within a Play: The Dramatist's Conception of his Art: Shakespeare to Anouilh* (New Haven, Conn., 1958).

Nicoll, Allardyce, *Stuart Masques and the Renaissance Stage* (London, 1938).

——, *A History of English Drama, 1600–1900*, vol. V: *Late Nineteenth Century*

Drama, 1850–1900 (Cambridge, 2nd edn, 1959).

Penzel, F., *Theatre Lighting before Electricity* (Middletown, Conn., 1978).

Pinter, Harold, 'Writing for the Theatre', *Evergreen Review*, 33 (1964) 80–2.

Planché, J.R., *Recollections and Reflections* (London, 1872) 2 vols.

Pulling, Christopher, *They Were Singing* (London, 1952).

Quennell, Peter (ed.), *Mayhew's London* (London, 1969).

Rees, Terence, *Theatre Lighting in the Age of Gas* (London, 1978).

Rice, Elmer, *Minority Report* (London, 1963).

Righter, Anne, *Shakespeare and the Idea of the Play* (London, 1962).

Rink, Peter, *Pirandello: Six Characters in Search of an Author* (Milton Keynes, 1977).

Robey, George, *Looking Back on Life* (London, 1933).

Roose-Evans, James, *Experimental Theatre from Stanislavsky to Today* (New York, 1971).

Rose, Clarkson, *Red Plush and Grease Paint* (London, 1964).

Rotha, Paul, *Rotha on Film* (London, 1958).

Rowell, George (ed.), *Victorian Dramatic Criticism* (London, 1971).

Salt, Barry, 'Film Form, 1900–06', *Sight and Sound*, 47 (1978) 147–53.

Scott, Harold, *The Early Doors* (London, 1946).

Senelick, Laurence, 'A Brief Life and Times of the Victorian Music-Hall', *Harvard Library Bulletin*, 19 (1971) 375–98.

Sewell, Elizabeth, *The Field of Nonsense* (London, 1952).

Sinden, Margaret, *Gerhart Hauptmann: The Prose Plays* (London, 1957).

Southern, Richard, *The Victorian Theatre: A Pictorial Survey* (Newton Abbot, 1970).

Speaight, George (ed.), *Bawdy Songs of the Early Music Hall* (Newton Abbot, 1975).

Stanley, Harry, *'Can You Hear Me Mother?: Sandy Powell's Lifetime of Music Hall* (London, 1975).

Stoker, Bram, *Personal Reminiscences of Henry Irving* (London, 1907).

Sussex, Elizabeth, *The Rise and Fall of British Documentary: The Story of the Film Movement Founded by John Grierson* (Berkeley, Calif. 1975).

Thorne, Guy, *The Great Acceptance: The Life Story of F. N. Charrington* (London, 1913).

Tynan, Kenneth, *Tynan on Theatre* (Harmondsworth, 1964).

US: The Book of the Royal Shakespeare Theatre Production (London, 1968).

Vicinus, Martha, *The Industrial Muse* (London, 1974).

Wandor, Michelene, 'Sexual Politics and the Strategy of Socialist Theatre', *Theatre Quarterly*, 9, 36 (1980) 28–30.

Wells, Stanley, *Literature and Drama, with Special Reference to Shakespeare and his Contemporaries* (London, 1970).

Willet, John, *The Theatre of Bertolt Brecht* (London, 1967).

——, *Brecht on Theatre* (London, 1964).

Wilson, A.E., *Prime Minister of Mirth* (London, 1956).

Wilson, Richard, *Studying Drama: An Introduction: 'Silence'* (Milton Keynes, 1976).

Worsley, Francis, *ITMA* (London, 1948).

Yates, W.E., *Nestroy: Satire and Parody in Viennese Popular Comedy* (Cambridge, 1972).

Index

Plays are indexed under their own titles and not under names of their authors. Alternative titles of plays are not usually indexed. Only in exceptional cases are characters of plays indexed. The Select Bibliography, the table forming Appendix I, and bibliographical references in the notes are not indexed. Many of the topic headings will also be found in *Popular Appeal in English Drama to 1850*.

183